A.S

THE ROAD TO LIFE
(AN EPIC OF EDUCATION)

With affectionate devotion to our friend and teacher MAXIM GORKY

In Three Parts

Part One

Foreign Languages Publishing House
Moscow 1955, Second Edition

Reprinted in the USA, 2014, by Red Star Publishers
www.RedStarPublishers.org

Translated from the Russian by Ivy and Tatiana Litvinov

Illustrations: selected from photographs
taken by Makarenko at the Maxim Gorky Colony

A. S. MAKARENKO
(1888-1939)

Anton Semyonovich Makarenko was born on March 13, 1888, in the town of Belopolye, in Kharkov Gubernia, the Ukraine. His father, Semyon Grigoryevich, was a painter in the railway workshops. Tatiana Mikhailovna, his mother, a woman with high standards for herself and for others, was a good and loving wife and mother.

The Makarenkos were united by ties of deep, undemonstrative affection, and each of the family had his or her well-defined responsibilities. Honesty, a sense of duty and human dignity – these qualities were inculcated in Anton Makarenko from childhood.

Anton learned to read at the age of five. When he was twelve years old he was sent to the city secondary school. The Makarenkos were poor, and when his father took Anton to this school, which was attended by the children of petty employees and shopkeepers, he told him:

"These schools were not made for the likes of us, but you just show them. Nothing but full marks! Understand?"

And the son faithfully fulfilled his father's orders. Throughout his school years, and later in the Pedagogical Institute, Anton Makarenko always stood at the head of his class.

After the six-year course of study at the city secondary school, he entered a normal school. When he received his teacher's diploma he began to work at the school for railwaymen's children in the settlement of Kryukoyo, where his family then lived. A Makarenko Memorial Museum was opened there in 1951.

The first years of Anton Makarenko's pedagogical work coincided with the period of the first Russian revolution.

"In the short period of only three years of revolution (1905-07) the working class and the peasantry received a rich political education, such as they could not have received in thirty years of ordinary peaceful development. A few years of revolution made clear what could not be made clear in the course of decades of peaceful development."[*]

It was in these very years that Makarenko's world outlook took shape. Recalling this period in later life, he said: "The understanding of history came to us through the medium of Bolshevik education and revolutionary events.... In the railway school where I taught, the atmosphere was infinitely purer than in other places; working-class society,

---

[*] *History of the Communist Party of the Soviet Union (Bolsheviks), Short Course, p. 150.*

truly proletarian society, kept the school firmly in its hands."

This working-class society, from the ranks of which Anton Makarenko himself came, and in which he worked, greatly facilitated his theoretical and political development as a Marxist.

Then and later, a big role in the shaping of Makarenko's outlook was played by Maxim Gorky. "Gorky taught us," he said, "to *feel* that history, he infected us with the wrath and the passion, and with the great confident optimism and joy, of his demand: 'Let the storm break in all its fury!'"

In 1914 Anton Makarenko entered the Poltava Pedagogical Institute to qualify himself as a teacher in the secondary schools. He was one of the Institute's best students. He read widely and frequently delivered detailed and vivid lectures on problems of education. He always remembered his teachers with gratitude. "...Many became Bolsheviks, and many of them laid down their lives on the fronts of the Civil War.... They were real human beings, and they instilled in us the loftiest human aspirations. It was they who helped me to realize the most important of pedagogical principles – how to combine with the most exacting demands upon the pupil the utmost respect for his personality."

Anton Makarenko graduated from the Poltava Institute with a gold medal.

On September 1, 1917, he was appointed head of a secondary school, which post he occupied when the Great October Revolution broke out. "After the October Revolution," wrote Makarenko, "wide horizons opened before me. We pedagogues were fairly intoxicated by these horizons."

It was then that Makarenko began his vigorous search for new forms and methods of education, new paths in pedagogics.

In the autumn of 1920 the Gubernia Department of Public Education entrusted Anton Makarenko with the organization of a colony for homeless children, later named the Maxim Gorky Labour Colony. The colony was given forty hectares of land with several dilapidated buildings, some six kilometres from the town of Poltava. Before the October Revolution this had been a colony for juvenile delinquents. When Makarenko took over, it was in a ransacked state: neighbourhood kulaks had removed even the windowpanes, doors and stoves, and dug out the fruit trees.

After two months of hard work one of the dormitories was made habitable. Part of the equipment of the former colony was recovered.

The first group of the colony's charges arrived in December that year. Realizing that any far-reaching demands were out of the question at the start, Makarenko worked with them gradually, but firmly. His first step in building up a collective was to form a group of the most active and willing lads to patrol the forest against illegal cutters of timber. "The guarding of the state forest," said Makarenko, "considerably raised us in our own eyes, provided us with extremely entertaining work, and, finally, brought us in no small gain." In the early years the pupils, "grown savage in their own egoism," caused Anton Makarenko many a bitter moment, although, as he was later to write, "little by little the embryo of the collective conceived in our midst the first winter grew and developed."

Makarenko did not believe in pedagogical miracles. Better than anyone else, he knew, from long years of experience, the tremendous efforts the educator had to expend in fanning the pupils' momentary sparks of duty, honour, discipline and industry into a vitalizing flame. Producing these sparks was easy enough, but though often bright they died out quickly. It was difficult to awaken consciousness, but more difficult to develop and channelize strength of character, particularly when the pupil's entire previous life had taught him laxity.

It was to the collective that Makarenko ascribed the leading role in educational work. His motto was education in the collective, through the collective and for the collective.

After a visit to the colony, Maxim Gorky wrote in his article "Across the Soviet Union" (1929): "Who is it that has been able to change in such an unrecognizable way, to re-educate, hundreds of children so brutally and humiliatingly mauled by life? The organizer and head of the colony is A. S. Makarenko. He is indisputably a talented educator. " And in one of his letters to Makarenko, Gorky said: "You are doing splendid work, and it should yield magnificent fruit.... An amazing man, you are, just the kind Russia needs."

In 1927 Anton Makarenko was appointed head of the Dzerzhinsky Labour Commune, a newly-founded institution for homeless children and adolescents on the outskirts of Kharkov. From 1928, when he gave up his duties at the Gorky Colony, to 1935 he devoted all his energies to the Dzerzhinsky Commune, the number of whose charges grew to 600.

Makarenko's pedagogical system was built up, proved and improved during the years in the Gorky Colony (1920-28). This was a pedagogical laboratory, as it were, while in the Dzerzhinsky Commune the system, now fully formed, was confidently applied. Here the principle of combining productive labour and schooling, the principle of unity of mental, character, physical and aesthetic education and polytechnical instruction, was brought to a high degree of perfection.

In the commune, work activities as a character-building factor were arranged on new lines, differing from those at the Gorky Colony. While in the colony they were based on agricultural occupations and handicraft workshops (sewing, shoemaking, carpentry, etc.) serving the colony's needs, the Dzerzhinsky Commune had, in addition, industrial forms of labour at its own modern plants equipped with precision machinery.

The commune members worked and received a secondary school education at the same time; many of them later passed the entrance examinations for higher schools with flying colours.

During his sixteen years of educational work at the Gorky Colony and the Dzerzhinsky Commune Anton Makarenko reared some 3,000 fine citizens and devoted patriots of the Socialist Homeland. They are doing good work today in various fields – as engineers, officers of the Soviet Army, doctors, teachers, actors, and so on.

Anton Makarenko was not only a remarkable teacher but a profound theoretician who made a major contribution to Soviet pedagogics.

Basing himself on the teachings of Lenin and Stalin on communist education, he developed his pedagogical system in a trenchant battle with bourgeois and petty-bourgeois pedagogical theories, hostile to Marxism-Leninism. He ridiculed and rejected the anarchistic "theory of free education," showing that it led to laxity, lack of initiative, inability to meet difficulties, etc. He vigorously fought the pseudoscience of pedology, which made its chief law the fatalistic predetermination of child personality by heredity and an immutable environment, and which displayed an exaggerated interest not only in the child's past but in its ancestors, too. What interested Makarenko was not the child's past but its future. He combated the pedologist "law" of fatalistic predetermination because of heredity by theoretically substantiating the tremendous influence of correct education and demonstrating this influence in practice. He refuted the artificial and defective pedologist methods of studying children (by intelligence tests, farfetched questionnaires) and knew how to probe the child's personality by pedagogical observation. He was adamant in his criticism of early 20th century experimental pedagogics for its biological tendencies, and fought, also, the metaphysical theories which built pedagogical "laws" on a purely speculative foundation divorced from real life, as, for example, the reactionary' pedagogical system of the German pedologist Herbart.

In place of these various theories Anton Makarenko built up a truly Marxist-Leninist system of educational methods. His disquisition on "pedagogical logic" is a model of the treatment of educational problems from the philosophical standpoint of dialectical materialism.

Pedagogical logic, says Makarenko, is determined by educational goals, and these are not immutable but change as society changes. The present goal, he wrote at the beginning of the 'thirties, is the development of such traits of character as are "necessary to the Soviet State in the era of the dictatorship of the proletariat, of the establishment of classless society." No special Makarenko system existed, he said, stressing that his was a Soviet system. Indeed, he proceeded from the teachings of Marx, Engels, Lenin and Stalin on society, on the aim and the role of communist education, and the essence of communist ethics. Makarenko's pedagogics is permeated through and through with Stalinist humanism. One of Makarenko's fundamental premises, as has already been noted, was a combination of the most exacting demands upon the pupil with utmost respect for his individuality. His entire pedagogical system is imbued with Bolshevik confidence in man's vast potentialities, with great optimism, and faith in the creative powers of people organized in a collective. Makarenko's system could have arisen only in the conditions created by the Great October Socialist Revolution, when the problem of the relationship between society and the individual received a correct solution for the first time in history.

Makarenko was an innovator in education. He worked out a new and original approach to the methodological foundations of pedagogy; a new understanding of discipline, as "discipline of combating and surmounting difficulties"; and a system of methods in character building. He devoted great attention to the problem of upbringing in the family, and gave many valuable instructions in this field. To him we owe the first detailed elaboration of the educational significance of the collective. Another innovation was his remarkably profound "system of perspectives," the essence of which he defined in the following words: "Man must have something joyful ahead of him to live for. The true stimulus in human life is the morrow's joy. In pedagogical technique this not too distant joy is one of the most important objects to be worked for. In the first place the joy itself has to be organized, brought to life, and converted into a possibility. Next, primitive sources of satisfaction must be steadily converted into more complex and humanly significant joys.... To educate a man is to furnish him with a perspective leading to the morrow's joy." When properly applied by the educator, the system of perspectives keeps the collective in a buoyant, joyous mood, holds a clear-cut purpose before the children, strengthens their confidence in their own powers, and spurs them to strive for ever greater achievements.

Anton Makarenko is the author of a number of literary works dealing with education, among them *The Road to Life, Flags on the Tow-*

ers, 1930 Marches On and *A Book for Parents*. He left behind a literary legacy of more than 100 separate works.

The Road to Life in which Makarenko describes life in the Gorky Colony (or, more correctly, the building up of the colony), and his pedagogical system, was begun in 1925 and completed in 1935. Maxim Gorky much admired this book, which he called "one of the best examples of Soviet literature."

As a work of literature dealing with education, the book has no equal in the world. This book, revealing the vast forces and potentialities inherent in Man the Fighter, a book of intense humanism, is immensely popular among Soviet readers. And no wonder, for it arouses the will to life and activity, shows how "the aspiring soul marches ever further and further, soars ever higher and higher." The reader is filled with the immense joy of a life of toil, and in the innumerable examples of the spiritual growth of the members of a children's collective, he sees how the ideas of communist education are being carried out.

In *The Road to Life* Anton Makarenko shows how the individual, burdened by the legacy of the old world, may be made over in the conditions of Soviet life, conditions in which, for the first time, each individual has been given the opportunity for happiness in union with others, in comradely and joyous work together for the welfare of the Homeland.

The language of the book is vivid, full of imagery, truth and humour, and gives subtle psychological descriptions of the pupils and teachers in the colony. Gorky said that Makarenko "knew how to describe each colonist in a few words, and this as if a photograph of each character were made."

In speaking of his former pupils, upon whom he bestowed such warm affection, Makarenko expresses his feelings in words that ring with emotion:

"My Gorkyites also grew up, and were scattered all over the Soviet Union, so that now I should find difficulty in gathering them together, even in my imagination. There's no getting hold of engineer Zadorov, who has become absorbed by some vast Turkmenistan construction work; and neither Vershnev, Medical Officer to the Special Far Eastern Army, nor Burun, a doctor in Yaroslavl, can be called for an interview. Even Nisinov and Zoren, those kids, even they have flown away from me, rustling their wings, but these wings are no longer the tender sprouts of my pedagogical sympathy, they are the steel wings of Soviet airplanes."

Flags on the Towers, a novel in three parts, constituting something like a sequel to *The Road to Life* though it is a perfectly independent story, was published in the magazine *Krasnaya Nov* in 1938. It describes the life and achievements of a collective that has completely affirmed itself – the Dzerzhinsky Commune. Makarenko gives much from his own biography through the personality of the main character, Zakharov.

A year earlier, in 1937, *A Book for Parents* was published. This is a literary work devoted to problems of upbringing in the family.

From 1937 to 1939 Makarenko wrote a number of stories and articles. His fertile literary activities are notable not only for variety of subject matter, their full and timely response to the events and aspects of life in the Socialist Homeland; it is not merely his unusual literary energy which is so amazing, but also the wide range of fields of literature he covered: he appears before his readers simultaneously as a novelist, a writer for and about children, a literary critic, a journalist, and – last but not least – a specialist in the theory of education.

Anton Makarenko placed high demands on his literary talent. Here is how he expressed his literary credo in the *Literaturnaya Gazeta* in 1939:

"I pledge that my literary work will be honest and truthful, free from distortion or deception. Wherever I see a fresh conquest, it is my duty to be the first to raise the flag of triumph, in order to cheer on the fighters and enhearten the pusillanimous and the falterers. Wherever I see a rift, it is my duty to be the first to sound the alarm, in order to enable the courage of my own people to mend the rift at the first opportunity. Wherever I see a foe, it is my duty to be the first to expose his true physiognomy, in order that the foe be destroyed as soon as possible.... Thus the work of the writer is by no means a tranquil occupation, and its field of action is the whole front of the socialist offensive."

In recognition of Anton Makarenko's great services in the sphere of literature, the Soviet Government decorated him, on February 1, 1939, with the Order of the Red Banner of Labour.

The glorious, indefatigable life of Anton Makarenko came to an abrupt end on April 1, 1939. He died suddenly, in the train, on his way back to Moscow from a country home for writers not far from the capital. In his absorption in literary and public activities Makarenko did not spare himself, and his constitution was undermined by many years of strenuous toil.

Innumerable former pupils – now commanders in the Soviet Army, engineers, doctors, fellows of colleges, teachers, journalists, students in military schools – came from all over the country to the graveside of this splendid man and noble citizen. They took their places in the guard of honour around his coffin like members of a big, affectionate, and now orphaned family....

Research into Makarenko's rich pedagogical legacy and posthumous publication of his numerous articles and lectures were begun in 1940. His literary works, as well as his *Lectures on Child Education,* which are devoted to the principles of upbringing in the family, have gone through many editions. Besides, the Academy of Pedagogical Sciences of the R.S.F.S.R. has put out a two-volume edition of Makarenko's selected pedagogical writings and is issuing a seven-volume edition of his complete works. Various aspects of Makarenko's work have been treated in dissertations presented for scientific degrees. Teachers and directors of Soviet schools and children's homes use his ideas and principles as a guide in their educational work.

Professor Y. Medinsky
Member of the Academy of Pedagogical
Sciences of the R.S.F.S.R.

CONTENTS

Introduction		*III*
1.	A CONVERSATION WITH THE CHIEF OF THE GUBERNIA DEPARTMENT OF PUBLIC EDUCATION	3
2.	THE INGLORIOUS BEGINNINGS OF THE GORKY COLONY	6
3.	A DESCRIPTION OF OUR PRIMARY NEEDS	17
4.	OPERATIONS ON THE HOME FRONT	26
5.	MATTERS OF STATE IMPORTANCE	34
6.	THE CAPTURE OF THE IRON TANK	41
7.	"EVERYBODY'S GOOD FOR SOMETHING!"	47
8.	CHARACTER AND CULTURE	55
9.	"THE AGE OF CHIVALRY IS NOT DEAD IN THE UKRAINE"	60
10.	"HEROES OF SOCIAL EDUCATION"	75
11.	THE APOTHEOSIS OF THE SEED-DRILL	82
12.	BRATCHENKO AND THE DISTRICT COMMISSAR FOR SUPPLIES	89
13.	OSADCHY	98
14.	INKPOTS AS GOOD-WILL PROMOTERS	105
15.	"OURS IS A BEAUTY!"	111
16.	GABER SOUP	120
17.	SHARIN ON THE WARPATH	128
18.	A LINK-UP WITH THE VILLAGE	135
19.	A GAME OF FORFEITS	141
20.	A HORSE FOR A HARVESTER	150
21.	HORRID OLD MEN	165
22.	AMPUTATION	178
23.	SELECTED SEED	184
24.	SEMYON'S WAY OF SORROWS	193
25.	REGIMENTAL PEDAGOGICS	201
26.	THE MONSTERS OF THE NEW COLONY	209
27.	THE STORMING OF THE KOMSOMOL	219
28.	THE CEREMONIAL MARCH BEGINS	228

1
A CONVERSATION WITH THE CHIEF OF THE GUBERNIA DEPARTMENT OF PUBLIC EDUCATION

September of the year 1920 I was summoned by the Chief of the Gubernia Department of Public Education.

"Look here, my friend," he said. "I'm told you're raising hell about this here... er... this... gubsovnarkhoz" [Gubernia Economic Council. – Tr.] place you've been allotted for your school!"

"It's enough to make anyone raise hell," I replied. "Raise hell? I could sit down and cry! Is that a Craft School? A reeking, filthy hole like that? Is that your idea of a school?"

"Oh, yes! I know what you'd like! Us to erect a new building, put in new desks, and you just move in and do your stuff! But it's not the building that matters, my friend – what matters is the creation of the new man, and you educational chaps do nothing but carp. 'The building won't do, and the tables aren't right!' You haven't got the... er... spirit, the revolutionary spirit, you know. You're one of those White-collar workers, that's what you are!"

"Well, I don't wear a white collar, anyhow!"

"All right – *you* don't! But you're all a pack of lousy intellectuals. Here am I, looking everywhere for a *man* – and there's such a great work to be done! These homeless kids have increased and multiplied till you can hardly move for them in the streets, and they even break into the houses. And all I get for an answer is: 'It's *your* job, "it's the responsibility of the Department of Public Education'... all right, then, what about it?"

"What about what?"

"You know very well what! No one wants to take it on! Whoever I ask, they turn me down – 'No, thanks – we don't want to get our throats cut!' All you chaps want is your comfortable study and your darling books... you and your eyeglasses!"

I laughed.

"Now it's my glasses!"

"That's just what I say – you only want to read your books, and when you're confronted with a real live human being, you can only squall: 'He'll cut my throat – your real live human being!' Intellectuals!"

The Chief of the Gubernia Department of Public Education kept darting angry glances at me from his small black eyes, and showering imprecations through his walrus moustache upon the whole of the teaching fraternity.

But he was wrong, the Chief of the Gubernia Department of Public Education.

"Now, listen!" I began.

"What's the good of listening? What can you have to tell me? I know what you're going to say: 'If only we could do like they do over there... er... in America!...' I've just read a book about it – someone shoved it on to me. Reforma-... what d'you call them? Oh, yes, reformatories! Well, we haven't got any here yet!"

"Do let me say something!"

"Go ahead, then! I'm listening!"

"Before the Revolution there were ways of dealing with waifs, weren't there? They had reform schools for juvenile delinquents...."

"That won't do for us! What they had before the Revolution won't do for us!"

'Quite right! So we have to find new methods for the creation of the new man."

"New methods! You're right there!"

"And no one knows where to begin."

"And you don't either?"

"And I don't!"

"There's some chaps right here in this Gubernia Department of Public Education who know!"

"But they don't mean to do anything about it."

"You're right they don't – damn them! You're right, there!"

"And if I were to take it up, they'd make things impossible for me. Whatever I did, they'd say: 'That's not the way!'"

"They would, the swine! You're right, there!"

"And you'd believe *them* – not me!"

"No, I wouldn't! I'd say: 'You should have done it yourselves!'"

"And supposing I really do make a muddle?"

The Chief of the Gubernia Department of Public Education banged on the table with his fist.

"You and your 'make-a-muddle'! What are you driving at? D'you think I don't understand? Muddle or no muddle, the work's got to be done. We'll have to judge by results. The main thing isn't just a colony for juvenile delinquents, but you know – er... social re-education. We've got to create the new man, you know – our sort of man. *That's* your job! Anyhow, we've all got to learn, and you'll learn. I like the way you said to my face, 'I don't know!' Very well, then!"

"And have you got a place? After all, we can't do without buildings, you know!"

"There is a place! A wonderful place, old man! There used to be a reform school for juvenile delinquents in that very place. It's quite near – about six kilometres. And it's fine there – woods, fields... you'll be keeping cows!"

"And what about people?"

"I suppose you think I keep them in my pocket! Perhaps you'ld like a car, too!"

"And money?"

Money we've got! Here you are!"

He produced a bundle of notes from the drawer of his desk.

"A hundred and fifty million. This is for all sorts of organizational expenses, and any furniture you need."

"Are the cows included?" "The cows can wait. There aren't any windowpanes. You draw us up an estimate for the coming year."

"It's a bit awkward, somehow. Oughtn't I to go and have a look at the place first?"

"I've done that! D'you think you'll see thing I missed? All you need to do is to move in!"

"All right!" I said, with a sigh of relief, for I was convinced at the moment that nothing could be worse than those rooms of the Economic Council.

"You're a trump!" Said the Chief of the Gubernia Department of Public Education. "Go ahead! It's a glorious cause!"

2
THE INGLORIOUS BEGINNINGS OF THE GORKY COLONY

Six kilometres from Poltava, springing out of sandy hillocks, there is a pine forest of some 200 hectares, bordered by the smooth, endlessy gleaming cobblestones of the highroad to Kharkov. In a corner of a 40-hectare clearing in the forest, a perfect square is formed by a group of uncompromisingly symmetrical brick buildings. This is to he the new colony for juvenile delinquents.

The sandy, sloping courtyard merges in a wide glade extending towards a reed-fringed lake, on the opposite bank of which may be discerned the dwellings and wattle fences of a kulak farmstead. Beyond these, etched against the sky, is a straight line of ancient birch trees and a huddle of thatched roofs.

Before the Revolution there had been a colony for juvenile delinquents in this place, but in 1917 its inmates all ran away, leaving behind them extremely faint vestiges of an educational system. Judging by the contents of the dilapidated registers, the educational staff had been chiefly recruited from retired non-commissioned officers, whose main duty it was never to take their eyes off their charges, either during work or recreation, and at night to sleep next to them in an adjoining room.

According to the local peasantry, the educational methods of these tutors were not very subtle, being in practice limited to that simplest of all pedagogical apparatus – the rod.

Material traces of the former colony were still further to seek, its neighbours having carried and carted away to their own barns and outhouses everything in the way of furniture, stores, and workshop equipment on which they could lay their hands. Among other valuables they even removed the orchard. But there was not the slightest indication of a spirit of vandalism in all this. The fruit trees had not been cut down, but simply uprooted and replanted elsewhere, the windowpanes not broken, but taken carefully out of their frames, the doors hacked by no ruthless axe, but gently lifted off their hinges, the stoves removed brick by brick. The only article of furniture left was a sideboard in the apartment of the former director.

"How is it that the sideboard was left behind?" I asked Luka Semyonovich Verkhola, a neighbour who had come from the farmstead to have a look at the new bosses.

"Well, you see, *our* people had no use for this cupboard. It wouldn't have gone through their doors – too high, and too wide. And there would be no point in taking it to pieces."

The sheds were crammed with odd articles, but there was nothing of any practical use in them. Following a hot scent I managed to retrieve a few things which had been stolen quite recently. Thus I recovered an old seed-drill, eight rickety joiners' benches, a brass bell, and a thirty-year-old cob, an erstwhile fiery Kirghiz steed.

Kalina Ivanovich, manager of supplies, who was already on the spot when I arrived, greeted me with the question:

"Are you the pedagogical director?"

I was soon to learn that Kalina Ivanovich spoke with a Ukrainian accent, although he refused, on principle, to recognize the Ukrainian language. There were many Ukrainian words in his lexicon, and he pronounced his g's in the southern manner.

"Are you the pedagogical director?"

Me? I'm the director of the colony.

"No, you're not!" said he, taking his pipe out of his mouth. "You're the pedagogical director, and I'm the supply manager."

Picture to yourself Vrubel's "Pan," but Pan gone quite bald, with only a tuft of hair over each ear. Shave off Pan's goatee, trim his moustache in the episcopal manner, stick a pie stem between his teeth, and Pan becomes Kalina Ivanovich Serdyuk. He was a remarkably versatile individual for so modest a post as that of manager of supplies in a children's colony. Of his fifty-odd years, which lad been spent in the most varied activities, he was proud to recall only two phases – his youth, when he had been a private in the Keksholm Infantry Regiment of the Guards, and his superintendence, in 1918, of the evacuation of Mirgorod during the German offensive.

Kalina Ivanovich became the first object of my educational zeal. It was the very abundance and variety of his views which constituted my greatest difficulty. With impartial fervour, he damned the bourgeoisie and the Bolsheviks, the Russians and the Jews, Russian slackness and German punctiliousness. But out of his blue eyes there shone such a zest for living, and he seemed so responsive and so full of life, that I did not grudge expending a little of my pedagogical energy on him. I started on his education the very first day, beginning with our very first encounter.

"Comrade Serdyuk, surely you don't imagine a colony can get on without a director! After all, somebody has to be responsible for everything!"

Kalina Ivanovich again removed his pipe, and said, with a courteous inclination of the head in my direction:

"So you want to be the director! And you want me to be so-to-speak your subordinate!"

"Not necessarily! I could be your subordinate if you prefer it that way."

"Well, I've never been taught pedagogics. I don't claim what isn't mine by rights! Still, you're only a young man and you want an old man like me to be at your beck and call. And that's not right, either. But I haven't got enough book learning to be the director – besides, I don't want to be!"

Kalina Ivanovich stalked away in a huff. All day he seemed dejected, and in the evening he came into my room quite heartbroken.

"I've moved a bed and a table in here. They're the best I could find," he said.

"Thanks."

"I've been thinking and thinking what we're to do about this here colony. And I've decided that you'd better be the director and I'll be so-to-speak your subordinate."

"We'll get on all right, Kalina Ivanovich!"

"I think so, too. After all, it doesn't take a genius to put a sole on a boot. We'll manage. And you, since you're an educated man, will be so-to-speak the director."

We set about our work. The thirty-year-old cob was raised to its feet by the judicious use of props. Kalina Ivanovich clambered into a sort of phaeton, kindly provided by one of our neighbours, and the whole remarkable contraption set out for the town at the rate of two kilometres an hour. The organizational period had begun.

The task set for the organizational period was a most appropriate one – to wit, the accumulation of the material values required for the creation of the new man. Kalina Ivanovich and I spent whole days in town during the first two months, he driving there, I going on foot. He considered it beneath his dignity to walk, and I could not stand the languid pace of our Kirghiz steed.

During these two months we managed, with the help of experts from the villages, to get one of the barracks of the old colony into some sort of shape, putting in windowpanes, repairing stoves, hanging new doors.

We had only one victory on the "external front," but it was a notable one: we succeeded in wangling 150 poods of rye flour out of the Food Commissariat of the First Reserve Army. And this was all we managed to "accumulate" in the way of material values.

But when I came to compare what had actually been done, with my ideals in the sphere of material culture, I realized that even if I had achieved a hundred times as much, I should have fallen just as short of my aim. And so, bowing to the inevitable, I declared the organizational period concluded. Kalina Ivanovich was quite of my way of thinking.

"What can we expect to find here," he exclaimed, "when those parasites produce nothing but cigarette lighters? First they lay the land waste, and then they ask us to 'organize'! We'll have to do as Ilya Muromets did!"

"Ilya Muromets?"

"Yes, Ilya Muromets! Maybe you've heard of him! They've made a hero of him – a bogatyr – the parasites! But I say he was just a tramp – a loafer, going sleigh riding in the summer!"

"All right, then! Let's be like Muromets. We could do worse! But who'll be Solovei, the highwayman?"

"There'll be no lack of them – don't you worry!"

Two teachers arrived at the colony – Ekaterina Grigoryevna, and Lydia Petrovna. I had by that time almost despaired of finding teachers; no one seemed anxious to devote himself to the task of creating the new man in our forest – everyone was afraid of our "tramps," and no one believed our plans would come to any good. And then one day at a conference of village schoolteachers, in response to my efforts at persuasive eloquence, two real live people came forward. I was glad they were women. It seemed to me that the "elevating feminine influence" was just what was needed to round out our system.

Lydia Petrovna was extremely young, hardly more than a schoolgirl. She had only just graduated from high school, and was fresh from the maternal nest. The Chief of the Gubernia Department of Public Education, while putting his signature to her appointment, asked me:

"What do you want with a girl like that? She doesn't know a thing!"

"She's just what I was looking for. D'you know I sometimes think book learning is not the chief thing just now. This Lydochka is an unspoiled little thing, and I regard her as a kind of yeast to leaven our dough."

"Aren't you being a bit farfetched? All right, here you are!"

Ekaterina Grigoryevna, on the other hand, was a seasoned pedagogue. She wasn't so very much older than Lydochka, but Lydochka clung to her as a child clings to its mother. Ekaterina Grigoryevna had a grave beauty of countenance, emphasized by black eyebrows almost masculine in their straightness. She was always neat, in clothes that had been preserved, as by a miracle, and Kalina Ivanovich justly observed, after making her acquaintance:

"You've got to watch your step with a girl like that!"

Now everything was in readiness.

On the fourth of December our first sis charges arrived at the colony, presenting me with a fantastic packet bearing five huge seals. This packet contained their "records." Four of them had been sent to us for housebreaking while bearing arms. These were about eighteen years old. The other two, who were a little younger, had been accused of theft. Our new charges were splendidly attired, in the smartest of riding breeches and cavalry boots. They wore their hair in the height of fashion. These were no mere street arabs. Their names were Zadorov, Burun, Volokhov, Bendyuk, Gud, and Taranets.

We received them with the utmost cordiality. The whole morning went in preparations for a gala dinner; the cook bound her hair with a fillet of dazzling whiteness; in the dormitory, festive tables were spread in the space unoccupied by the beds; we had no tablecloths, but brand-new sheets provided effective substitutes. All the members of our incipient colony were gathered there. Kalina Ivanovich turned up in honour of the occasion in a green velvet jacket instead of his usual stained grey coat.

I made a speech about the new life of toil, and the need for forgetting the past and pressing ever onward. The newcomers paid scant attention to my words, whispering to one another and allowing their sardonic glances to rove over the camp beds with their worn quilts, and the unpainted window frames and doors. While I was in the middle of my speech, Zadorov suddenly exclaimed loudly to another boy:

"You're the one who let us in for all this!"

We devoted the rest of the day to drawing up plans for our future life. The newcomers, however, listened to my proposals with courteous indifference, eager to get the whole thing over.

And the next morning a much-perturbed Lydia Petrovna came to me with the complaint:

"I can't manage them! When I told them to fetch water from the lake, one of them – the one with his hair done so smartly – started tugging on his boot, letting the toe swing right up to my face, and all he said was: 'Look how tight the bootmaker has made them!' "

The first days they weren't even rude, they merely ignored us. Towards evening they would saunter away, returning only in the morning and acknowledging my pathetic expostulations with discreet smiles. And then, a week later, Bendvuk was arrested by a detective from the Gubernia Criminal Investigation Department for robbery with murder the previous night. Lydochka, frightened out of her wits by this event, retreated to her room for a good cry only emerging every now and then to ask of all and sundry: "What does it mean? I don't understand! Did he just go out and kill somebody?"

Ekaterina Grigoryevna, smiling gravely and knitting her brows, exclaimed:

"I don't know, Anton Semyonovich, I really don't know! Perhaps we'd better just go away! I don't seem to be able to find the right approach."

The lonely forest surrounding the colony, the empty shells of our buildings, our dozen camp beds, the axes and spades which were almost our only tools, the half-dozen boys who were in frank opposition not only to our pedagogical system, but to the very principles of human culture itself – all this was as unlike as possible to any scholastic experience any of us had ever had.

The long winter evenings in the colony were distinctly uncanny. Two oil lamps, one in the dormitory, the other in my room, afforded our only illumination. The teachers and Kalina Ivanovich were reduced to thee time-honoured system of our forebears – a wick floating in a saucer of oil. The chimney of my lamp glass was broken at the top, and the lower part was always grimy with soot, owing to Kalina Ivanovich's habit of poking nearly half a newspaper down it to light his pipe.

The snowstorms started early that year, and the yard was soon blocked with drifting snow, through which it was nobody's business to clear paths. I asked the boys to do this, but Zadorov said:

"That's easy enough, but wouldn't it be better to wait till the end of the winter? What's the good of us clearing it away when it's sure to snow again? See?"

Bestowing a smile of angelic sweetness upon me, he joined a friend, as if oblivious of my very existence. It could be seen at a glance that Zadorov was the child of educated parents. He spoke correctly, and his face had that youthful refinement only found among those who have had a well-nurtured childhood. Volokhov belonged to quite another category. His wide mouth, spreading nose, and wide-set eyes, composed, with the puffy mobility of his features, the physiognomy of a typical "tough" Volokhov, his hands as always deep in the pockets of his riding breeches, sauntered up to me:

"Well, you've had your answer," he drawled.

I went out of the dormitory, my rage congealing into a hard lump in my chest. But paths had to be cleared, and my suppressed fury called imperatively for the outlet of action.

"Let's go and clear away the snow!" I said having sought out Kalina Ivanovich.

"What? Have I come here to be a navvy? And those chaps?"

He motioned in the direction of the dormitory. "The highwaymen?"

"They won't!"

"The parasites! Come on, then!"

Kalina Ivanovich and I had almost finished the first path when Volokhov and Taranets came along it for their nightly sally townwards.

"Atta boy!" cried Taranets gaily.

"And high time, too!" added Volokhov.

Kalina Ivanovich blocked their way.

"What d'you mean 'high time'?" he spluttered. "Just because you, you blighters, don't want to work, you think I'm going to do it for you! You shan't use this path, you parasites! You go through the snow, or I'll bash your head in with this shovel!"

Kalina Ivanovich brandished the spade fiercely, but the next moment it had flown into a distant snowdrift, while his pipe catapulted in another direction, and the astonished Kalina Ivanovich stood there, blinking, at the departing youths.

"You can go and get the shovel yourself!" they shouted, proceeding on their way with gales of laughter.

"I'll quit, hang me if I don't! I'm not going to work here any more!" said Kalina Ivanovich, and he went back to his room, leaving the spade in the snowdrift.

Life at the colony became melancholy and gruesome. Cries of "Help, help!" were heard on the Kharkov road night after night, and the plundered villagers were always begging for succour in the most tragic accents. I procured myself a revolver from the Chief of the Gubernia Department of Public Education, by way of protection from our own particular knights of the road, but concealed from him the situation at our colony. I had not as yet given up hope of coming to some sort of an understanding with my charges.

These first months of the existence of the colony, as well as being a time of despair and futile effort for myself and my colleagues, were also a time of ardent research. In the whole of my previous existence I had not read so many books on education as I did that winter of 1920.

It was the time of Wrangel and the Polish war. Wrangel was quite near, just outside Novomirgorod: and quite near to us, in Cherkassy, was the Polish army, while all over the Ukraine roamed the "atamans," and many of those around us were still going about under the blue-and-yellow spell of Petlyura's banners. But in our wilderness we endeavoured, our chins propped on our hands, to shut out the thunder of great events, and devoted ourselves to the study of pedagogics.

The chief outcome of all this reading was a firm, well-founded conviction that the books had yielded me very little in the way of science or theory, and that I should have to bring my own theories out of the sum total of the actual phenomena, as displayed in everyday life.

At first I felt, rather than understood, that what I needed was not a set of abstract formulae, which I should anyhow have been unable to apply, but immediate analysis of the situation, followed by immediate action.

I was well aware that I should have to hurry, that I could not afford to lose a single day. The colony was becoming more and more like a den of thieves and cutthroats. The attitude of the boys to their teachers was rapidly crystallizing into habitual insolence and frank hooliganism. By now they were bandying dirty stories in front of the women teachers, rudely demanding their dinner, throwing plates about the dining room, making open play with their Finnish knives, and inquiring facetiously into the extent of every body's possessions, with jeering remarks such as: "You never know what might come in handy!"

They flatly refused to cut down trees for firewood, breaking up the wooden roof of a shed under the very nose of Kalina Ivanovich, joking and laughing good-humouredly the while.

'It'll last our time!" they cried gaily.

Kalina Ivanovich, scattering constellations of sparks from his pipe, threw out his arms in despair:

"What's the good of talking to them, the parasites!" he cried. "Who taught them to break up what other people have built? Their parents, the parasites, ought to go to quod for it!"

And then, one day, the storm broke. I suddenly lost my footing on the tight rope of pedagogical practice. One wintry morning I asked Zadorov to chop some wood for the kitchen stove, receiving the usual cheerfully insolent reply: "Do it thyself! God knows there are plenty of you here!"

It was the first time any of the boys addressed me with the familiar 'thou." Desperate with rage and indignation, driven to utter exasperation by the experiences of the previous months, I raised my hand and dealt Zadorov a blow full in the face. I hit him so hard that he lost his balance end fell against the stove. Again I struck him, seizing him by the collar and actually lifting him off his feet. And then I struck him the third time.

I saw to my astonishment that he was simply aghast. Pale as death, he kept putting on and taking off his cap with trembling hands. Perhaps I would have gone on hitting him, if he had not begun to whimper out: "Forgive me, Anton Semyonovich!"

My rage was so wild and unbridled that a word of resistance would have set me rushing at the whole pack of them, ready for murder, ready to wipe out this gang of thugs. An iron poker had somehow found its way into my hand. The other five huddled speechless around their beds. Burun was nervously adjusting his clothes.

Turning towards them, I rapped with the poker against the foot of one of the beds.

"Either you all go this minute to work in the woods, or you leave the colony, and to hell with you!"

With this I left the room.

Going to the shed in which our tools were kept, I took up an axe, and grimly watched the boys, who had trooped nearer me, select axes and saws. It did pass through my mind that it might be as well not to put axes into the boys' hands on such a day, but it was too late – they had taken everything they needed. But I was at the end of my tether. I was ready for anything, resolving only that I would not sell my life cheap. Besides, there was a revolver in my pocket.

We set out for the forest. Kalina Ivanovich, overtaking me, whispered in profound excitement: "What's up? For God's sake, what has made them so obliging all of a sudden?"

I looked abstractly into Pan's blue eyes and replied:

"A bad business, old man! For the first time in my life I've struck my fellow man."

"God almighty!" exclaimed Kalina Ivanovich, "and what if they complain?"

"If that were all!"

To my astonishment, however, everything went off swimmingly. The boys and I worked away till dinnertime, cutting down the more stunted pine trees. They were a bit sulky, but the bracing frosty lair, the splendid, snow-crowned pines, and the fellowship of toil, mingling with the rhythm of axe and saw, did their work.

When a halt was called, all self-consciously dipped into my proffered store of coarse tobacco, and Zadorov, sending a puff of smoke towards the pine tops, suddenly burst out laughing:

"That was a good one!"

It was quite a pleasure to look at his rosy, laughing visage, and I couldn't help smiling back at him.

"What? The work?" I asked.

"The work's all right. I meant the way you licked me!"

He was a strong, strapping lad, and could certainly afford to laugh. I was astonished at myself for having dared to lay hands on such a Hercules.

With another peal of laughter, he picked up his axe and went up to a tree:

"What a joke! Oh, what a joke!"

We had dinner all together, with good appetites, bandying jokes, and nobody mentioned the occurrence of the morning.

Still feeling slightly embarrassed, but determined not to relax my authority, I firmly issued orders after dinner.

Volokhov grinned, but Zadorov came up to me and said, with a grave look: "We're not such bad chaps, Anton Semyonovich! Everything will be all right! We understand...."

3
A DESCRIPTION OF OUR PRIMARY NEEDS

The next day I said to the boys: "The dormitory must be kept clean! You must appoint a dormitory monitor. You can only go to town with my permission. If anyone goes without it, he needn't trouble to come back, or I won't let him in.

"I say!" exclaimed Volokhav... couldn't you let us down a little more lightly?"

"Well, boys, you can choose for yourselves," I said. "That's all I can do! There's got to be discipline in the colony. If you don't like it, find somewhere else to go to. But those who stay will submit to discipline. Whatever you think, we're not going to run a thieves den here."

"Shake!" said Zadorov, extending his hand towards me· "You're right! You, Volokhov, shut up! You're a fool about this sort of thing. Anyhow we have to stay here for la while. And it's better than quod, isn't it?"

"And is attending school compulsory?" asked Volokhov.

"Certainly!"

And if I don't wish to study? What good'll it do me?"

"School is compulsory. You've got to attend whether you like it, or not. Zadorov called you a fool just now. You must learn and grow wise."

Volokhov shook his head comically, exclaiming:

We're in for it now!"

The incident with Zadorov proved to be a turning point in discipline. I have to admit that I was beset by no qualms of conscience. Very well – I had struck one of my pupils. Keenly as I felt the pedagologial impropriety, the illegality of my action, at the same time I realized that the purity of our pedagogical conscience would have to be subordinated to the immediate task before me. I firmly decided to be a dictator if other methods failed. Not long after I came to loggerheads with Volokhov, who, while monitor, had failed to clean up the dormitory, and refused to do so on being reprimanded.

"Don't drive me to extremes," I said, looking sternly at him. "Do the room!"

"And if I don't you'll give me one in the eye, will you? You have no right to!"

I seized him by the collar, dragged him towards me, and, with the fullest sincerity, hissed into his face:

"Listen! I give you fair warning! I shan't give you one in the eye – I'll mark you for life! Then you can complain. If I go to prison for it, it's no business of yours."

Volokhov wriggled out of my grasp, exclaiming plaintively:

"No sense in going to prison for a little thing like that! I'll tidy the room, damn you!"

"Don't you dare to talk to me like that!" I roared at him.

"Well, how d'you want to be talked to? Go to – – "

"Go on! Swear!" Suddenly he burst out laughing, with a baffled gesture.

"What a fellow!" he cried. "All right, I'll tidy the room, don't shout at me!"

It should not be thought that I believed, even for a moment, that I had discovered a sovereign disciplinary method in the use of physical force. The Zadorov incident had cost me more than it had cost Zadorov himself. I was in constant fear of falling into the habit of taking the line of least resistance. Lydia Petrovna criticized me with frank severity:

"So you've discovered a method at last? Just like in the old seminary, isn't it?"

"Leave me alone, Lydochka!"

"No, but really! Are we to beat them up? May I, too? Or is it your monopoly?"

"I'll let you know a little later, Lydochka. I don't yet know myself. Give me time!"

"All right! I can wait."

Ekaterina Grigoryevna went about with a frown on her brows for some days, addressing me with distant politeness. Five days passed before she asked me, with her grave smile:

"Well, how are you feeling?"

"Thanks! I'm all right."

"D'you know what's the most distressing feature of this affair?"

"Distressing?" "Yes. It is that the boys speak of your exploit with enthusiasm. They are all but in love with you, especially Zadorov. What does it mean – I don't understand! Could it come from a habit of servitude?"

I thought for a while before answering, and then said:

"No, it isn't that. It has nothing to do with servitude. It must he something else. Let's look deeper: after all, Zadorov is stronger than I am, he could have crippled me with a single blow. And he fears nothing, any more than Burun and the rest do. In this whole affair it's not the beating they remember, it's the passion, the fury of a human being. They know very well I needn't have beaten them, I could easily have sent Zadorov back to the Commission as incorrigible, and made things unpleasant for them in all sorts of ways. But I didn't do any of this; instead I chose a way which was dangerous for myself, but it was a human, not a bureaucratic way. And after all they do really need our colony. Things are not so simple. And they see how we work for them. They're human beings, too. And this is a most important factor."

"You may be right," said Ekaterina Grigoryevna thoughtfully.

But this was no time for philosophical musings. A week later, in February 1921, I went to town in a furniture cart and brought back some fifteen real waifs, in real rags. What with scrubbing them, getting them fitted out somehow or other, and curing them of the itch, they gave us plenty to do. By March we had thirty boys at the colony. Most of them were in a terrible state of neglect, savage beings who were by no means hopeful material for the fulfilment of the social-educational ideal. So far they seemed entirely devoid of that creativeness which is said to bring the child's mental processes so close in type to those of the scientist.

Our colony had become richer in teachers too. By March we had a regular Pedagogical Council. To the astonishment of the whole colony Ivan Ivanovich Osipov, and his wife Natalya Markovna, brought with them quite a lot of property in the form of couches, chairs, cupboards, and all sorts of raiment and dishes. Our ill-clad charges watched with profound interest the depositing of all these goods at the door of the Osipov abode. This interest was far from abstract, and I was extremely afraid that this glorious display might find its way to the stalls of the market.

A week later the marked interest taken in the possessions of the Osipovs was diverted to the arrival of a housekeeper. This functionary was an extremely good natured, garrulous, simple old soul. Her inventory, while not so valuable as that of the Osipovs, included some extremely titillating items. To wit: large quantities of flour, jars full of jam and other cornestibles, a number of neat little boxes, and certain bags which the trained eyes of our boys knew, by their contours, to contain all manner of good things. The housekeeper arranged her room very cosily, according to the canons of an old woman, placing her sundry bags and boxes in corners and on shelves which seemed to have been destined for them from the beginning of time, and very soon the friendliest footing had been established between her and some of our boys. This friendship was founded on the principle of mutual advantage: the boys brought her firewood and tended her samovar, in exchange for which services she would treat them to an occasional cup of tea and entertain them with her worldly wisdom. There was really nothing for a housekeeper to do at our colony, and I used to puzzle over her appointment.

Decidedly there was no need of a housekeeper at the colony. We were incredibly poor. Apart from the few rooms in which the staff was installed, we had only been able, on the whole premises, to put into repair one barge dormitory, with two cylindrical iron stoves. In this room there were thirty camp beds, and three tables, at which the boys ate, and did their lessons. Another large dormitory, a dining room, two classrooms, and an office, awaited their turn to be put into repair.

We had one and a half changes of bed clothes, and no other linen at all. Almost our only contact with wearing apparel consisted in endless appeals to the Department of Public Education, and other departments.

The Chief of the Gubernia Department of public Education who had so confidently called the colony into being, had been transferred to another job, and his successor, who bad more important work to do, displayed little interest in us.

The atmosphere at the Gubernia Department of Public Education was far from propitious to our dreams of prosperity. At that time the Gunernia Department of Public Education consisted in a conglomeration of rooms big and little, and all sorts of individuals, but the true pedagogical creative units were not so much rooms or people, as tables. Rickety, with peeling surfaces, once red or black, these erstwhile desks, dressing tables and card tables, surrounded by equally heterogeneous chairs, represented the various departments, as testified to by notices hung on the walls over each table. Most of the tables were deserted, since the human appendage of any given table was as a rule not so much the head of his department as bookkeeper or something else in some other commissariat. Should a figure suddenly happen to appear behind any of the tables – all those waiting their turn would make a rush at him. The ensuing conversations were restricted to inquiries as to whether this was the right department, or another should he applied to – and if so why, and which one? And if this was not the right department, why had the comrade who was at that table over there last Saturday, said it was? After successfully elucidating these points, the head of the department hastened to weigh anchor, and disappeared with the rapidity of a shooting star.

Our faltering perambulations around the tables got us nowhere. And so, in the winter of 1921, our colony was not much like an educational establishment. Tattered padded jackets barely covered the boys' naked bodies; but seldom could the remains of a crumbling shirt be made out beneath a jacket. The first batch of boys, who had arrived so well-dressed, did not long stand out among the others: chopping wood, kitchen duty and work in the laundry, educational as all these tasks were, had disastrous effects upon clothing. By March our boys might have evoked the envy of an actor playing the part of the Miller in Dargomyzhsky's *Water Pixy*. Very few of them had boots, most of them winding strips of cotton or linen, kept on with string, round their feet. And even in this primitive form of footwear there was a shortage.

Our food known as kondyor [aA thin millet gruel – Tr.]. Other forms of norishment were not to be counted on. In those days there were various categories of food rations – normal rations, increased rations, nations for delicate individuals, rations for healthy individuals, rations for "defective" children, sanatorium rations, hospital rations. By the exercise of the most subtle diplomacy, by begging, by strategy, through the appeal of our wretched looks, even by hints at the danger of a revolt among the boys, we sometimes angled a sanatorium ration, or some other augmented allowance. Such rations ostensibly included milk, fats galore, and white bread. Of course we got nothing of the sort, but we did get extra allowance of black bread and some groats for a time. Every month or so we suffered a strategic defeat, which would degrade us to the condition of ordinary mortals again, and then we had to start all over again weaving our intricate web of open and secret diplomacy. Sometimes we actually managed to get meat, smoked fish, and candy rations, but this only made it harder to bear when it subsequently appeared that only mental defectives, and not moral defectives, were entitled to such luxuries.

Occasionally, overstepping the limits of the strictly pedagogical sphere, we made sallies into outlying domains, such as the Gubernia Commissariat for Supplies, or the Food Commissariat of the First Reserve Army, or some other more or less appropriate authority. The Department of Public Education severely discountenanced such irregular proceedings, and our sallies had to be made in secret.

All we had to do was to arm ourselves with a paper inscribed with the simple but expressive legend: "The Colony for Juvenile Delinquents requests one hundred poods of rye flour for the use of its inmates."

At the colony itself we never used words like "delinquent," and our colony never bore such a title. In those days we were known as "moral defectives." But such a title, being too suggestive of educational authorities, would not have done when approaching outside departments.

Armed with my paper, I would station myself in the corridor of an appropriate department, just outside the door of the main office. A perpetual stream of visitors was always passing through this door. Sometimes the office was so crowded that anyone who liked could get in. Once inside, one only had to elbow one's way through the crowd towards the official seated at the table, and silently insert one's paper between his hands.

The heads of supply departments were as a rule but little versed in the intricacies of pedagogics, and would often fail to see any connection between "juvenile delinquents" and the educational system. Moreover, the emotional impact of the very words "juvenile delinquents" was an impressive one. It was therefore but seldom that an official would glance sharply at us with the words: "What made you come to us? Apply to your Department of Public Education."

More often this is what happened: the official, after due thought, would propound a series of questions.

"Who's supposed to supply you – the prison authorities?"

"Well, no, the prison authorities don't supply us. Our boys are miners, you see.

"Who does then?"

"Well, you see, that hasn't yet been established."

"How d'you mean 'hasn't been established'? Isn't that rather strange?"

At this point in the proceedings the official, jotting a few words on his pad, would tell us to come again in a week's time.

"In that case," I would suggest, "perhaps you could just let us have twenty poods to go on with."

"I can't give you twenty – you can have five for the present. And I'll investigate the matter as soon as I can."

Five poods was inadequate, and the conversation had taken a turn by no means in accordance with our plans which, naturally, had not provided for investigations of any sort.

The only outcome of such interviews which was acceptable to the Gorky Colony, was for the official, without putting any inconvenient questions, to receive our paper in silence, scribbling across one corner of it the single word: "Granted."

When this happened I would rush headlong back to the colony.

"Kalina Ivanovich! An order! A hundred poods! Quick, get hold of some men and go and fetch it before they have time to make investigations."

Kalina Ivanovich would stoop gleefully over the paper.

"A hundred poods! Fancy that! Where does it come from?"

"Can't you see? The Gubernia Commissariat for Supplies for the Gubernia Department for Jurisdiction!"

"Whatever does that mean? But never mind – we're not particular where it comes from!"

The primary need of man is food. The clothing situation was not, therefore, so depressing to us as the food problem. Our charges were perpetually hungry, and this complicated to a considerable extent the task of their moral re-education. And they were only able to satisfy their appetite to a very small extent by private enterprise.

One of the principal forms of their private food industry was fishing. This was a strenuous occupation in winter. The easiest method was to pillage the yateri (nets in the form of a four-faceted pyramid) set up in a neighbouring stream and in our lake by the inhabitants of the hamlet. The instinct of self-preservation, and a certain common sense in regard to their own practical interests which is inherent in human nature, restrained the boys from carrying off the actual nets, but a day came hen this golden rule was broken by one of them.

This was Taranets. Sixteen years of age, he was from an old-established family of thieves, slender, pock-marked, gay, witty. He was a splendid organizer, and a most enterprising individual, but he had little respect for the interests of the collective. Having stolen several yateri from the river, he brought them into the colony. The owners of the nets came in his wake, and the affair culminated in a great row. After this the farmers began to keep watch over their nets, and our fishermen rarely managed to plunder them. Not long after, however, Taranets and a few other boys became the proud possessors of nets of their own, presented to them by a mysterious "friend in the town." With the aid of these nets our fisheries soon became a flourishing concern. At first fish was enjoyed by the privileged few, but towards the end of the winter Taranets imprudently decided to include me among the elect.

He came to my room with a plate of fried fish.

"I've brought you some fish."

"So I see, but I'm not going to accept it."

"Why not?" "Because it wouldn't be right. Everyone in the colony ought to get some."

Taranets flushed with indignation.

"Why should they? I get the nets, I catch the fish, I get soaked through in the river, and now I'm to share it with everyone!"

"All right, take your fish away, I didn't get any nets, and I didn't get soaked though."

"But this is a present."

"And I'm not going to accept it. I don't like the whole business. There's something wrong."

"What's wrong?"

"I'll tell you what: you didn't buy the nets, did you? You say they were given to you'"

"That's right!"

'And who were thy meant for? Only for you? Or for the whole colony?"

"What do you mean – the whole colony? They were given to me."

And I consider that they were meant for me and for all of us. Whose frying pans do you use? Your own? No – everyone's! And the sunflower oil you wheedle out of the cook – whose is that, d'you think? Everyones, of course! And the wood, the stove, the pails? Well – what have you to say to that? I have only to confiscate your yateri, and that would be the end of it. But it's your uncomradely spirit that's worst of all. What if the nets are yours – you have your comrades to think of. Anyone can catch fish."

"All right," said Taranets, "have it your own way. But do have some fish!"

I accepted the fish, and from that day, everyone took a turn at fishing, and the catch was sent to the kitchen.

Another unofficial means of procuring food consisted in visits to the market. Every day Kalina Ivanovich would harness Laddie, our Kirghiz, and set forth to procure provisions, an onslaught on the respective departments. Two or three of the boys who had reasons of their own for going to town – for medical treatment perhaps, or to appear before some commission – would insist on accompanying him, to help him by holding Laddie's head when necessary. These lucky ones would return from the town with full stomachs, and usually brought something good for their comrades with them. There was not a single case of anyone getting run in at the market. The spoils obtained during these sallies were given a legitimate aspect: "My aunt gave it to me," "I met a friend," and so on. I tried not to insult any member of our colony by base suspicions, and invariably accepted these explanations. What good could my distrust do, anyhow? The famished, grubby lads, wildly searching for food, did not seem to me suitable material for the propagation of morals of any sort, on such trifling provocation was the snatching of a bublik [rings of cracknel dough – tr.], or a pair of boot-soles from a market stall.

Our unutterable poverty had its good side: everyone – director, teachers and pupils – was equally hungry and equally needy. Our salaries were worth very little in those days, and all had to put up with the same wretched kondyor and go about in almost the same tattered condition. All through the winter I had practically no soles to my boots, and bits of my portyanki [strips of cloth or linen bound round foot and ankle, and worn instead of sack inside high boots. – Tr.] were always sticking out. The one exception was Ekaterina Grigoryevna, in her scrupulously brushed and tended dresses.

4

OPERATIONS ON THE HOME FRONT

In February, a bundle of notes almost equivalent to my six months' salary disappeared from one of my drawers.

At that time my room was office, teachers' room, accountant's office, and pay desk, since I fulfilled the corresponding functions in my own person. The bundle of crisp banknotes had disappeared from a locked drawer which bore not the slightest traces of having been forced.

I informed the boy's of this the same evening, asking them to return the money, pointing out that I could adduce no proof of theft, and might easily have been accused of embezzlement. The boys heard me out in grim silence, and dispersed. After this meeting I was waylaid in the dark courtyard on the way to my room in the wing by two of the boys – Taranets and a slight, agile lad named Gud.

"We know who took the money," whispered Taranets, "only we couldn't say so in front of everyone; we don't know where it's hidden. And if we peached, he'd run away with the money."

"Who was it?"

"There's a chap –" began Taranets, but Gud shot him a lowering glance, obviously not approving of his tactics.

"What's the good of talking? He ought to have his mug pushed in."

"And who's going to do it?" retorted Taranets. "You? He could knock you into a cocked hat!"

"Why not tell me who it was. I'll speak to him myself," I said.

"That wouldn't do!"

Taranets was all for a conspiratorial secrecy.

"Well, just as you like," I said, shrugging my shoulders. And I went off to bed.

The next morning Gud found the money in the stable. Someone had stuffed it between the bar of the narrow window, and the notes lay scattered all over the place. Gud, in a frenzy of joy, came running up to me with his fists full of crumpled banknotes in wild disorder.

In his ecstasy Gud capered all over the colony, the other boys were radiant, and kept running into my room to have a look at me. Only Taranets strode about, his head held proudly erect. I refrained from questioning either him or Gud about their activities subsequent to our conversation of the previous night.

Two days later someone wrenched the padlocks off the door of the cellar, and made off with a few pounds of lard – our entire stock of fats, and the padlocks themselves. A day or two later the storeroom window was taken out, and some sweets we had been saving up for the anniversary of the February Revolution, together with a few jars of cart grease, were missing. The cart grease was worth its weight in gold to us.

Kalina Ivanovich actually began to lose flesh; turning his wan visage upon one boy after another, and puffing smoke into their faces, he tried to reason with them:

"Look here! It's all for you, you sons-of-bitches! You're robbing yourselves, you parasites!"

Taranets evidently knew more about it than anyone else, but would say nothing outright, it apparently not suiting his book to give the show away. The boys expressed themselves freely about it, but it was the sporting aspect which appealed to them. They could not be brought round to the view that it was themselves who were being robbed.

In the dormitory I shouted at them in bitter rage:

"Who do you think you are? Are you human beings, or are you – ?"

"We're gangsters!" called a voice from a bed at the other end of the room. "Gangsters-that's what we are!"

"Shucks! You're not Gangsters! You're just sneak thieves, stealing from one another! Now you haven't any lard, and be hanged to you! There'll be no sweets for the anniversary. No one's going to give us any more. You can go without – I don't care!"

"But what can we do, Anton Semyonovich? We don't know who did it. You don't know yourself, and no more do we!"

I had known all along that my urgings would be useless. The thief was obviously one of the bigger boys, of whom all the rest went in fear.

The next day I took two of the boys with me into town to try to rangle another fat ration. It took us several days, but in the end we did get some lard. They even issued us a fresh supply of sweets after haranguing us at length for our inability to hold on to what we had already been given. When we got back, we spent the evenings in an exhaustive narration of our adventures. At last the lard was brought to the colony and stored in the cellar. The same night it was stolen.

I was almost glad when this happened. Now, I thought, the common, collective nature of our interests will assert itself, and arouse greater zeal in the matter of clearing up the thefts. As a matter of fact, though all the boys seemed downcast, there was no special display of zeal, and after the first impression had passed, they fell again under the spell of the sporting interest: who was it that worked so adroitly?

A few days later a horse-collar was missing, and now we couldn't even go into town. We had to go from house to house begging the loan of one for a few days.

Thefts had become everyday occurrences. Every morning something or other would be found to be missing: an axe, a saw, a pot or a pan, a sheet, a saddle strap, a pair of reins, provisions. I tried not going to bed, pacing the yard with my revolver handy, but of course I couldn't keep this up more than two or three nights. I asked Osipov to stand guard for one night, but he showed such terror at the prospect that I never brought it up again.

My suspicions fell on many of the boys, not excluding Gud and Taranets. But I could produce no evidence whatsoever, and was compelled to keep my suspicions to myself.

Zadorov, laughing uproariously, asked me facetiously:

"Did you really think, Anton Semyonovich, that it would be all work, work in a labour colony, and not a spot of fun? Just you wait – there's more to come! And what d'you mean to do to the one you catch?"

"Send him to prison."

"Is that all? I thought you intended to beat him up."

One night he came out into the yard, fully dressed.

"I'll walk up and down with you for a bit."

"See that the thieves don't have it in for you, that's all!"

"Oh, they know you're on watch tonight, and they won't go out stealing. So that's all right."

"You're afraid of them, Zadorov, aren't you? Own up, now!"

"Afraid of the thieves? Of course I am! But me being afraid or not isn't the point – you know yourself, Anton Semyonovich, that it's not the thing to peach on one's pals."

"But it's you yourself who is being robbed."

"Me? There's nothing of mine here."

"But you live here."

"You call this living, Anton Semyonovich? Is this life? Nothing will come of this colony of yours. You might as well give it up! You'll see, as soon as they've stolen all there is to be stolen, they'll run away. You should simply engage a couple of hefty watchmen with rifles."

"I'm not going to engage any watchmen with rifles."

"Why ever not?" asked Zadorov, astonished.

"Watchmen have to be paid and we're poor enough as it is; and what is more important — you've got to learn to realize that you yourselves are the owners."

The idea of hiring night watchmen was suggested by many of the boys. There was a regular debate held on the subject in the dormitory.

Anton Bratchenko, the best of our second batch of boys, argued as follows:

"While there's a watchman on guard, no one will go out stealing, and if anyone does, he'll get a load of shot you-know-where. And after walking about with it for a month he won't try any more tricks."

He was opposed by Kostya Vetovsky, a good-looking boy whose specialty in the world-at-large had been searching people's rooms with forged warrants. His was but a secondary part in these searches, the principal roles belonging to adults. Kostya himself, as attested in his "record," had never stolen anything, his interest in these operations being purely theoretical. Thieves he had alas despised. I had long noted the subtle and complex nature of this lad. What amazed me was the way he got on with the roughest of the boys, and his acknowledged authority on political matters.

"Anton Semyonovich is right," he insisted. "There mustn't be any watchmen. We don't all understand yet, but soon we shall realize that there must be no stealing in the colony. Even now lots of our chaps understand that. Soon we shall begin to stand guard ourselves. Shan't we, Burun?" he exclaimed, suddenly turning to Burun.

"Why not? There's no harm in standing guard," replied Burun.

In February our housekeeper resigned her post in the colony, I having found her a place in a hospital. One Sunday Laddie was driven up to her doorstep, and all her former cronies and the participants of her philosophical tea parties, began busily piling her innumerable bags and boxes on the sledge. The good old soul, swaying serenely atop of her treasures, set out at Laddie's habitual two kilometres an hour to take up her new life.

But Laddie returned late that same night, bringing back the old woman, who burst sobbing and crying into my room: she had been robbed of almost all her worldly possessions. Her cronies and other helpers had not put all her boxes and bags on to the sledge, but had carried some off – it was a flagrant case of robbery. I at once aroused Kalina Ivanovich, Zadorov and Taranets, and together we searched the colony through and through. Such a lot had been stolen that it had not been possible to hide everything properly. The housekeeper's treasures were found among bushes, in the lofts of outhouses, under the steps of a porch, and even simply pushed beneath beds and behind cupboards. And she certainly was a rich old woman: we found about a dozen new tablecloths, a quantity of sheets and towels, some silver spoons, various little glass receptacles, a bracelet, some earrings, and trifles of all sorts.

The old woman sat weeping in my room, which gradually filled with suspects – her former cronies and allies.

At first the boys denied everything, but after I shouted at them a bit the horizon began to clear. The old lady's friends turned out not to have been the principal thieves. They had restricted themselves to a few souvenirs, such as a napkin or a sugar bowl. Burun was found to have been the chief actor in the whole business. This discovery amazed everyone, especially me. From the very first, Burun had seemed the most reliable of all the boys, invariably grave, reserved, but friendly, and one of the best and most painstaking of our scholars. I was overwhelmed by the scope and thoroughness of his proceedings: he had stowed away the old woman's property by the bale. There could be no doubt that all the previous thefts in the colony had been the work of his hands.

At last I had arrived at the source of the evil! I brought Burun before a "People's Court" – the first to be held in the history of our colony.

In the dormitory, seated on beds and tables, were ranged the ragged and grim-visaged jury. The rays from the oil lamp lit up the tense faces of the boys, and the pale countenance of Burun, who, with his heavy, awkward frame and thick neck, looked like a typical American gangster.

In firm, indignant tones I described the crime to the boys: to have robbed an old woman, whose only happiness consisted in her wretched possessions, to have robbed one ho had shown more affection for the boys than anyone else in the colony, just when she had turned to tem for aid – surely anyone capable of this must have lost all human semblance, he must be, not simply a beast, but a skunk! A man should he able to respect himself, should be strong and proud, and not rob feeble old women of all.

Whatever the cause – whether my speech made a great impression, or whether the boys were sufficiently aroused anyhow – Burun became the object of a united and vehement attack. Little, shock-headed Bratchenko extended his arms towards Burun:

"Well! What can you say for yourself? You ought to be put behind bars, you ought to be thrown into quod! All through you we've gone hungry – it was you who took Anton Semyonovich's money!"

Burun made a sudden protest. "Anton Semyonovich's money? Prove it if you can!"

"Don't you worry about that!"

"Prove it then!"

"So you didn't take it – it wasn't you!"

"So it was me, was it?"

"Of course it was you!"

"I took Anton Semyonovich's money? Who's going to prove it?"

From the back of the room came the voice of Taranets:

"I am!"

Burun as thunderstruck. Turning towards Taranets, he seemed to he going to make a rebuttal, but changing his mind, only said:

"Well, what if I did? I put it back, didn't I?" Somewhat to my surprise the boys burst out laughing. They found the altercation highly entertaining. Taranets bore himself like a hero. Stepping forward he declared:

"But still he shouldn't be expelled. We've all of us done what we oughtn't to. But there'd be no objection to giving him a thorough licking."

Everyone fell silent. Burun let his unhurried glance travel over the pock-marked face of Taranets.

"I'd like to see you do it! What are you trying so hard for, anyway? You'll never be made manager of the colony, however you try! Anton will give me a licking, if necessary and it's none of your business."

Vetkovsky jumped up.

"What d'you mean 'none of our business': Fellows – is it, or is it not our business?"

"It is, it is!" shouted the boys. "We'll beat him up ourselves, and we'll do it better than Anton could!"

Someone was already making a rush at Burun. Bratchenko was shaking his fists in his very face, bawling. "You ought to be flogged, you ought!"

Zadorov whispered in my ear: "Take him away, or they'll beat him up!"

I dragged Bratchenko away from Burun. Zadorov shoved two or three of the other boys out of the way. With difficulty we put a stop to the din.

"Let Burun speak! Let him tell us!" cried Bratchenko.

Burun hung his head.

"There's nothing to tell. You're right, all of you! Let me go with Anton Semyonovich! Let him punish me as he thinks fit!"

Silence. I moved towards the door, fearing to allow the rage welling up within me to overflow. The boys dispersed to right and left to make way for me and Burun.

We crossed the dark yard picking our way among the snowdrifts in silence, I in front, he following.

My state of mind was deplorable. I regarded Burun as the very scum of humanity. I did not know what to do with him. He had been sent to the colony as one of a gang of thieves, most of whom – the adults – had been shot. He was seventeen years old.

Burun stood silently just inside the door. Seated at the table, I restrained myself with difficulty from throwing some heavy article at him, and thus putting an end to the interview.

At last Burun lifted his head, looked steadily into my eyes and said slowly, stressing every word, and scarcely able to repress his sobs:

"I... will... never... steal... again!"

"You're a liar! That's what you promised the Commission!"

"That was the Commission! And this is you! Give me any punishment you like, only don't expel me from the colony."

"And what is it you like about the colony?"

"I like it here. There's the lessons I want to learn. And if I stole, it was because I was always hungry."

"Very well! You'll stray under lock and key for three days and get nothing but bread and water. And don't you lay a finger on Taranets!"

"All right!"

Burun spent three days shut up in the little room next to the dormitory, that very room in which the tutors had slept in the former reform school. I didn't lock him up, he having given his word not to go out of the room without my permission. The first day I did send him nothing but bread and water, but the next day I took pity on him and sent a dinner to him. Burun attempted a proud refusal, but I shouted at him:

Come off that – I don't have any of your airs!"

He smiled faintly, shrugged his shoulders, and took up his spoon.

Burun kept his word. He never stole any thing again, either in the colony, or anywhere else.

5

MATTERS OF STATE IMPORTANCE

While our boys had been brought to regard the property of the colony with something like indifference, there were outside elements which took the deepest interest in it.

The main forces of these elements stationed themselves along the Kharkov highroad. Hardly a night passed without somebody being robbed on this road. A string of carts belonging to the local inhabitants would be held up by a single shot from a sawn-off rifle, and the robbers, without wasting words, would thrust the hand unencumbered by a rifle down the fronts of the women's dresses, while their greatly perturbed husbands, tapping the sided of their high hoots with the handles of their whips, would exclaim in astonishment: "Who would have thought it! We put our money in the safest place we knew – in our wives' dresses. And just look – they make straight for their bosoms!

What may be called collective robbery of this kind was seldom accompanied by bloodshed. The husbands, after having stood still for the time laid down by the robbers, would return to their senses, and come to the colony with graphic accounts of the occurrence. Collecting a posse armed with palings, I taking my revolver, we would rush to the highroad and make a thorough search in the adjoining woods. Only once was our search crowned with success; about half a kilometre from the road we came upon a small group hiding in a forest snowdrift. They answered the shouts of our lads with a single shot, and dispersed in all directions, but we managed to capture one, and take him back to the colony. Neither rifle nor loot was found on him, and he hotly denied all accusations. When handed over to the Gubernia Criminal Investigation Department, however, he was found to be a notorious bandit, and shortly after, the whole gang was arrested. The Gubernia Executive Committee expressed its appreciation to the Gorky Colony.

But the robberies on the highroad went on as before. Towards the end of the winter our boys began to come upon indications of some "sticky business" perpetrated in the night. Once we caught sight of an arm protruding out of the snow between the pine trees. Digging around it, we found the body of a woman, killed by a shot in the face. Another time, in the bushes just beside the road, we found a dead man, in a waggoner's coat, with his skull broken in.

We awoke one morning to see two men dangling from the trees at the outskirts of the forest. While awaiting the arrival of the coroner, they hung thus for two whole days, staring at the colony with bulging eyes.

Far from displaying any fear in regard to such phenomena, the colonists did not attempt to conceal their interest in them. In the spring, when the snow had melted, they would scour the woods for skulls gnawed clean by foxes, mount them on sticks, and carry them into the colony for the express purpose of scaring Lydia Petrovna. As it was, the teachers lived in perpetual terror, trembling in their beds lest at any moment a gang of robbers should burst into the colony, and a massacre begin. The Osipovs, whom general opinion credited with possessions worth stealing, were the most terrified of all.

One evening towards the end of February, when our cart, loaded with all sorts of provisions, was crawling home from the town at its usual rate, it was held up just at the turning leading to the colony. On the cart were grain and sugar, which for some reason did not appeal to the highwaymen. Kalina Ivanovich had no valuables on him but his pipe. This circumstance aroused the righteous indignation of the robbers, who struck Kalina Ivanovich over the head, so that he fell into the snow, where he lay till they disappeared. Gud, who was always entrusted with the care of Laddie, remained a passive witness of the incident. When they got back to the colony, they both poured detailed accounts of the adventure into our ears, Kalina Ivanovich stressing the dramatic side, while Gud emphasized the comic aspect. But a unanimous resolution was passed, henceforward always to send an escort from the colony to meet the cart on its way home.

We stuck to this resolution for two years. And we gave these sallies along the highroad la military name – "straddling the road."

An escort usually consisted of about ten persons. Sometimes I would be one of them, as had a revolver. I couldn't trust all and sundry with it, and without a revolver our posse was felt to be scarcely strong enough. To Zadorov alone I would occasionally entrust the revolver, which he would proudly strap over his rags.

Road duty was an extremely interesting occupation. We would dispose ourselves over one and a half kilometres of the road, from the bridge over the river, to the turning leading to the colony. The boys tried to keep themselves warm by jumping about in the snow, shouting to one another the while, so as not to lose contact, and striking terror of sudden death into the soul of the belated traveller in the dusk. Homeward-faring villagers, whipping up their horses, dashed silently past regularly recurring figures of a most sinister aspect. Sovkhoz directors and other representatives of authority swept by on their rattling carts, taking care to let the boys see their double-barrelled guns and sawn-off rifles; pedestrians lingered by the bridge in the hope of enlisting the support of numbers in the form of fellow wayfarers.

When I was with them, the boys never got tough, or scared travellers, but without my restraining influence they sometimes got out of hand, and Zadorov insisted on my accompanying them, even though it meant giving up the revolver I started going out with the escort every time, but I let Zadorov carry the revolver, not wishing to deprive him of his well-earned enjoyment.

When our Laddie came into sight we would greet him with shouts of "Halt! Hands up!" But Kalina Ivanovich would only smile and start puffing at his pipe with exaggerated satisfaction. His pipe lasted him the whole way, and the familiar saying: "the hours passed unnoticed" was fully applicable here.

The escort would gradually fall into line behind Laddie, and enter the grounds of the colony in a gay crowd, eagerly inquiring of Kalina Ivanovich the latest items of news with regard to provisions.

This same winter we went in for operations the importance of which extended far beyond the interests of the colony – operations of national importance. The forest guard came to our colony and asked us to help to keep watch in the woods, there being too much illicit felling going on for his staff to cope with.

The guarding of the state forest considerably raised us in our own estimation, provided us with extremely interesting work, and ultimately brought us in no small profit. Night. Day will soon be breaking, but it is still quite dark. I am waked by a tap on my window. Opening my eyes I can just make out through the frosty patterns on the windowpane, a nose pressed flat against it, and a tousled head.

"What's up?"

"Anton Semyonovich, they're cutting down trees in the woods!"

Lighting my improvised lamp, I dress rapidly, pick up my revolver and double-barrelled gun, and go out.

On the doorstep on one such night were those ardent lovers of nocturnal adventure – Burun, and a guileless little chap named Shelaputin. Burun took over the gun and we entered the wood.

"Where are they?"

"Listen!"

We came to a stop. At first I could hear nothing, but gradually I began to make out, amidst the confused sounds of the night, and the sound of our own breathing, the dull thud-thud of steel against wood. We followed the sound, stooping to avoid detection, the branches of young pine trees scratching our faces, knocking off my glasses, and scattering snow over us. Every now and then the sound of the axe would cease, so that we didn't know which direction to take and had to wait patiently for it to begin again. And ever and anon the sounds would be repeated, getting louder and nearer every minute.

We tried to approach as quietly as possible, so as not to frighten away the thief. Burun lumbered along with a certain bear-like agility, the diminutive Shelaputin tripping after him, pulling his jacket closer to keep himself warm. I took up the rear.

At last we reached our goal. We posted ourselves behind the trunk of a pine tree, just in time to see a tall slender tree quivering throughout its length – at its base a belted figure. After a few tentative, fumbling strokes the wielder of the axe straightened himself, glanced round, and again resumed his felling. We were now about five yards away from him. Burun, holding the gun in readiness, muzzle upwards, looked at me and held his breath. Shelaputin, crouching beside me, leaned against my shoulder and whispered:

"May I? Is it time?"

I nodded. Shelaputin gave Burun's coat sleeve a tug.

The shot rang out with a terrific explosion, resounding through the trees.

Instinctively the man with the axe squatted down. Silence. We went up to him. Shelaputin knew his job, and the axe was already in his hands. Burun cried out in cheerful greetings:

"Ah! Moussi Karpovich! Good morning!"

He patted Moussi Karpovich on the shoulder, but Moussi Karpovich was unable to utter a single word in response. Trembling from head to foot, he kept mechanically flicking the snowflakes from the left sleeve of his coal.

"Where's your horse?" I asked.

Moussi Karpovich was still unable to speak, and Burun answered for him:

"There it is! Hi, you! Come over here!"

Only then did I observe, through the screen of pine branches, a horse's head and the shaft-bow of a farm cart.

Burun took Moussi Karpovich by the arm. "This way to the ambulance, Moussi Karpovich!" he said gaily.

At last Moussi Karpovich began to manifest signs of life. Taking off his cap, he passed his hand over his hair, whispering without looking at us: "My God! My God!"

Together we moved towards the sleigh. The sleigh was slowly turned, and soon we were moving over deep tracks now almost hidden by feathery snow. Our driver, a lad of fourteen or so, in an enormous cap and outsize boots, made clucking sounds to the horse, and shook the reins mournfully. He kept snuffling, and seemed thoroughly upset.

On nearing the outskirts of the wood Burun took the reins from the lad.

"You're going the wrong way!" he exclaimed. "If you were carrying a load, it would be the right way, but as you're only driving your Dad, this is the way."

"To the colony?" questioned the lad, but Burun did not give him back the reins, and turned the horse's head in the direction of the colony.

Day was beginning to break.

Suddenly Moussi Karpovich halted the horse by twitching at the reins over Burun's arm, at the same time, with his free hand, taking off his cap.

"Anton Semyonovich!" he pleaded. "Let me go! It's the very first time! We have no fire wood.... Do let me go!"

Burun angrily shook Moussi Karpovich's hand off the reins, but did not send the horse on, waiting to see what I was going to say.

No, no, Moussi Karpovich!" I said. "That won't do! We'll have to draw up a deposition. This is an affair of State – you know that!"

Shelaputin's silvery treble rose towards the dawn:

"And it's not the first time either! It's not the first time, but the third! Once your Vassili was caught, and the next time...."

Burun's hoarse baritone cut across the silver music of the treble:

"What's the good of us hanging about here? You, Andrei, get away home! You're just small fry! Go and tell your mother, Dad's been caught. Let her get something ready to send to him."

Andrei, frightened out of his wits, scrambled down from the cart and ran at top speed towards the farmstead. We started on our way again. Just as we entered the colony grounds we encountered a group of lads setting out to meet us.

"Oh, oh! We thought you were being murdered, and we decided to come out and save you."

"The operation has been carried out with complete success!" laughed Burun.

Everyone crowded into my room. Moussi Karpovich, profoundly dejected, sat on a chair facing me. Burun took up his seat on the window-sill, still holding the gun. Shelaputin whispered the gruesome details of the night's adventure into the ears of his pals. Two of the boys were sitting on my bed, and the rest were ranged on benches, all absorbed in watching the process of the taking of a deposition.

The deposition was drawn up in heart-rending detail.

"You have twelve desyatins [about 2.7 acres] of land, haven't you? And three horses?"

"Horses!" groaned Moussi Karpovich. "You can't call that one a horse! It's only a two-year old."

"A three-year old!" insisted Burun, patting Moussi Karpovich kindly on the shoulder.

I went on writing:

"The cut was six inches deep...."

Moussi Karpovich flung out his arms: "Ah, now Anton Semyonovich! For God's sake! How d'you make that out? It was barely four!"

Suddenly Shelaputin, breaking off in the middle of his whispered narrative, measured about half a metre with his extended arms, and grinned cheekily into Moussi Karpovich's face.

"Like this?" he cried. "This is how deep it was, isn't it?"

Moussi Karpovich, pretending not to notice the interruption, submissively followed with his eyes the movements of my pen.

The deposition was completed. On leaving Moussi Karpovich shook hands with me with an air of injured innocence, and extended his hand to Burun as the eldest of the boys present.

"You shouldn't be doing this, lads," he said. "We've all got to live!"

Burun answered him with facetious courtesy: "Don't mention it! Always happy to oblige!" Then he was struck by a sudden thought:

"I say, Anton Semyonovich! What about the tree?"

This set us all to thinking. After all, the tree was almost felled, by tomorrow somebody would be sure to finish it off and take it away. Without waiting to hear the outcome of our musings, Burun made for the door. On his way out he flung a remark over his shoulder at the now thoroughly vanquished Moussi Karpovich:

"Don't you worry – we'll bring the horse back! Who's going with me, lads? All right – six will be enough. Is there a rope there, Moussi Karpovich?"

"It's tied to the sleigh."

Everyone went out. An hour later a long pine tree was brought into the colony. This was our time-honoured tradition, remained in the colony. For a very long time to come, whenever inventories are being checked, we shall say to one another:

"Where is Moussi Karpovich's axe?"

It was not so much moral expostulations or occasional outbursts of wrath, as this fascinating and vital struggle with hostile elements which fostered the first shy growth of a healthy collective spirit. Of an evening we would hold lengthy discussions, laughing our fill, sometimes embroidering upon the subjects of our adventures, and drawing ever closer to one another in the thick of these adventures, till we gradually became that integral unit known as the Gorky Colony.

6
THE CAPTURE OF THE IRON TANK

All this time our colony was gradually consolidating the material side of its existence. Neither extreme poverty, vermin, nor frost-bitten toes, could prevent our indulging in dreams of happier future. Despite the fact that our middle-aged Laddie and ancient seed-drill offered little hope for the development of agriculture, all our dreams revolved around farming. But so far these were only dreams. Laddie's horse-power was so inadequate to agricultural requirements that it was only by the wildest flight of fancy that he could be pictured drawing a plough. Besides, along with all the rest of us, Laddie was under nourished. It was with the greatest difficulty that we obtained straw for him – not to mention hay. All through the winter, driving him was a prolonged torture, and Kalina Ivanovich got a chronic pain in his right arm from the threatening motions with the whip without which Laddie refused to budge.

To crown all, the very soil on which our colony stood was unsuited to agricultural purposes. It as little better than sand, which a breath of wind sent shelving into dunes.

Even at this distance of time I am unable to understand how it was, situated as we were, that we dared to embark upon so wild a venture – one which was, nevertheless, destined to put us on our feet.

It all began in the most fantastic manner.

Fortune suddenly smiled upon us, and we obtained an order for oak logs. They had to be fetched straight from the woods where they were felled. Although these particular woods were within the boundary of our Village Soviet, we had never been so far in that direction before.

Having arranged to go there with two of our neighbours from the farmstead, they providing the horses, we set of on our travels into a strange land. When we got to the place, Kalina Ivanovich and I turned our attention to a distant line of poplars towering above the reeds of the frozen stream. Leaving the drivers among the fallen trees to load their sleighs and argue as to the probability of the logs falling off on the way, we crossed the ice, climbed a hill by a sort of avenue on the other side of the river, and found ourselves in a kingdom of the dead. Before us, in the most ruinous condition, stood almost a dozen buildings of varying sizes – houses, sheds, huts, outhouses, and the like. All were in about the same stage of dilapidation. Where once there had been stoves, there now lay heaps of bricks and lumps of clay, half-covered with snow. Floors, doors, windows, staircases, had all disappeared. Many of the partitions and ceilings were shattered, and here and there brick walls and foundations had been removed bodily. All that remained of the vast stables were the walls back and front, above which there towered, in blank melancholy, a remarkable iron tank or cistern which looked as if it had been freshly painted. On the whole estate this tank alone seemed to be imbued with life – everything else was stone-dead.

On one side of the yard stood a new two-storey house, left unstuccoed, but with some pretensions to style. Its lofty, spacious chambers retained fragments of plaster moulding and marble window-sills. At the opposite end of the yard there was a new stable built of hollow concrete. Even the most dilapidated of the buildings amazed us on closer examination by their solid workmanship, huge oak beams, sinewy ties, and slender rafters, and by the precision of all vertical lines. That powerful economic frame had not died of senility and disease, but had been violently destroyed in its prime.

Kalina Ivanovich groaned at the sight of so much wealth.

"Just look at it all!" he cried. "A river, garden – and what meadows!"

The river bounded the estate on three sides, gliding past that hill which was such a rarity on our plains. The orchard sloped towards the river in three terraces, the first planted with cherry trees, the second with apple trees and pear trees, and the lowest thickly covered with black currant hushes.

In a yard on the other side of the main building was a large, five-storey mill, its sails going full swing. From the workers at the mill we learned that the estate had belonged to the brothers Trepke, who had fled with Denikin's army, abandoning their houses with all that was in them at the time. All movable property had long ago found its a to the neighbouring village or Goncharovka and nearby farmsteads, and now the houses themselves were on their way out. Kalina Ivanovich was moved to eloquence.

"Savages!" he burst out. "Swine! Idiot! Look at all this property! Dwellings! Stables! Why couldn't you have lived here, sons-of-bitches? You could have moved in, farmed the place, drunk your coffee – but all you can think of is hacking at this frame with an axe. And what for? All because you must boil your precious dumplings, and you're too lazy to chop wood.... May the dumplings stick in your throats, you fools, you idiots! They'll go to their grave just as they are – no revolution will help the likes of them! Oh, the swine, oh, the rotters, the cursed blockheads! What the hell!"

Here Kalina Ivanovich turned to a passing worker from the mill.

"Could you tell me, Comrade," he asked, "how to get that tank up there? The one sticking up over the stable. It'll he ruined here, anyhow without doing any good to anyone."

"That tank? Damned if I know! The Village Soviet is responsible for everything here."

"I see. Well, that's something!" said Kalina Ivanovich, and he set out for home.

Striding home behind our neighbours' sleighs, over the smooth surface of the road, which was already beginning to yield to the influence of impending spring, Kalina Ivanovich indulged in daydreams: wouldn't it be nice if we could get hold of that tank, move it to the colony, and set it up in the attic over the laundry, thus converting the laundry into a steam bath?

The next morning, before setting out again for the forest, Kalina Ivanovich buttonholed me. "Do write me a paper for that there Village Soviet, there's a good chap! They no more need a rank than a dog needs hip pockets! And for us it would mean a steam bath."

To please him I gave Kalina Ivanovich a paper. Towards evening he returned, almost beside himself with rage.

"The parasites! They look at everything theoretically, they're incapable of a practical point of view! They say – drat them! – this here tank is state property. Did you ever hear of such idiots! Write me out another paper – I'll go straight to the Volost Executive Committee."

"How are you going to get there? It's twenty kilometres away. What'll you go in?"

"I know someone who's going that way, he'll give me a lift."

Kalina Ivanovich's plan for a steam bath appealed to everyone at the colony, but nobody believed he would be able to obtain the tank.

"Let's make one without it. We can make a wooden tank."

"A lot you understand! If people made tanks of iron, it means they knew what they were about! And I mean to get it, if I have to choke it out of them!"

"And how do you mean to get it over here? Is Laddie to haul it?"

"That'll be all right! Where there's a trough there'll always be pigs!"

Kalina Ivanovich came back from the Volost Executive Committee crosser than ever, and seemed to have forgotten all words which were not oaths.

Throughout the next week he followed me about, begging me, to the accompaniment of laughter from the boys, for yet another "paper to the Uyezd Executive Committee."

Leave me alone, Kalina Ivanovich! "I cried. "I have other things to think of besides this tank of yours!"

"Do write me out a paper!" he insisted. "It can't hurt you! Do you grudge the paper, or what? Just you write it out, and I'll bring you the tank."

I wrote out this paper, too, for Kalina Ivanovich. Thrusting it into his pocket, he at last relaxed into a smile.

"There can't be such an idiotic law – letting good property go to ruin, and no one lifting a finger! We're not living under the tsarist regime any more!"

But Kalina Ivanovich returned late in the evening from the Uyezd Executive Committee and did not put in an appearance either in the dormitory or in my room. He did not come to see me till the next morning, when he was coldly supercilious, aloofly dignified, fixing his eye upon a distant point out of the window.

"Nothing will come of it," he said tersely, handing me back the paper.

Right across our minutely detailed application was written curtly, in red ink, the one word, decisive and heartbreakingly final – "Refuse." Kalina Ivanovich brooded long and passionately over this reverse. For almost two weeks he lost his delightful elderly sprightliness.

The following Sunday, when March was dealing drastically with the remains of the snow, I invited some or the boys to come for a walk with me. They scraped together some warm garments, and we set out for... the Trepke estate.

"What if we move our colony over here!" I mused aloud.

"Over here?"

"To these houses."

"But they're not habitable!"

"We could put them into repair."

Zadorov burst out laughing and started spinning around the yard.

"We have three houses waiting to be repaired," he reminded me, "and we haven't been able to get them done all the winter."

"I know! But supposing we could get this place put into repair?"

"Oh! That would be some colony! A river – a garden – and a mill!"

We scrambled about among the ruins and let our fancy soar: here we'd have a dormitory, here a dining room, this would make a capital club, and there would be the school-rooms....

We came home exhausted but full of energy. In the dormitory a noisy discussion of the details of our future colony was held. Before separating for the night, Ekaterina Grigoryevna said:

"D'you know what, boys, it's not healthy to indulge in daydreams. It's not the Bolshevik way!" An awkward silence ensued in the dormitory. I cast a wild glance at Ekaterina Grigoryevna, and declared, bringing my fist down on the table with a bang:

"I'm telling you! In a month's time that estate will be ours! Is that the Bolshevik way?" The lads burst out laughing and cheering. I laughed with them, and so did Ekaterina Grigoryevna.

All through the night I sat up preparing a statement for the Gubernia Executive Committee.

A week later the Chief of the Gubernia Department of Public Education sent for me.

"Not a bad idea, that! Let's go and have a look at the place!"

Another week passed, and our project was being discussed before the Gubernia Executive Committee.

It appeared that the authorities had had this estate on their minds for quite a time. I availed myself of the opportunity to tell them of the poverty and neglected state of our colony, of our lack of prospects, and of the living collective which had nevertheless sprung up among us.

The chairman of the Gubernia Executive Committee said:

"The place wants a master, and here are people who want to get to work. Let them have it!" And here was I – an order in my hands for the former Trepke estate, comprising sixty desyatins of arable land, and my estimate for repairs approved. I stood in the middle of the dormitory hardly able to believe it was not all a dream, and around me an excited crowd of boys, a whirlwind of enthusiasm, a forest of uplifted arms...

"Do let us see it!" they begged.

Ekaterina Grigoryevna entered. The boys rushed at her, overflowing with good-natured raillery, Shelaputin's shrill treble ringing out:

"Is that the Bolshevik way, or what? Just you tell us!"

"What's the matter? What's happened?"

"Is this the Bolshevik way? Only look!"

No one was happier about it all than Kalina Ivanovich.

"You're a trump," he said, "it's like the preachers say: 'ask and ye shall find, knock and it shall be opened unto you' and thou shalt receive–' "

"A smack in the jaw!" interolated Zadorov.

"That's not a smack in the jaw," said Kalina Ivanovich, turning to him, "that's an order."

You knocked for a tank, and all you got was a smack in the face. But this is an affair of state importance, not just something we asked for."

"You're too young to interpret the scriptures," said Kalina Ivanovich jocosely – nothing could have put him out at this moment.

The very next Sunday he accompanied me and a crowd of boys to inspect our new domain. Kalina Ivanovich's pipe sent triumphant puffs of smoke into the face of every brick in the Trepke ruins. He strutted proudly past the tank.

"When are we going to move the tank?" asked Burun with perfect gravity.

"Why should we move it, the parasite?" said Kalina Ivanovich. "We'll find a use for it here. These stables have been built according to the last word in technique, you know!"

7
"EVERYBODY'S GOOD FOR SOMETHING!"

We could not immediately translate into the language of facts our jubilations on coming into the Trepke heritage. The release of the money ad material required was, for one reason or another, delayed. But the main obstacle was the Yolomak, a small but mischievous stream. Its course lay between our colony and the Trepke estate, and in April it showed itself to be a formidable representative of the elements. At first it flooded its banks with slow obstinacy, only to retire still more slowly within its modest limits, leaving behind it fresh disaster – mud impassable either by man or beast.

"Trepke," as we had begun to call our new acquisition, remained, therefore, a set of ruins for a long time to come. In the meantime the boys revelled in the coming of spring. In the morning, after breakfast, while waiting for the bell to summon them to work, they would range themselves outside the barn, basking in the sunlight, exposing their chests to its rays, and strewing the yard with their carelessly flung jackets. They were capable of sitting in the sun without speaking for hours on end, making up for the winter months when it had been so hard to keep warm, even in the dormitory.

The sound of the bell compelled them to get up and shuffle reluctantly to their respective places, but even during work they would find pretexts and means to warm their sides in the sun every now and then.

In the beginning of April, Vaska Poleshchuk ran away. He was not what you would call a prepossessing member of the colony. I had come across him in December, at one of the tables in the Department of Public Education – a dirty, ragged lad surrounded by a small crowd. The Department for Defective Juveniles had declared him a mental defective, and was sending him to a home for such boys. The tatterdemalion protested, weeping that he was not mad at all, that they had got him to town by a trick, telling him they were taking him to Krasnodar, where they had promised to put him into a school.

"What are you yelling for?" I asked him.
"They say I'm mad!"
"Allright – I heard you! Stop bawling, and come with me."
"How are we going?"
"On our two feet! Come on!"

The little chap's countenance was not exactly an index of intelligence. But he exuded energy, and I thought to myself. "What the hell! Everybody's good for something!"

The Department for Defective Juveniles was glad to be relieved of its charge, and we set out at a brisk march for the colony. On the way he unfolded the usual tale, beginning with the death of parents and dire poverty. His name was Vaska Poleshchuk. He was, in his own words, "a casualty," having taken part in the storming of Perekop.

On his first day in the colony he went completely mum, and neither teachers nor boys could get a word out of him. Probably it had been something of this sort which had forced the pundits to the conclusion that Poleshchuk was a defective.

The other boys were intrigued by his silence, and asked my leave to apply methods of their own to him – only give him a good fright, they said, and he'd talk all right. I flatly forbade any such measures. I already regretted having brought this mute into the colony.

And then, Poleshchuk suddenly began to talk, without the slightest apparent provocation. It may have been simply the warm spring day, fragrant with the exhalations which the sun drew from the still humid earth. He talked with shrill energy, accompanying his words with bursts of laughter, and sudden leaps. He would not leave my side for days on end, chattering endlessly about the delights of life in the Red Army, and about Commander Zubata.

"What a man! His eyes so black, so blue – when he looks at you, you go all cold! When he was at Perekop our own chaps were afraid of him...."

"You keep on and on about Zubata," the boys said. "Do you know his address?"

"How do you mean – address?"

"His address – do you know where to write to him?"

"No, I don't. Why should I write I'll just go to Nikoliayev, and I'll find him there."

"He'll send you packing!"

"He won't either! It was the other one who sent me away. He was the one who said: 'what's the use of our troubling ourselves with this nitwit?' I'm not a nitwit, am I?"

For days on end Poleshchuk chattered to all and sundry about Zubata – his good looks, his courage, and how he never used really bad language when he swore.

"Do you mean to bolt?" the boys asked him.

Poleshehuk would cast a glance in my direction and fall into a reverie. He evidently thought long over this, and when the rest had forgotten all about him, and were deep in some other subject, he would suddenly get hold of the boy who'd put the question to him, and ask:

"Would Anton be angry?"

"What about?"

"Well – if I were to bolt?"

"I should think he would! After all the trouble he took about you!"

Vaska fell into his reverie again.

And one day, just after breakfast, Shehaputin came running into my room.

"Vaska's not anywhere in the colony. He didn't have breakfast – he's bolted! Gone to Zubata!"

The lads clustered around me in the yard. They wanted to see how I was going to take Vaska's departure.

"Poleshchuk did run away, after all...."

"It's the spring....

"He's gone to the Crimea...."

"Not the Crimea – Nikolaev...."

"If we went to the station, we might still catch him!"

Vaska might be nothing to boast of, but his defection impressed me painfully. It was embittering to have to admit that here as one who could not accept our modest offering, and had gone in quest of something better. At the same time I knew well enough that our poverty-stricken colony was not calculated to attach people to us.

To the boys I said:

"To hell with him! If he's gone – he's gone! We have other things to think of."

In April, Kalina Ivanovich began to plough. This was made possible by the most unexpected event. The Commission for Juvenile Delinquency had a horse thief – a juvenile one – brought before it. The culprit was sent to some place or other, but the owner of the horse was not to be found. The Commission went through a week of agony, not being accustomed to deal with such cumbersome material evidence as a horse. Then came Kalina Ivanovich to the Commission, beheld the sorry plight of the unoffending beast, forlorn in the middle of the cobbled yard, seized its bridle without a word and led it to the colony, pursued by the relieved sighs of the members of the Commission. At the colony Kalina Ivanovich was greeted with cries of rapture and astonishment. Gud took the bridle from Kalina Ivanovich into his trembling hands, while into the wide spaces of his soul the exhortation of Kalina Ivanovich sank deep:

"Take care, now! She's not to be treated like you treat one another! She's only an animal – she can't speak. She can't complain, you know that yourselves! But if you tease her, and she gives you a kick on the noddle, it'll be no use going bawling to Anton Semyonovich! You can bawl your heart out, but it won't help you. And I'll break your skull for you!"

The rest of us clustered around this solemn group, and no one dreamed of resenting the terrible threats hanging over Gud's head. Kalina Ivanovich stood beaming, pipe in mouth, while delivering this intimidating oration. The horse was a chestnut, still fairly young, and well nourished.

Kalina Ivanovich and some of the lads busied themselves for several days in the shed. With the aid of hammers, screwdrivers, and odd bits of iron, and to the accompaniment of endless sententious harangues, they managed to patch up some sort of a plough from odds and ends found among the refuse left by the former colony.

At last the blissful moment arrived when Burun and Zadorov followed the plough. Kalina Ivanovich kept up with them, exclaiming:

"Oh, the parasites! They can't even plough – there's a fault, and there, and there!" The lads retorted good-naturedly:

"Show us the way yourself, Kalina Ivanovich! You've probably never ploughed a furrow in your life!"

Kalina Ivanovich, taking his pipe out of his mouth, looked as fierce as he could:

"Me? I've never ploughed? You don't need to have ploughed yourself! You've got to understand! I can see when you go wrong – and you can't!"

Gud and Bratchenko accompanied them. Gud watched the ploughmen furtively to see they didn't maltreat the horse, while Bratchenko simply followed Red with his enamoured gaze. He had appointed himself stableboy under the aegis of Gud.

Some of the older lads had begun fiddling about with the old seed-drill in the shed. Sofron Golovan was shouting at them, filling their impressionable souls with admiration for his vast technical erudition.

Sofron Golovan possessed certain vivid characteristics which distinguished him among his fellow mortals. Of enormous stature, full of animal spirits always a little tipsy but never really drunk, he had his own opinions about everything under the sun, and wonderfully ignorant ones they were. Golovan was an extraordinary mixture of kulak and blacksmith: he owned two huts, three horses, two cows and a smithy. For all his kulak wealth, however, he was an able smith, and his hands were much clearer than his head. Sofron's smithy stood right on highroad, next to the inn, and it was to this topographical situation that the Golovan family owed its rise to fortune.

Golovan came to the colony on the invitation of Kalina Ivanovich. Tools of a sort were found in our sheds, though the smithy itself was in a broken-down condition. Sofron offered to bring with him his own anvil and forge, as well as a few additional tools, and to work in the capacity of instructor. He was even ready to repair the smithy at his own expense. At first I could not understand this eagerness to help us, but my mind was cleared by Kalina Ivanovich during his evening "report."

Thrusting a scrap of newspaper down my lamp chimney to light his pipe, Kalina Ivanovich said:

"That parasite Sofron has a good reason for wanting to come to us. The muzhiks are alter him, you know, and he's afraid they'll confiscate his smithy; and if he stays here, you know, it'll look as if he's working for the Soviets."

"What shall we do about him?" I asked.

"Let him stay! Who else would come to us? Where could we find a forge? And the tools? We have nowhere to lodge an instructor – if we used one of the huts, we'd have to call in carpenters. And after all–" Kalina Ivanovich screwed up his eyelids. "What if he is a kulak? He'll work just as well as if he was an honest man."

Kalina Ivanovich, who had been thoughtfully sending puffs of smoke towards my low ceiling, suddenly broke into a smile:

"The muzhiks, the parasites, will confiscate his smith anyhow, and what good will that do anyone? It'll just stand idle. We might as well have a smithy – Sofron will get what's coming to him, anyhow. We'll string him along, and send him about his business when we've done with him. 'This here is a Soviet institution,' we'll tell him, 'and you, you son-of-a-bitch, you're nothing but a bloodsucker, you're an exploiter of the people.' Ho-ho-ho...!"

We had by now received a part of the money for repairing the estate, but it came to so little that our ingenuity was taxed to the utmost. Everything had to be done by ourselves, and we needed a smithy and a carpenter's shop of our own. Joiners' benches of a sort we had, tools we bought, and soon we acquired a carpentry instructor. Under his guidance the lads fell energetically to sawing boards brought from the town, making window frames and doors for the new colony. Unfortunately the technical level of our carpenters was so low that the process of making windows and doors for our new life was at first excruciatingly difficult. Our work in the smithy – and there was plenty of it – was at first nothing to boast of, either. Sofron was in no hurry to bring the reconstruction phase of the Soviet state to an end, though the pay he got as instructor was not much, and on pay day he would demonstratively send one of the boys with his whole salary to an old woman who ran a still, for "three bottles of the best."

I knew nothing about this for some time. I was jus then altogether under the spell of the magic words: staples, hinge plates, hinges, latches.... The boys were just as excited as I was by the sudden expansion of our work. Very soon carpenters and locksmiths cropped up among them, and we actually found ourselves with a little money to spend.

We were thrilled by the animation which the smithy brought with it. At eight o'clock the cheerful ring of the anvil resounded throughout the colony; laughter was always coming from the smithy, around the wide-open doors of which two or three villagers were invariably hanging about, discussing farming, taxation, Verkhola, the chairman of the Kombed, [Poor Peasants' Committee – Tr.] fodder, and our seed-drill. We shed the farmers' horses, put tires on their cart wheels, and repaired their ploughs. We charged the poorer peasants half rates, and this served as a starting point for endless discussions on social justice and injustice.

Sofron offered to make us a gig. Some sort of a body was dug up from beneath the rubbish in which the sheds of the colony abounded. Kalina Ivanovich brought a couple of axles from the town. For two whole days these axles were beaten on the anvil by hammers big and small. At last Sofron announced that the gig was quite ready but for the springs and heels. And we had neither springs nor wheels. I looked for secondhand springs all over the town, while Kalina Ivanovich set out on a long journey into the depths of the country.

He was away a whole week, and brought back two pairs of brand-new wheel rims and a veritable budget of impressions, the main one being: what ignorant folk these muzhiks are.

One day, Sofron brought with him Kozyr – an inhabitant of the farmstead. He was a quiet, courteous man with a perpetual bright smile, much addicted to making the sign of the cross. He had only recently been discharged from a lunatic asylum, and trembled all over whenever his wife's name was mentioned, for she it was who had been the cause of the incorrect diagnosis of the gubernia psychiatrists. Kozyr was a wheelwright. He could scarcely contain his delight at being asked to make four wheels. The circumstances of his home life, and his own ascetic leanings, prompted him to make us a purely practical proposal: "Comrades – (God forgive me!) – you sent for the old man, didn't you? And now supposing I stay here and live with you?"

"But we have nowhere to put you!"

"Don't let that worry you! I'll find a place for myself. The Lord will help me! It's summer now, and when winter comes we'll manage somehow. I can live in that shed over there, I'll be quite comfortable!"

"All right – you can stay!"

Kozyr crossed himself and attacked the practical side of the question immediately.

"We'll get rims! Kalina Ivanovich couldn't, but I know how to set about it. The rims will come to us – the muzhiks will bring them themselves, you'll see! God won't let us want!"

"But we don't need any more rims, Pop!"

"Don't need them – don't need them? God bless my soul! You may not need them, but others do! How can a muzhik live without a wheel? You can sell them and make money, and the boys will be the gainers."

Kalina Ivanovich laughed, and supported Kozyr's supplications.

"Let him stay, damn him! Nature's such a grand thing you know – even a human being may be of some use!"

Kozyr became a favourite throughout the colony. He took up his quarters in the little room nest to the dormitories. Here he was perfectly safe from his wife, who was indeed a virago. The boys hugely enjoyed defending Kozyr from her incursions. This lady invariably made her appearance at the colony in a whirlwind of shrieks and oaths. Demanding her husband's return to the bosom of her family, she accused me, the boys, the Soviet government, and "that tramp Sofron," of destroying her domestic felicity. With unconcealed irony the boys would assure her that Kozyr was no good as a husband, and that the making of wheels was of far greater importance than domestic felicity. Kozyr himself would sit huddled up in his little room all the time, patiently waiting for the attack to be finally beaten off. It was only when the voice of the injured spouse could be heard from the other side of the lake, whence mere snatches of her pious wishes for him could be made out – "...sons-of-... damn your..." – that Kozyr would emerge from his sanctuary: "The Lord deliver us, my sons! What a disorderly female'."

Unfavourable though the atmosphere was, the wheel trade bean to show profits. Kozyr, merely by crossing himself, managed to do good business; without the slightest effort on our part, the rims rolled in, and we did not have to pay money down for them. Kozyr was indeed a splendid wheelwright, and the work of his hands was famous far beyond the precincts of our district.

Our life had become more complicated and a great deal brighter. Kalina Ivanovich did, after all, sow some five desyatins of our fields with oats, Red graced our stable, in our yard stood the new gig, its sole defect being its extraordinary height: it reared itself almost seven feet above the ground, and to the passenger inside it always seemed that, while there undoubtedly was a horse in front, it must be somewhere far, far below the top of the gig.

Our activities developed to such an extent, that we began to feel our lack of manpower. We had hurriedly to repair another building for use as a dormitory, and it was not long before reinforcements arrived. These were of a quite different nature from any we had so far received.

By this time great numbers of the atamans had been liquidated, and many of their youthful followers, whose military and piratical roles had been confined to the function of grooms or cook boys, were sent to the colony. It was owing to this historical circumstance that the colony's membership was enriched by names like Karabanov, Prikhodko, Goles, Soroka, Vershnev, and Mityagin.

8
CHARACTER AND CULTURE

The arrival of the new members at our colony shook our far from stable collective to its foundations, and we once again relapsed into our old bad ways.

Our original members had only been brought to recognize law and order on the most elementary level. And the newcomers, complete strangers to discipline, were still less disposed to submit to any law and order whatsoever. It should, however, be stated that there was never again any open resistance or display of hooliganism towards the teachers. It is to be presumed that Zadorov, Burun, Taranets and others, managed to give the newcomers a concise history of the first days of the Gorky Colony. Both veterans and novices realized that the teaching staff was not a force hostile to themselves. The chief reason for the prevalence o this spirit should undoubtedly be sought in the work of the teachers themselves, work so selfless and so obviously onerous, that it evoked instinctive respect. And so the boys, with extremely rare exceptions, were always on good terms with us, bowed to the necessity of working and studying in the school, thoroughly realizing that it was to our mutual advantage. Slothfulness and shrinking from hardships assumed purely biological forms, and never that of protest.

We ourselves faced the fact that any improvement in our situation came from a purely external form of discipline, and implied not the slightest, not even the most primitive, culture.

But the reason for the boys' consenting to live amidst our poverty, and take part in toil which was distinctly arduous, without running away, must of course be sought not merely on the educational level. There was nothing particularly attractive in the life of the streets during the year 1921. Our gubernia was not on the list of starvation districts, but for all that, conditions in the town itself were extremely severe, and there certainly was hunger. Besides, in the first years our boys were not real waifs, hardened to roving the streets. The greater part of our lads came from homes with which they had only recently broken their ties.

At the same time, the colonists, while presenting the most vivid characteristics, were on the lowest possible cultural level. These were precisely the types selected for our colony, which was specially intended for difficult cases. The overwhelming majority of them were semiliterate or completely illiterate, they were almost all inured to filth and vermin, and their attitude to their fellow man had hardened into the pseudo-heroic pose of aggressive self-defence.

A few individuals of a somewhat higher degree of intelligence – Zadorov, Burun, Vetkovsky, Bratchenko, and, among the later arrivals, Karabanov and Mityagin – stood out in the crowd; the rest only gradually and slowly approached the acquisitions of human culture, and the poorer and hungrier we were, the longer it took them.

During our first year one of our greatest vexations was their perpetual tendency to quarrel among themselves, the appalling weakness of the ties which must exist in any collective, but which in their case broke down every minute over the merest trifles. To a great extent this arose not so much from enmity, as from this same pseudo-heroic pose, undiluted by the slightest political consciousness. Although many of them had dwelt in the tents of their class enemies, they had not the slightest awareness of belonging to any particular class. We had hardly any children of workers, the proletariat was for them something remote and unknown, while most of them harboured profound scorn for agricultural labour, or rather not so much for the labour, as for the labourer's scheme of life and mentality. Hence there remained a wide field for all sorts of eccentricity, for the manifestation of personalities sunk in semibarbarity, demoralized by spiritual loneliness. Although in its general outlines the picture was melancholy enough, the sprouts of the collective spirit which had begun to show themselves during that first winter burgeoned mysteriously in our community, and these sprouts had to be cherished at all costs – no alien growths must be allowed to smother their tender verdure. I consider my chief merit to lie in the fact that I remarked this important development at the time, and estimated it at its proper value. Tending these first shoots turned out to be a process of such arduousness and length that, had I been able to foresee it, I would probably have taken fright and thrown up the sponge. The saving factor was that – incorrigible optimist as I am! – I always believed myself to he within an inch of victory.

Every day of my life during this period was a medley of faith, rejoicings, and despair.

Everything would seem toe going swimmingly. The teachers had done their day's work, had finished reading aloud, chatting, or otherwise entertaining their charges, and, wishing them good night, had gone to their own rooms. The kids were in peaceful mood, getting ready to go to bed. In my room the last beats of the pulse of the day's work were throbbing to a close: Kalina Ivanovich was sitting there, propounding his usual axioms, a few of the more inquisitive boys were hanging around, Bratchenko and Gud were standing at the door waiting ran opportunity for their routine attack upon Kalina Ivanovich on the question of fodder, when suddenly the air was rent with cries:

"The fellows are knifing each other!"

I rushed headlong from the room. The dormitory was in an uproar. In one, corner were two ferocious groups of frenzied individuals. Threatening gestures and leaps were mingled with the foulest of oaths. Somebody was boxing somebody else's ear, Burun was wrenching a Finnish knife from one of the heroes, and from the other side of the room arose voices of protest:

"Who asked you to interfere? D'you want me to give you what-for?"

Seated on the side of a bed, surrounded by a crowd of sympathizers, a wounded hero was silently bandaging his bleeding hand with a piece of rag torn from a sheet.

Just behind me Kalina Ivanovich was whispering in frightened tones: "Hurry! Hurry! They'll cut each other's throats, the parasites!" I had made it my rule never to try and separate, or shout down combatants, so I stood silently in the doorway, observing the scene. Little by little the boys became aware of my presence and fell silent. The sudden silence sobered the most turbulent spirits among them. Knives were stowed away, fists were dropped, and swearing was checked in mid-flight. But I still maintained silence, though inwardly seething with rage and hatred for this whole savage world. It was the hatred of impotence, for I knew very well that today would not be the last time.

At last a heavy, uncanny silence reigned in the dormitory. Even the muffled sound of tense breathing died down.

Then it was that I broke out in a fit of veritable human fury, strong in the conviction that I was doing the right thing.

"Knives on the table! And quick about it, damn you!"

Knives were piled up on the table: Finnish knives, kitchen knives, filched for the purpose of reprisals, penknives, and home-made blades fashioned in the smithy.

Silence continued to hang over the dormitory. At the table stood Zadorov, smiling – dear, engaging Zadorov, who now seemed to me the only kindred spirit I had. I rapped out another curt order:

"Any bludgeons?"

"I have one here. I took it away," said Zadorov.

They all stood round, hanging their heads.

"To bed!"

I did not leave the dormitory till everyone was in bed.

The next day the kids avoided all mention of the row of the night before. I also made not the slightest reference to it.

A month or two elapsed, during which, here and there, in remote corners, the fires of individual feuds smouldered, rapidly extinguished by the collective itself whenever they gave signs of bursting into flame. Then there would suddenly be another violent explosion, and again infuriated boys, losing all human semblance, would chase one another with knives in their hands.

It was on one such evening that I realized I should have to tighten the screws. After a fight, I ordered Chobot, one of the most indefatigable knights of the Finnish knife, to go to my room.

He went like a lamb. Once in my room, I said to him:

"You'll have to quit!"

"Where'll I go?"

"I advise you to go where you can knife other people. Just because your comrade wouldn't give up his place to you in the dining room, you jabbed a knife into him, today. Very well, then, find yourself a place where differences are settled with knives."

"When am I to go?"

"Tomorrow morning."

He went out morosely. The next morning, during breakfast, all the boys came to me with the request: let Chobot stay – they would answer for him.

"What guarantee have you?"

This they could not understand.

"How are you going to answer for him? Suppose he does use his knife again – what could you do about it?"

"Then you can expel him!"

"So you've no guarantee! No – he must quit!"

After breakfast, Chobot himself came up to me with the words:

"Goodbye, Anton Semyonovich! Thanks for the lesson!"

"Goodbye, and no ill feelings. If things are too hard, come back. But not before a fortnight."

A month later he returned, gaunt and pale faced.

"I've come back, like you said." "You didn't find a place to suit you?" He smiled.

"Didn't I? There are such places. I'll stay in the colony, and I won't use a knife."

The boys greeted us affectionately in the dormitory.

"So you did forgive him. We said you would!"

9

"THE AGE OF CHIVALRY IS NOT DEAD IN THE UKRAINE"

One Sunday, Osadchy got drunk. He was brought to me for disturbing the peace in the dormitory. Osadchy slat in my room, emitting an uninterrupted flow of nonsensical drunken grievances. It was useless to argue with him. I left him there and told him to lie down and sleep it off. He meekly complied.

On entering the dormitory I caught a whiff of spirits. Many of the kids were obviously trying to keep out of my way. Not wishing to make a row by looking for the culprits, I merely said:

"Osadchy is not the only one who is drunk. A few others have had a drop."

Several days later there were again drunken members in the colony. Some of these kept out of my way, but others, on the contrary, came to me in a fit of drunken remorse, and, cheerfully garrulous, made me declarations of love.

They did not conceal the fact that they had been visiting in the farmstead.

In the evening, talks about the evils of drunkenness were held in the dormitory, the culprits vowed they would never drink again, and I pretended to be satisfied, not even punishing anyone. I had accumulated a small store of experience by now, and knew very well that, in the struggle against drunkenness, it was no good hitting out at the colonists – there were others who had to be dealt with.

And these others were not far to seek.

We were surrounded by an ocean of samogon [vodka made in illicit stills – *Tr.*]. Drunken individuals – employees and peasants – were frequently at the colony. I had just learned, moreover, that Golovan was in the habit of sending the boys out for drink. He did not even take the trouble to deny it.

"Well, and what if I did?"

Kalina Ivanovich, who never touched drink, bawled Golovan out:

"Don't you know what the Soviet government is, you parasite? Do you think the Soviet government exists for you to swill homebrew?"

Golovan moved awkwardly on his rickety creaking chair, and endeavoured to excuse himself.

"Well, what about it? Who doesn't drink? I ask you! Everyone has a still, and everyone drinks as much as he wants. Let the Soviet government stop drinking itself!"

"What Soviet government?"

"All of them! They drink in the town, and they drink in the villages."

"D'you know who sells samogon here?" I asked Sofron.

"How do I know? I never bought any myself. If you want any – you send someone. Why do you ask? Are you going to confiscate it?"

"What d'you think? Certainly I am!"

"Oho! Look what a lot the militia confiscated, and all no good!"

The next day I went to the town and obtained a mandate for a ruthless war against illicit stills anywhere on the territory covered by our Village Soviet.

That evening Kalina Ivanovich and I took council together. Kalina Ivanovich was sceptically inclined.

"Don't get mixed up in that dirty business," he advised me. "I tell you, they're all as thick as thieves – the chairman of the Village Soviet – you know, Grechany – is one of them. And look where you will in the homestead, they're almost all Grechanys! You know what those people are – they don't use horses for ploughing, they use oxen. Look here, now – they have Goncharovka like this – – !" and Kalina Ivanovich held up a tightly clenched fist. "They've got it in their grip, the parasites, and there's not a thing you can do about it!"

"I don't understand you, Kalina Ivanovich. What's all this got to do with stills?"

"You're a funny guy, aren't you? And you an educated man! Don't you see they have all the power in their hands? Better not touch them, or they'll have your blood – you'll see if they don't!"

In the dormitory I said to the boys:

"I'm telling you, kids – I'm not going to have you drinking! And I'll crush that bunch of bootleggers in the farmsteads! Who wants to help?"

Most of them hesitated, but some fell my suggestion with enthusiasm.

"That's a great idea – a great idea!" said Karabanov, his black eyes blazing. "It's time somebody got after those kulaks!" I accepted the help of three of them – Zadorov, Volokhov, and Taranets.

Late on Saturday evening we drew up our strategic plans. By the light of my lamp we bent over the plan of the farmstead which I had made, Taranets thrusting his fingers into his mop of red hair, his freckled nose hovering over the paper.

"If we raid one hut, they'll have time to hide their stills in the others. Three isn't enough."

"Have they got stills in so many of the huts?"

"In almost every one! Moussi Grechany's, Andrei Karpovich's, Sergei Grechany, the chairman himself – they all brew! All the Verkhobas do it, and the women sell it in the town. We must have more of the fellows, or they'll beat us up, and that'll be an end of it."

Volokhov, who had been sitting yawning in the corner, suddenly spoke.

"Beat us up! Not they!" he said. "Take Kabanov and no one else, then no one will lay a finger on us. I know those kulaks. They're afraid of us chaps."

Volokhov took his part in the matter without enthusiasm. He still held himself aloof from me – he didn't like discipline, this kid! But he was deeply attached to Zadorov, and followed his lead without much bothering about principles.

Zadorov as usual smiled calmly and confidently. He had the gift of acting without wasting his energy, and without the loss of an ounce of his individuality. And now, as ever, I had confidence in no one so much as in Zadorov. I knew he was capable of any sacrifice which life might have in store for him, and would meet it as he met everything, without the loss of an ounce of his individuality And now he turned upon Taranets:

"Stop fidgeting, Fedor! Just tell us which hut we're to begin with, and where to go. And tomorrow we'll see. Volokhov's right, we must take Karabanov. He knows how to talk to those kulaks – he used to be one himself. And now let's go to bed, we've got to get up early tomorrow, before they're all drunk over there. Haven't we, Gritsko?"

"Um-h'm," slaid Volokhov, beaming.

We dispersed. Lydochka and Ekaterina Grigoryevna were strolling about the yard, and Lydochka called out to me:

"The kids say you're going to put the fear of God into the distillers. What put that into your head? Is that what you call pedagogical work? I call it a disgrace!"

"That's just what pedagogical work is," I replied. "Come along with us tomorrow!"

"D'you think I'm afraid? I'll be there! Just the same, it's *not* pedagogical work!"

"Will you really come?"

"That's what I said!"

Ekaterina Grigoryevna called me aside.

"What d'you want to take that child for?" she said.

"None of that!" called out Lydia Petrovna. "I'm going anyhow!"

And so our commission numbered five persons.

At seven a.m. we were knocking at the gate of Andrei Karpovich Grechany, our nearest neighbour. Our knock was the signal for an elaborate canine overture, which lasted five minutes.

The action itself, as was right and proper, only began after the overture. It began with the appearance upon the scene of Andrei Grechany, a little baldish man with a neatly clipped beard.

"What d'you want with us?" inquired Gaffer Andrei surily.

"You have an illicit still, we've come to destroy it," I told him. "I have a warrant from the Gubernia Militia."

"An illicit still!" repeated Gaffer Andrei in perturbed tones, letting his keen glance travel over our faces and the picturesque attire of our boys.

But at this point the canine orchestra crashed out fortissimo; Karabanov had edged his way behind the Gaffer to the black of the stage, after dealing a resounding blow with a stick, with which he had prudently provided himself, at a shaggy sandy dog, which followed up this opening with a deafening solo, at least two octaves higher than the usual canine range.

We dashed into the breach, scattering the dogs. Volokhov shouted at them in his powerful bass, and the dogs retreated far into the yard, underscoring further developments with the vague music of their aggrieved whinings. Karabanov was already inside the hut, and when we entered with the Gaffer, he triumphantly displayed what he had found – a still!

"There you are!"

Gaffer Andrei stamped about the hut, resplendent in a truly operatic-looking moleskin jacket.

"Did you brew yesterday?" asked Zadorov.

"Aye, we did," assented Gaffer Andrei, absent-mindedly fingering his beard, and glancing at Taranets, who was dragging out from under a bench in the near corner a gallon bottle of pinkish-violet nectar.

Gaffer Andrei suddenly flew into a rage and rushed at Taranets, considering, reasonably enough, that it would be easier to cope with him in the cluttered corner, with its jumble of benches, icons and table. And he did get hold of Taranets, who, however, calmly passed the bottle to Zadorov over the Gaffer's head, and all the Gaffer got for his pains was the maddeningly frank, winning smile of Taranets, and his mild: " 'smatter, Pop?"

"You ought to be ashamed!" cried Gaffer Andrei with warmth. "You ought to be ashamed of yourselves, going about the huts, and plundering! Even bringing your wenches with you! When will the people get some peace? When will you get what's coming to you?"

"Why, you're quite a poet, Gaffer!" said Karabanov in lively mimicry.

Leaning on his stick, he fell into a pose of elegant courtesy before the Gaffer.

"Get out of my hut!" shouted Gaffer Andrei, and snatching up huge iron prongs from beside the stove, he dealt Volokhov a clumsy blow on the shoulder.

Volokhov laughed and replaced the prongs, drawing the Gaffer's attention to a new development.

"Just you look over there!" The Gaffer glanced around and saw Taranets, the guileless smile still on his face, clambering down from the top of the stove with another gallon bottle of samogon. Gaffer Andrei, his head hanging, subsided on to a bench with a gesture of despair.

Lydochka seated herself beside him, saying kindly:

"Andrei Karpovich! You know it's illegal to run ia still! Besides, corn is wasted on it, while all around people are going hungry!"

"It's only shirkers who go hungry. Anyone who works won't come to want."

"And do you work, Gaffer?" asked Taranets from the stove, in his gay, ringing voice. "Isn't it Stepan Nechiporenko who works?"

"Stepan?"

"Yes, Stepan! You turned him out, you wouldn't pay him, you didn't give him his clothes, and now he's trying to get into the colony."

With a gay click of his tongue it the Gaffer, Taranets leaped from the stove.

"What are we to do with all this?" asked Zadorov.

"Break it all up outside!"

"The still, too?"

"The still, too!"

The Gaffer did not come out to the place of execution – he remained in the hut to listen to the succession of economic, psychological, and social arguments, so brilliantly propounded by Lydia Petrovna. The sole representatives of the proprietors in the yard were the dogs, squatting indignantly on their haunches at a safe distance, and it was only when we went out into the street that some of them uttered a belated, impotent protest.

Zadorov was thoughtful enough to call Lydochka out of the hut:

"Come along with us, or Gaffer Andrei'll make sausage meat of you!"

Lydochka came running out, elated by her chat with Gaffer Andrei.

"He took it all in!" she exclaimed. "He agrees it's a crime to run a still."

The boys replied with guffaws of laughter.

"He agrees, does he?" Karabanov asked, looking at Lydochka from between half-closed lids: "That's great! If you'd stayed beside him a little longer, perhaps he would have broken up the still himself! What d'you think?"

"Be thankful his old woman wasn't at home, said Taranets. "She's gone to church – to Goncharovka. But you'll have to have a talk with the Verkhola dame."

Luka Semyonovich Verkhola was continually at the colony on various errands, and we sometimes turned to him when in need – borrowing now a horse collar, now a cart, and now a barrel. Luka Semyonovich was a gifted diplomat, garrulous, accommodating, ubiquitous. He was very good-looking and kept his wavy red beard scrupulously clean and trimmed. He had three sons, of whom the eldest, Ivan, was famous ten kilometres around for his performance on the three-tiered Viennese accordion, and for the stunning caps he affected.

Luka Semyonovich gave us a cordial reception.

"Ah! my good neighbours!" he cried. "Welcome! Welcome! I've heard, I've heard! You're after the 'samovars'! That's fine! That's fine! Sit down! Sit on the bench, young man! Well, how goes it? Have you found masons for Trepke? If not, I shall be in Brigadirovka tomorrow, and I could bring you some. And what masons...! Why don't you sit down, young man? I haven't got any still – not I! I don't go in for that sort of thing. It's not allowed! What an idea! Since the Soviet government forbids it, I understand one can't do it! Don't be afraid, old woman – they're welcome guests!"

A bowl full to the brim with smetana [thick, sour cream – *Tr.*], and a dish heaped with cheesecakes made their appearance on the table. Without servility or undue deference, Luka Semyonovich invited us to partake of these dainties. He had a friendly, frank bass, and the manners of a worthy squire. I could see how our boys' hearts weakened at the sight of the cream – Volokhov and Taranets could not take their eyes off the lavish display. Zadorov stood in the doorway, blushing, smiling, fully aware that an impossible situation had been created. Karabanov sat next to me, and found a moment to whisper in my ear: "Oh, the son-of-a-bitch! Well, it can't be helped, you know! I'll have to take some – God knows I will! I can't help myself – God knows I can't!"

Luka Semyonovich pulled up a chair for Zadorov.

"Eat up, dear neighbours! Eat up! I could get you some drink, but the errand you are on...."

Zadorov seated himself opposite me, lowered his eyes, and stuffed half a cheesecake into his mouth, smearing his chin with the thick cream. Taranets was adorned from ear to ear with moustaches of cream; Volokhov bolted cake after cake without turning a hair.

"Bring some more cakes," said Luka Semyonovich to his wife. "Give us a tune, Ivan!"

"Service is going on in the church," objected his wife.

"That doesn't matter!" said Luka Semyonovich. "For our dear guests we can make an exception!"

The silent, sleek Ivan played "In the Moonlight." Karabanov almost fell under the table with laughing.

"Fine guests we are!" After the repast, the conversation was opened. Luka Semyonovich supported with great enthusiasm our plans regarding the Trepke estate, and was ready to come to our aid with all his practical resources.

"Don't you stick here in the woods!" he advised. "You get over there as quick as you can! The eye of the master is needed. And take over the mill – mind you, take over the mill! That Board they'ye got – it can't run a business like that! The peasants complain – how they complain! They need cake flour for Easter, for pies, and they've been going there day after day for a month, trying to get it. The peasant must have pies, and how can you make pies when you haven't got the chief thing – cake flour?"

"We're not strong enough to tackle the mill, yet," I said.

"What d'you mean 'not strong enough'? You can get help. You know how the people round here respect you! Everyone says – 'there's a fine fellow'!"

Just as this affecting climax was reached Taranets appeared in the doorway, and the hut echoed to the shrieks of the terrified housewife. In Taranets' hands was a part of a fine still – its most vital part – the coil. None of us had noticed Taranets slip away.

"I found it in the attic," said Taranets. "The stuff's there, too. It's still warm."

Luka Semyonovich gathered his beard into his fist, and looked solemn for the fraction of a second. But he brightened up immediately, approached Taranets, and stood in front of him with a smile on his face. Then, scratching behind his ear and winking at me, he said:

"That young man will go far! Well, since that's the way things are, I haven't a word to say. I'm not even offended. The law's the law! You'll be destroying it, I suppose! Well, then, you, Ivan – help them!"

But Verkholikha did not share her sage husband's respect for law and order. Tearing the coil out of Taranets' hands, she shrieked:

"Who's going to let you break it up? Who's going to let you? All you can do is to break a thing! Just try and make one! You lousy bums! Get out, before I break your skulls for you!" Verkholikha's harangue went on and on. Lydochka, up till now standing quietly in the corner, attempted to embark upon a calm discussion of the evils of home-brewed spirit. But Verkholikha was the possessor of a splendid pair of lungs. The bottles of home-brew were broken, Karabanov, in the middle of the yard, was finishing off the still with an iron bar, Luka Semyonovich was bidding us a gracious farewell, pressing us to come again and assuring us he was not in the least offended, Zadorov had shaken hands with Ivan, Ivan was grinding out a tune on his accordion, but Verkholikha went on shouting and bawling, finding ever new adjectives for the description of our conduct, and the outlining of our lamentable future. In the neighbouring yards the women folk stood stock-still, dogs barked and whined, tugging at the chains sliding along overhead wires strung across the yard, and the men, at work in the stables, shook their heads in consternation.

We rushed out into the street, Karabanov falling helplessly against a wattle fence.

"I shall die! My God, I shall die! Dear guests – oh, oh! Rot your guts with your smetana! Is your belly aching, Volokhov?"

That same day we destroyed six stills. Ourselves we suffered no casualties. It was only as we were leaving the last hut that we encountered Sergei Petrovich Grechany, the chairman of the Village Soviet. The chairman was like a Cossack chief, with his black, sleeked hair and waxed and curled moustache. Though quite young, he was the most successful farmer in the district, and was considered an extremely able man. He shouted to us from a little way off: "Hi, there! Stop a minute!"

We stood still.

"Good day to you! he cried. "The greetings of the season! May I ask what warrant you have for this violent interference – breaking up people's stills and all that! What right have you to go on like this?"

He gave an extra twist to his moustache, and looked searchingly at our unofficial countenances.

In silence I handed him my warrant for "violent interference." He turned it over and over in his hands, and gave it back to me in obvious displeasure.

"It's a permit, all right, but the people are annoyed. If just any colony can go on like this, who can tell what the consequences may be for the Soviet government? I myself keep trying to put an end to bootlegging."

"And yet you have a still yourself!" said Taranets quietly, his penetrating glance travelling impudently over the chairman's face.

The chairman cast a ferocious look at the ragged Taranets.

"You mind your own business!" he said. "Who do you think you are? From the colony? We'll carry this business to the highest authorities and then we'll see if a set of felons are to be allowed to insult local authorities with impunity!"

We parted – he in his direction, we in ours.

Our expedition had produced a good impression. The next day Zadorov said to our clients, grouped about the smithy:

"Next Sunday we'll do 'better – the whole colony – fifty of us – will come."

The villagers wagged their beards and hastened to agree:

"It's right, of course! Corn does go on it, and since it's prohibited, then it's right to put a stop to it."

There was no more drunkenness in the colony, but a new trouble arose – gambling We began to observe that some of the boys took no bread with their dinner, and that cleaning out the rooms or some other of the less pleasant duties were being done by the wrong persons.

"Why are you doing the room today, and not Ivanov?" "He asked me to do it for him!"

"He asked me to do it for him!"

Work done "by request" became an everyday phenomenon, and definite groups of such "petitioners" were formed. The number of boys not eating, but giving up their portions to their comrades, began to increase.

There can be no greater misfortune in a juvenile colony than gambling. The ordinary fare no longer suffices a gambler, who finds himself compelled to look for extra funds, the only means for which is theft. I lost no time in rushing to the attack against this foe.

Ovcharenko, a jolly, active lad, who had settled down with us nicely, suddenly ran away. My inquiries into the reasons for this were unavailing. The next day I came face to face with him in the town, in the thick of the street market, but plead with him as I might, he refused to return to the colony. He spoke to me in a way which betrayed his extreme embarrassment.

Gambling debts were regarded among our charges as debts of honour. A failure to pay such a debt entailed not merely a beating up or other form of violence, but public scorn.

On my returning to the settlement I questioned the boys in the evening.

"Why did Ovcharenko run away?"

"How do we know?" "You know very well!"

Silence.

That same night, calling Kalina Ivanovich to my assistance, I carried out a thorough search. The results astounded me: under pillows, in trunks, in boxes, in the very pockets of some of the boys, were found enormous quantities of sugar. Richest of all was Burun – in the trunk which with my permission he had made himself in the carpentry shop, over thirty pounds were found. But most interesting of all was what we found in the possession of Mityagin. Under his pillow, concealed in an old sheepskin cap, was fifty rubles in copper and silver coin.

Burun admitted frankly, with a look of extreme dejection:
"I won it at cards."
"From the other boys?"
"M'hm!"
Mityagin replied to all inquiries:
"I won't tell you!"

The biggest stores of sugar and various other articles, such as blouses, kerchiefs and handbags, were found in the room occupied by our three girl members – Olya, Raissa and Marusya. The girls refused to say to whom the things belonged. Olya and Marusya wept, but Raissa held her peace.

There were three girls at the colony. They had all been sent by the Commission for stealing from apartments. One of them – Olya Voronova – was (probably accidentally) involved in an ugly business, no rare occurrence in the lives of juvenile servants. Marusya Levchenko and Raissa Sokolova were extremely brazen and wanton, swearing and drinking with the boys, and taking part in the card playing, which usually went on in the girls' room. Marusya was, moreover, excruciatingly hysterical; she frequently insulted the other two, even beating them up, and was always quarrelling with the boys for the most absurd reasons, considering herself a "lost being," and replying to all admonitions with the monotonous phrase:

"What's the good? I'm done for, anyhow!"

Raissa, plump, slovenly, lazy, was a giggler, but far from stupid, and, comparatively speaking, not without education. She had once upon a time been to high school, and our women teachers wanted her to try and prepare for the Rabfak. [Workers faculty – *Tr.*] Her father had been a shoemaker in our town, but two years previously was stabbed to death in a drunken brawl; her mother drank and begged. Raissa assured us these were not her real parents, that she had been left on the Sokolov's doorstep as an infant, but the boys declared she was making this up.

"Soon she'll tell you her father was a prince." Raissa and Marusya maintained a certain independence towards the boys, among whom they enjoyed a measure of respect, as experienced "moils." It was on this account that they were entrusted with the important details of the dark machinations of Mityagin and others.

With the arrival of Mityagin, the gangster element in the colony increased both as to quantity and quality.

Mityagin was a practised thief, ingenious, daring and successful. And with all this he was exceedingly attractive. He was seventeen years old, or maybe a little older.

He bore on his countenance a "distinguishing mark" in the form of bushy, flaxen eyebrows. As he said himself this "distinguishing mark" frequently spoiled the success of his undertakings. It never entered into his head that he could go in for anything but stealing. On the very evening of his arrival at the colony, he spoke to me in the most frank and friendly manner.

"The chaps speak well of you, Anton Semyonovich."

"Well, what about it?"

"That's fine! If the chaps like you it's easier for them." "So you'll have to like me, too?"

"Oh, no! I shan't be long in the colony."

"Why not?"

"Why should I? I shall always be a thief."

"You can get out of the habit."

"I know, but I don't consider it worth while."

"You're just putting on airs, Mityagin!"

"No, I'm not! Stealing is fun! You only have to know how – and you mustn't rob just anyone! There's some swine who simply ask for it, and there are some people you mustn't rob."

"You're right there," I said. "But it's the one who steals, not the one who's robbed, who is the real sufferer."

"How d'you mean 'sufferer'?"

"I'll tell you! You get used to stealing and unused to work. You find everything easy, you get used to drinking, and there you are – nothing but a bum. Then you get into prison, and after prison somewhere else...."

"As if there aren't human beings in prison! Lots of people are worse off 'outside' than they are in prison. You never can tell!"

"Have you ever heard of the October Revolution?"

"OF course I have! I was with the Red Guard."

"Very well, then! Now there's going to be a better life for the people than in prison."

"That remains to be seen," said Mityagin thoughtfully. "There's a hell of a lot of lousy bums still going about. They'll get their own way, one way or another. Look at the bunch round the colony! Oho!"

When I broke up the colony's gambling organization, Mityagin refused to say where the money in his cap came from.

"Did you steal it?"

He smiled: "What a funny chap you are, Anton Semyonovich!" he said. "Naturally I didn't buy it! There's plenty of suckers left in the world. All this money was brought by suckers to one place, and handed over, with bowing and scraping, to fat-bellied rogues. So why should I be sqeamish? I might just as well take it myself! All right – I took it! The trouble is, there's nowhere to hide anything in your colony! I never thought you'd search the place..."

"Very well! I shall take this money for the colony. We'll take a deposition here and now, and debit ourselves with it.

Just now we won't speak about you."

I spoke to the boys about the thefts.

"I flatly forbid gambling. You're not going to play cards any more. Playing cards means robbing your comrades."

"Let them not play, then!"

"They play because they are fools. Lots of the members of our colony are going hungry, not eating sugar and bread. Ovcharenko left the colony all because of this gambling, and now he's roving about the thieves market, crying."

"Yes – that was a bad business with Ovcharenko," said Mityagin.

"It seems," I continued, "that there's no one in the colony to protect a weaker comrade. So I shall have to do it myself. I won't have boys going hungry and ruining their health just because they get a rotten deal. I won't have it! Choose for yourselves! Don't suppose I enjoy having to search your dormitories! But after I saw Ovcharenko in the town – crying and going to his ruin – I decided I wouldn't stand on ceremony with you. If you like, let's come to an agreement that there shall be no more gambling. Can you give your word of honour? Only I'm afraid your word of honour isn't worth much. Burun gave his word...."

Burun pushed forward.

"It's not true, Anton Semyonovich!" he cried. "You ought to be ashamed to tell lies! If you're going to tell lies, then we – I never said a word about cards!"

"Sorry! You're quite right. It was my fault for not taking your promise not to play cards at the same time. And samogon, too..."

"I don't drink samogon."

"All right! That'll do! What about it, now?"

Karabanov moved slowly to the front. Irresistibly vivid and elegant, he was, as usual, posing just a little. In the steppe he had imbibed some of the massive strength of the steppe bullock, a strength rendered still more effective by his manner of holding it in check.

"Fellows! It's as clear as daylight! We can't go on robbing our comrades at cards. Whether you get sore with me, or not, I'm coming out against gambling! So now you know: I won't peach about anything else, but about gambling, I will! Or I'll punish anyone I catch playing cards, myself. I saw Ovcharenko go. It was like sending a chap to his grave. And Ovcharenko, you know, has no gift for stealing. It was Burun and Raissa who cleaned him out. Let them go and look for him is what I say! And don't let them come back until they've found him!"

Burun agreed heartily, but added: "What the hell do I want Raissa for? I'll find him myself."

The kids began talking all together. Everyone was pleased with the agreement arrived at. Burun confiscated all cards and threw them with his own hands into the pail. Kalina Ivanovich cheerfully gathered up the hoards of sugar. "Thanks, kids!" he said. "That's a great economy."

Mityagin saw me out of the dormitory.

"Am I to quit?" he asked.

"You can stay a bit longer," I said wearily.

"I shall go on stealing just the same."

"All right – to hell with you! Steal, then! It's your look-out!"

Startled, he left me.

The next morning, Burun set off for town, to look for Ovcharenko. The boys tagged after him, dragging Raissa with them. Karabanov clapped Burun on the shoulder, bawling all over the colony:

"The age of chivalry is not dead in the Ukraine!"

Zadorov, grinning, stuck his head out of the smithy. He turned to m, in his usual easy, confidential way, exclaiming:

"Lousy bums – but they're a swell lot, really."

"And who d'you think you are?" asked Karabanov fiercely.

"Former hereditary bum, and now Alexander Zadorov, blacksmith to the Maxim Gorky Labour Colony!" he said, drawing himself up to attention.

"At ease!" said Karabanov, strutting past the smithy.

In the evening Burun brought back Ovcharenko, famished, but deeply content.

10
"HEROES OF SOCIAL EDUCATION"

There were five, including myself. We were known as "the heroes of social education." Not only did we never call ourselves by this name, it did not so much as occur to us that we were doing anything specially heroic – neither in the early days of the colony's existence, not later, when it celebrated its eighth anniversary.

The word "heroes" was used not only about the Gorky Colony, but in our secret hearts we considered such words as mere catchwords to raise the morale of workers in children's homes and colonies. For at that time Soviet life, and the revolutionary movement, were fraught with heroism, while our own work was only too prosaic in essence and achievements.

We were just ordinary mortals, with any amount of shortcomings. We didn't even really know our own business: our working day was crammed with error, diffident movements, confused thinking. And ahead was impenetrable mist, through which we could only make out, with the utmost difficulty, the vague outlines of our future pedagogical life.

Every step we took could have been criticized from any point of view, for our every step was unplanned. There was nothing incontrovertible in our work. And when we began to argue, matters grew still worse – for no truths were ever born of these arguments.

There were only two points as to which no doubt ever arose: one was our firm resolve never to throw up the work, but to carry it to some sort of a conclusion, even if that conclusion should be failure; the other was our everyday life – our life in and around the colony.

When the Osipovs first came to the colony, they had felt a shuddering aversion for its inmates. According to our regulations, the teacher on duty had to have dinner with the boys. Both Ivan Ivanovich and his wife firmly declared that they were not going to sit at the table with the boys, being, as they said, unable to conquer their fastidiousness.

"We'll see, "I said.

During his evening duty in the dormitory, Ivan Ivanovich would never sit on one of the beds, and as there was nothing else to sit on he spent his evening duty on his feet. Ivan Ivanovich and his wife would wonder how I could sit on these verminous beds.

"That's nothing," I told them. "Everything will come right in the end. We'll get rid of the lice, or find some other way..."

Three months later, Ivan Ivanovich was not only eating heartily at the same table with the boys, but actually stopped bringing his own spoon to table with him, selecting a wooden spoon from the pile in the middle of the table, and contenting himself with merely passing his fingers over it. And in the dormitory of an evening, Ivan Ivanovich, seated on a bed surrounded by a lively bunch of boys, would take part in the game of "Thief and Informer." For the purpose of this game all the players were dealt out tickets inscribed "thief," "informer," "investigator," "judge" or "executioner." The one drawing the lot marked "informer" was armed with an improvised lash, and had to guess who was the thief. Each in turn stretched out his hand, and the informer had to single out the thief with a flick of the lash on the suspect's palm. He just as often hit upon the judge or the investigator, which honest citizens, insulted by his suspicions, in their turn smote the informer on his own palm, according to the established tariff for such affronts. When the informer succeeded in discovering the thief, his sufferings were at an end, and those of the thief began. The judge pronounced the sentence – five hot ones, ten hot ones, five cold ones. The executioner then seized the lash and carried out the sentence.

Since the parts taken by the players were constantly changing, the thief in one round becoming the judge or the executioner in the next, the main charm of the game consisted in the alternation of suffering and revenge. A harsh judge or ruthless executioner, on becoming informer or thief, got his own back from the reigning judge or executioner, who now remembered against him his former sentences and inflictions.

Ekaterina Grigoryevna and Lydia Petrovna also took part in this game, but the boys treated them chivalrously, merely assigning three or four cold ones, while the executioner, with the mildest expression in the world, just stroked the soft feminine palm with his lash.

When I played with them the boys would show the utmost curiosity as to my powers of endurance, so there was nothing for it but to brave it out. As judge I gave sentences which horrified even the executioners, and when it was my turn to carry out a sentence, I would cause the victim to forget his pride and call out:

"Anton Semyonovich – that's too much!"

To make up for this I was given it hot. I always went home with a swollen left hand – it was considered infra dig to change one's hand, and I needed my right hand for writing with.

Ivan Ivanovich Osipov, from sheer cowardice, adopted effeminate tactics, and at first the boys treated him gently. One day I told Ivan Ivanovich that these tactics were erroneous: our boys must grow up to be brave and daring. They must not fear danger, still less physical pain. Ivan Ivanovich did not agree with me.

One evening when we were both taking part in the game, I sentenced him, in my capacity as judge, to twelve hot ones, and in the next round, as executioner, ruthlessly slashed his palm with the whistling lash. He lost his temper, and revenged himself on me when his turn came. My devotees could not leave such conduct on the part of Ivan Ivanovich unrevenged, and one of them reduced him to the ignominy of changing his hand.

The next evening Ivan Ivanovich endeavoured to wriggle out of this barbarous game, but was shamed into participation again by the irony of the boys, and henceforward came through the ordeal with flying colours, neither cringing, when judge, nor showing the white feather when informer or thief.

The Osipovs frequently complained that they took lice home with them.

"It's in the dormitories that we must bet rid of the lice," I told them, "not in our own rooms."

And we did our best. With great efforts we obtained two changes of linen and two suits, for everyone. These suits were a mass of patches, but they could be steamed, and hardly any lice remained in them, nevertheless it took us some time to get rid of the lice entirely, owing to the constant arrival of newcomers and our contacts with the villagers.

The work of the staff was officially divided into main duty, work duty and evening duty. In addition to these, the teachers gave lessons in the mornings. Main duty was a kind of hard labour from five a. m. till the bell went for bedtime. The teacher on main duty had to see to the routine of the whole day, check the issue of provisions, superintend the fulfilment of tasks, look into conflicts, reconcile combatants, conciliate objectors, order supplies, check the contents of Kalina Ivanovich's storeroom, and see that linen and clothing were changed. Work while on main duty was so overwhelming, that by the beginning of our second year, some of our senior pupils, a red band on their sleeves, began to assist the teachers.

The teacher on work duty simply took part in any current work, particularly where a greater number of boys were engaged, or where there were many newcomers. The teacher's role was that of actual participation in any work on hand – anything else would have been impossible in our conditions. The teachers worked in the workshop, in the forest, felling timber, in the fields, and in the truck garden, and also wherever repairing of inventory was going on. Evening duty was little more than a formality, for in the evenings all the teachers, whether on duty or not, gathered together in the dormitories. There was no heroism in this, for we had nowhere else to go. It was not very cosy in our empty rooms, illuminated at night only by the floating wicks, whereas after evening tea we knew that we were impatiently awaited by the colonists, with their merry faces and keen eyes, with their endless fund of stories, true and untrue, with their incessant questions on topical, philosophical, political and literary subjects, with their games, from "Cat and Mouse" to "Thief and Informer." Here the events of our life were discussed, our peasant neighbours subjected to searching analysis, and nice points as to repairs, and our future, happy life in the new colony debated.

Sometimes Mityagin would spin a yarn. He was a great hand at tales, relating them with skill, not without an admixture of the theatrical element and rich mimicry. Mityagin was fond of the little ones, and his stories rejoiced their hearts. There was hardly ever anything magical in his stories, which were mostly about foolish peasants and wise peasants, reckless aristocrats, cunning craftsman, daring ingenious thieves, bedevilled policemen, brave, victorious soldiers and clumsy, heavy-witted priests.

We often arranged reading sessions of an evening in the dormitories. From the very first we had begun to get a library together, and I had begun to buy books, and beg for them in private houses. By the end of the winter we had almost all the Russian classics, and a number of political and agricultural publications. I managed to collect from the chaotic warehouses of the Gubernia Department of Public Education a quantity of popular works on various branches of science.

Many of our charges were fond of reading, but by no means all were capable of mastering the contents of a book. We therefore held reading sessions, in which, as a rule, everyone took part. The reader was either Zadorov, whose diction was irreproachable, or myself. During the first winter we read a great deal of Pushkin, Korolenko, Mamin-Sibiryak, and Veresayev – but most of all we read Gorky.

Gorky's works made a strong, though dual, impression. It was Gorky's romanticism which appealed to Karabanov, Taranets, Volokhov, and some others, who took no interest in the author's analytical side. With glowing eyes they listened to *Makar Chudra*, gasped and shook their fists at the character of Ignat Gordeyev, but were bored by the tragedy of *Gaffer Arkhip* and *Lyonka*. Karabanov was particularly fond of the scene in which the old Gordeyev looks on at the destruction of his "Boyarinya" by the breaking ice. Semyon, with set face, exclaimed in melodramatic tones: "There's a man for you! Oh, if everyone was like that!"

He listened to the account of Ilya's death in *The Three* with equal enthusiasm.

"Great fellow! Great fellow! Dashing out his brains against a stone – there's a death for you!"

Mityagin, Zadorov, and Burun laughed indulgently at the enthusiasm of our romantics, wounding them in their tenderest spots.

"You fellows listen, but you don't hear anything!"

"*I* don't hear anything?"

"Ah, but what is it you hear – what's there so fine in dashing one's brains out? He's a fool, that Ilya, a rotter! Some dame gives him a sour look, and he melts into tears. If I'd been him, I'd have throttled another of those merchants – they ought all to be throttled, your Gordeyev too!"

The opposing sides only agreed in their estimation of Luka, in *The Lower Depths*.

"Say what you like!" exclaimed Karabanov, wagging his head. "Such old chaps do a lot of harm. Buzz-buzz-buzz, and suddenly disappear.... I know that sort."

"That old Luka was a knowing one," said Mityagin. "It's all very well for him – he understands everything, he gets his own way everywhere. Now cheating, now stealing, now acting the dear old man. He'll always be all right, himself."

Childhood and *My Apprenticeship* made a strong impression on all of them. They listened with bated breath, begging for the reading to go on: "at least till twelve." At first they didn't believe me when I told them the story of Maxim Gorky's own life. They were stunned by the story, suddenly struck by the idea:

"So Gorky was like us! I say, that's fine!"

This idea moved them profoundly and joyfully.

Maxim Gorky's life seemed to become part of our life. Various episodes in it provided us with examples for comparison, a fund of nicknames, a background for debate, and a scale for the measurement of human values.

When, three kilometres away, the Korolenko Children's Colony was organized, our boys wasted little time on envying them.

"Korolenko's just the name for those kids! We're the Gorky boys!"

Kalina Ivanovich was of the same opinion.

"I met that Korolenko, and even had a talk with him – he was a respectable man. And you – you're tramps both in theory and practice!"

We were called the Gorky Colony without any official nomination or confirmation. In the town they gradually got used to our calling ourselves by this name, and raised no objections to our new seals and rubber stamps bearing it. Unfortunately we could not at first correspond with Alexei Maximovich, no one in our town knowing his address. It was only in 1925 that we read, in an illustrated weekly, an article on Gorky's life in Italy; in this article his name was given in its Italian version – "Massimo Gorky." We then sent him, on the off-chance of his getting it, our first letter, bearing the artlessly concise address: Italia, Sorrento, Massimo Gorky.

Both seniors and juniors were enthusiasts for Gorky's tales and Gorky's biography, although most of the juniors were illiterate.

We had about a dozen juniors, aged ten years and upwards. Each member of this little crowd was lively, slippery, light-lingered, invariably and inconceivably grubby. They always arrived at the colony in the most lamentable condition – skinny, rickety, scrofulous. Ekaterina Grigoryevna, our self-appointed medical officer and sick nurse, had her hands full with them. Despite her austerity, they all gravitated towards her. She knew how to scold them in a motherly way, knew all their weaknesses, never believed what they said (an achievement I could never attain), never overlooked a single offence, and displayed frank indignation at every breach of discipline.

But no one else could talk so simply and with such human feeling to a little chap – about life, his mother, about his becoming a sailor, a Red Army commander, or an engineer. No one else could so plumb the depths of the terrible injuries which a blind accursed fate had inflicted upon these little chaps. Moreover, she found ways of feeding them up, infringing, on the sly, all the rules and regulations of the supply department, and conquering with a kind word the rigid officialdom of Kalina Ivanovich.

The older boys, who noticed the contact between Ekaterina Grigoryevna and the youngest of our inmates, respected it, and invariably agreed with the utmost good humour and indulgence to fulfil any little request of Ekaterina Grigoryna – to see that a little chap washed himself properly, soaping himself all over, that another did not smoke, that clothes were not torn, that such a one did not fight with Petya, and so on; It was largely thanks to Ekaterina Grigoryevna that the older boys in the colony grew fond of the little ones, and treated them like younger brothers – affectionately, strictly and considerately.

11

THE APOTHEOSIS OF THE SEED-DRILL

A firewood detachment. The driver of the first cart is Anton Bratchenko, and second from right in the background is Semyon Karabanov

It was becoming increasingly evident that our colony was ill-adapted to farming, and our gaze was ever turning towards the new place, to the banks of the Kolomak, where the spring was awakening the orchards to such luxuriant blossoming, and the soil gleamed from its own richness.

But work on repairs in the new colony progressed at a snail's pace. The only carpenters whom we could afford to employ knew how to build log cabins, but were at a loss when confronted with buildings of a more complex design. Glass was not to be obtained for any amount of money, and we had no money. By the end of the summer, however, two or three of the larger buildings were put into some sort of shape, but could not be occupied for lack of window-panes. We were able to get a few small annexes completed, but these were needed for the housing of carpenters, bricklayers, stovemakers, and watchmen. There would have been no point in moving the boys into them, anyhow, without workshops, and with no real work on the and to do as yet.

Our boys visited the new colony every day, however, for a considerable part of the work was being done by them. In the summer, about ten boys made themselves improvised shelters and worked in the orchards. They sent cartloads of apples and pears back to the original colony. As a result of their efforts, the Trepke orchards began to look quite presentable, though there was still room for improvement. The inhabitants of Goncharovka were greatly perturbed by the arrival of new masters at the Trepke ruins, especially when they saw how disreputable, ragged, and little imposing these new masters were. To my dismay, our order for sixty desyatins turned out to be a mere scrap of paper, since all the arable land on the Trepke estate, including the area which had been allotted to us, had been under cultivation by the local peasantry since 1917.

In the town they only smiled at our perplexity.

"If you have an order, it means the land belongs to you. Just go into the fields and start ploughing!"

But Sergei Petrovich Grechany, the chairman of the Village Soviet, was of a different opinion.

"You know how it is, when a hard-working peasant gets and in strict accordance with the law," he explained. "He begins to till it. Those who write out all these orders and papers are simply stabbing the toiler in the back. And I advise you not to butt in with that order of yours!"

Since the footpaths to the new colony led only to the bank of the Kolomak, we made our own ferry, and our boys took it in turns to act as boatman. But to carry loads, or to ride or drive there, we had to take a roundabout way, and use the bridge into Goncharovka, where we encountered no little hostility. The village lads would jeer at the sight of our humble turnout.

"Hi, you – ragamuffins! Don't shake your lice over our bridge! You'd better keep out of here – we'll make Trepke too hot to hold you, you'll see!"

We installed ourselves in Goncharovka, not as peaceful neighbours, but as conquerors. And if in this, our military situation, we had not stood firm, or had shown ourselves unequal to the contest, we would inevitably have lost estate, grounds and all. The peasants knew that the dispute would be settled not in the offices, but right there in the fields. They had been ploughing the Trepke and for three years and had established a kind of proscriptive right to it and it was on this that they based their claim. It was necessary for them to extend the duration of this right at all costs, for their entire hopes rested on these tactics.

In much the same way, our only hope was to start farming the and as soon as possible.

In the summer, surveyors came to mark our boundaries, but, not daring to take their instruments into the fields, they merely pointed out to us on a map the ditches, banks, and thickets, according to which we could measure our land. Armed with the surveyor's deed, I went to Goncharovka with some of the older boys.

The chairman of the Village Soviet was now our old friend Luka Semyonovich Verkhola. He received us courteously, invited us to sit down, but would not so much as glance at the surveyor's deed.

"Dear comrades," he said. "There's nothing I can do for you. Our muzhiks have been tilling this and for a long time. I can't offend the muzhiks. Ask for and somewhere else!"

When the peasants went out into our fields and started ploughing them, I hung out a notice to the effect that the colony would not pay for the ploughing of its land.

I did not believe myself in the measures taken, for my heart sank at the realization that the land was to be taken from peasants, hard-working peasants, for whom it was as necessary as air.

And then, a few evenings later, Zadorov led a stranger up to me in the dormitory – a youth from the village. Zadorov seemed greatly excited.

"Listen to him – just you listen to him!" he exclaimed.

Karabanov, catching his excitement, was performing steps from the hopak [Ukrainian folkdance – *Tr.*], and yelling all over the dormitory: "He, ho! Now we'll show Verkhola what's what!"

The boys clustered round us.

The youth turned out to be a member of the Komsomol from Goncharovka.

"Are there many Komsomols in Goncharovka?" I asked him.

"There's only three of us."

"Only three?"

"We have a hard time of it, I can tell you!" he continued. "The village is under the thumb of the kulaks – the farmsteads, you know, take the lead. Our fellows have sent me to tell you to come over as soon as possible – then we'll show them! Your lads are a determined lot. If only we had a few like that!"

"But we don't know what to do about this land business."

"That's just what I've come about. Take the land by force. Pay no attention to that red-haired devil of a Luka. Do you know who's farming the land allotted to you?"

"Who?"

"Tell us, Spiridon! Tell us!"

Spiridon began checking off the names on his fingers.

"Grechany – Andrei Karpovich...."

"Gaffer Andrei! But he has land this side!"

"Very well, then.... Petro Grechany, Onopri Grechany, Stomukha – the one who lives next to the church... oh, yes, Seryoga.., Stomukhia, Yavtukh, and Luka Semyonovich himself. That's all – six of them!"

"Not really! How did it come about? And what about your Kombed?"

"Our Kombed is a small affair. It can be bought off with samogon. This is how it all happened: that land was to stay with the estate, it was to be used for something or other. And the Village Soviet is in their hands. So they just divided the land between themselves – that's all!"

"Now things will begin to get a move on!" shouted Karabanov. "Watch your step, Luka!"

One day, in the beginning of September, I was returning from town. It was about two o'clock in the afternoon. Our lofty gig was lumbering slowly ahead; Anton's discourse on the vagaries of Red buzzed dreamily past my ears. While listening to it I managed at the same time to think about various problems in connection with the colony.

All of a sudden Bratchenko fell silent. Looking fixedly ahead at a point some distance away on the road, he rose in his seat and whipped up the horse, making the carriage fly over the cobblestones with a terrible clatter. Anton went on whipping Red – a thing he never did – and shouted something to me. At last I was able to make out the words:

"Our chaps... with a seed-drill!"

At the turning towards the colony, we nearly ran into a seed-drill rushing at full speed, emitting strange metallic sounds the while. A pair of boys was tearing wildly ahead, terrified by the din of the unfamiliar chariot behind them. The seed-drill rolled ponderously over the highroad, rumbled over the sand, and then resumed its thunderous progress along the road to the colony. Anton, leaping from the gig to the ground and flinging the reins into my hands, rushed after the seed-drill, on which, hanging on to the taut reins, Karabanov and Prikhodko kept their balance as by a miracle. With the utmost difficulty, Anton managed to stop the strange vehicle.

Karabanov, breathless with excitement and exhaustion, told us what had happened.

"We were in the yard, piling bricks. Suddenly we saw a seed-drill with about five men following it – ever so grand! – driving into the fields. We went up to them. You go away!' we said. There were four of us – us two, and Chobot and... who else?"

"Soroka," said Prikhodko.

"That's right – Soroka! 'Go away!' I said. 'You're not going to sow here, anyhow!' Then one of them, a dark chap, looks like a gipsy, you know who I mean – lashed out at Chobot with his whip. Well, Chobot gave him a sock in the jaw. Suddenly we saw Burun rush up with a stick. I took one of the horses by the bridle, and the chairman rushed up and took hold of me by the front of my shirt...."

"Which chairman?"

" 'Which'? Ours, of course – that red-haired chap, Luka Semyonovich. Well, Prikhodko gave him a kick from behind, and he tumbled down with his nose in the earth. 'Get on to the seeder!' I shouted to Prikhodko, and off we went! When we were galloping into Goncharovkra, there were the village lads out in the street – what was I to do? I whipped up the horses, they galloped over the bridge, and there we were, on the highroad.... Three of our chaps are still there. I expect the muzhiks have given them a good beating up."

Karabanov was quivering all over with triumph. Prikhodko, imperturbably rolling himself a cigarette, was smiling quietly. I was picturing to myself the next chapters of this highly entertaining history: commissions, interrogations, investigations, and all that!

"Damn you all! You've got us into a mess again!"

Karabanov was profoundly dashed by my reaction.

"They began it...!"

"Very well, go back to the colony. We'll discuss it there."

We were met at the colony by Burun. His forehead was adorned with an enormous bruise, and he was surrounded by a crowd of laughing boys. Chobot and Soroka were washing at the water butt.

Karabanov seized Burun by the shoulders. "Well, so you got away from them! Good lad!"

"First they rushed after the seed-drill," said Burun, "then, seeing it was no good, they turned on us. How we ran!"

"And where are they?"

"We crossed in the boat, and they stood on the bank, swearing. We left them there."

"Are there any of our boys still over there?"

"Only kids – Toska and two others. Nobody will hurt them."

An hour later Luka Semyonovich came to the colony with two of the villagers. Our lads greeted them courteously: "Come for your seed-drill?"

It was almost impossible to move in my room for the crowd of interested spectators. The situation was an embarrassing one.

Luka Semyonovich, seating himself at the table, was the first to speak.

"Call those chaps who beat up me and my mates!" he demanded.

"Look here, Luka Semyonovich!" I said to him. "If you have been beaten up, go and complain wherever you like. I'm not going to call anyone just now. Tell me what it is you want, and what made you come to the colony!"

"So you refuse to call them?"

"I do!"

"Ha! You refuse, do you? Then we shall have to discuss it elsewhere."

"All right!"

"Who's going to give back the seed-drill?"

"'Give it back to whom?"

"There's the owner!" he said, pointing towards a dark, curly-haired morose fellow, evidently the one who Karabanov said looked like a gipsy.

"Is it your seed-drill?" I asked him.

"Yes, it is!"

"Well, then: the seed-drill I'll send to the District Militia, as seized during unlawful sowing on the property of others. And you, I'll ask to give me your name."

"My name? Grechany, Onopri! What d'you mean 'the property of others'? It's my and! It's always been mine...."

"Well, we won't go into that just now! Now we'll make out a deposition of unlawful entry, and beating up members of the colony while working in the fields."

Burun stepped forward.

"That's the one who nearly killed me," he said.

"You're not worth it! Kill you? You must be mad!"

The conversation went on in this strain for a long time. I forgot all about dinner and supper, the bell for going to bed had been rung, and still we sat there with the villagers, discussing the matter – now amicably, now with threats and excitement, now with elaborate irony.

I stood my ground, firmly refusing to surrender the seed-drill, and insisted on drawing up a deposition. Fortunately the villagers bore no traces of the fight on their persons, while our lads could point to bruises and scratches. It was Zadorov who put an end to further argument. Slapping the table with his hand, he made the following brief speech:

"That's enough, fellows! The land is ours, and you'd better not meddle with us. We're not going to let you into our fields. There are fifty of us – all determined lads!"

Luka Semyonovich thought long, and at last, stroking his beard, and grunting, said:

"All right, confound you! But you might at least pay us for the ploughing!"

"No," I said coldly. "I gave you fair warning!"

There was another pause.

"Well, then, give us back the drill."

"I will, if you sign the surveyor's deed!"

"All right. Give it here!"

After all, we did sow rye in the new colony that autumn. We were our own agricultural experts. Kalina Ivanovich knew very little about farming, and the rest of us knew still less, but everyone was eager to work with plough and seed-drill. Everyone, that is, but Bratchenko, who suffered pangs of jealousy for his beloved horses, anathematized the land, the rye, and our enthusiasm.

"Wheat isn't enough for them – they must have rye, too!" he grumbled.

By October, eight desyatins were a vivid green with young shoots. Kalina Ivanovich pointed proudly with his rubber-tipped staff towards some vague point in the east.

"We ought to sow lentils there," he said. "Splendid stuff, lentils!"

Red and Bandit toiled over the and to be sown with spring corn, and Zadorov would come home in the evenings, weary and dusty.

"To hell with it – this muzhik stuff is hard work! I'll go back to the smithy!"

Our work was half done when the snow overtook us. We thought this not so bad for beginners.

12
BRATCHENKO AND THE DISTRICT COMMISSAR FOR SUPPLIES

Colony members at work (1921)

Our farming developed along a path of miracles and sufferings. It was a miracle when Kalina Ivanovich managed to wangle an ancient cow, which he himself said must have been "born dry," from some department or other distributing its property; it was a mirjcle that we obtained from some purely agricultural department, quite unrelated to us, a no less ancient black mare – pot-bellied, lazy, subject to fits; it was a miracle that farm carts, arbas [a kind of bullock cart – *Tr.*], and even a phaeton, made their appearance in our shed. The phaeton, a two-horse one, was very beautiful in our eyes at that time, and exceedingly comfortable; but the miracle which would have been required to obtain matching horses for it was not forthcoming.

Gud having left the stables to go and work in the cobbler's workshop, the post of head groom was filled by Anton Bratchenko, an energetic individual whose vanity was so sensitive that he underwent moments of severe humiliation, seated on the box of the elegant vehicle behind the long-legged lanky Red, and the stocky, bandy-legged Bandit, as Anton had (quite unjustifiably!) christened the black mare. Bandit stumbled at every step, sometimes actually falling down, when our grand turnout had to be set to rights in the middle of the town, amidst the jeering remarks of other drivers, and of street urchins. Anton would often be provoked by these jibes to a fierce brawl with the unwelcome spectators, thus bringing still further discredit upon the stables of the Gorky Colony.

Anton Bratchenko was inordinately fond of a fight, could hold his own in a quarrel with any opponent, and was past master in the art of imprecation and innuendo, as well as possessing a considerable gift for mimicry.

Anton had never been a waif. His father worked in a bakery in the town. His mother, too, was alive, and he was the only son of his worthy parents. But from his earliest years Anton had felt an aversion for the domestic hearth, only coming home to sleep, and cultivating a wide circle of acquaintances among the street boys and thieves of the town. After distinguishing himself in a number of daring and entertaining adventures, and undergoing several short stretches in jail, he at last found himself at the colony. He was only fifteen, good-looking, curly-haired, blue-eyed, slender. He was extraordinarily gregarious, incapable of passing a single moment by himself. Somehow or other he had learned to read and write, and knew by heart volumes of adventure stories, but study he would not, and could only be kept in the classroom by main force. At first he would often leave the colony, always, however, returning in a day or two, without, apparently, feeling the slightest sense of guilt. He tried to overcome his roving inclinations. "Be as strict as possible with me," he would ask, "or else I'm sure to turn out a tramp, Anton Semyonovich!"

He never stole anything in the colony, and loved to stand up for the truth, but was quite unable to understand the logic of discipline, only accepting it to the extent that he found himself in agreement with the principle arising out of the circumstances of the moment.

He recognized no obligation to obey the rules of the colony, and made no secret of this. He did stand in a certain awe of me, it is true, but would never hear my admonitions out, interrupting me with a passionate speech, in which he would invariably accuse his innumerable enemies of all sorts of offences – such as sucking up to me, slander, or bad management – then, shaking his whip at absent foes, he would leave the room indignantly, slamming the door after him. He was intolerably rude to the teachers, but even in his rudeness there was a certain charm, and our teachers did not take offence. There was nothing brazen or even inimical in his bearing, for the passionate human note always prevailed, and he never quarrelled on selfish grounds.

Anton's conduct in the colony was ruled by his passion for horses and stable work. It would be hard to trace the origin of this passion. He was much more intelligent than the average inmate of the colony, and he used good townsman's Russian, merely seasoning his speech with occasional Ukrainian expressions by way of showing off. He tried to keep himself neat, read a great deal, and liked talking about books. This did not prevent him from spending almost his whole time in the stable, removing dung, perpetually harnessing and unharnessing the horses, polishing bridles and breechings, plaiting the whip; he was never too tired, in any weather, to drive to town, or to the new colony, in spite of the fact that he was in a perpetual state of semistarvation, for he was invariably late for dinner or supper, and if nobody remembered to leave him his share, he would never mention it himself.

His activities as stable boy were interspersed with incessant bickerings with Kalina Ivanovich, the blacksmiths, the storeroom monitors, and, above all, with anyone desirous of taking the horses out. He would only obey an order to harness the horses and go somewhere with them, after prolonged altercations, punctuated by accusations of cruelty to the horses, by reminders of occasions when Red and Bandit had come back with sores on their necks, and by demands for forage or shoeing iron. It was sometimes impossible to drive out of the colony for the simple reason that neither Anton nor the horses were to be found, and there was not the slightest indication of their whereabouts. After a painstaking search, in which half the colony participated, they might be found either in the Trepke grounds, or in a neighbouring meadow. Anton was always surrounded by two or three lads as infatuated with him as he was infatuated with the horses. These boys kept the horses well in hand, and scrupulous cleanliness prevailed in the stable – the floors swept, the harness in its right place, the carts in a straight row, a dead magpie hanging over each horse's head, the horses themselves well groomed, their manes plaited, their tails neatly tied.

Quite late one evening in June, some boys came running to me from the dormitory, exclaiming:

"Kozyr's ill – he's dying!"

"Dying?" "Yes, dying: he's burning hot and hardly breathes."

Ekaterina Grigoryevna corroborated their words, saying Kozyr had had a heart attack, and that a doctor must be found at once. I sent for Anton. He came, obviously determined to oppose in advance any order I was likely to give.

"Anton, put the horses to at once! You'll have to go to town immediately!"

Anton would not let me go on:

'I'm not going anywhere, and I won't let you have the horses! They've been worked off their feet all day – they haven't had a chance to cool down.... I'm not going to drive them!"

"Don't you understand it's for a doctor?"

"I don't care a straw who's sick! Red is sick too, and no one calls a doctor for him."

I fairly lost my temper.

"Give the stable over to Oprishko this minute! You're impossible to work with!"

"Let him have it, I don't care! We'll see how Oprishko manages! You believe anything people tell you – 'he's ill, he's dying,' and not the slightest consideration for the horses – let them die.... All right, let them – *I'm* not going to let you have them!"

"Did you hear me? You're not head groom any more, hand the stable over to Oprishko!"

"All right – I will! Let anyone have it who wants it. I won't live in the colony any more!"

"You can do as you like. Nobody's keeping you!"

Anton, with tears in his eyes, started fumbling in the depths of his pocket, and pulling out a bunch of keys, he put them on the table. Oprishko, Anton's right hand, came into the room and stared with amazement at his weeping chief. Bratchenko looked at him with scorn, made as if to say something, but only wiped his nose with his sleeve without a word and left the room.

He left the colony that very evening, not even going into the dormitory. Those who drove to town to fetch a doctor saw him striding along the road; he did not ask for a lift and waved away their invitation.

Two days later, in the evening, Oprishko burst into my room, crying, his face streaming with blood. Before I had time to ask him what it was all about, Lydia Petrovna, who was on duty that day, ran into the room in a state of great perturbation.

"Anton Semyonovich!" she cried. "Do go to the stable – Bratchenko is there, kicking up the most awful row!"

On our way to the stable we met the groom, the huge Fedorenko, making the woods resound with his bawling.

"What's the matter with you?" I asked.

"I... he... what right has he...? He beat me in the face with a pitchfork!"

"Who – Bratchenko?"

"Bratchenko! Bratchenko!"

At the stable I found Anton and another of our stable boys working away feverishly. Anton greeted me morosely, but seeing Oprishko behind me, forgot my presence altogether, and fell upon him.

"You stay away from here, or I'll lick you with the girth again! A fine driver you are! Look what he's done to Red!"

Snatching up a lantern, Anton dragged me up to Red. There really was a bad sore on Red's withers, which had been covered with a strip of clean cloth; Anton removed this gently, and put it back again.

"I've powdered it with xeroform," he said gravely.

"But what right have you to come to the stable without permission, dealing out reprisals, and beating people up?"

"You think I've done with him? He'd better keep out of my way – I'll beat him again!"

A crowd of boys stood laughing round the stable door. I had not the heart to be angry with Bratchenko – he was so sure that he and his horses were in the right!

"Look here, Anton," I said, "for beating up the boys you'll be under arrest in my room all the evening!"

"I have no time for that!"

"Will you shut up!" I shouted.

"All right, all right... so now I've got to stick about in some room!"

He spent the evening sulking over a book in my room.

In the winter of 1922, Anton and I had a bad time of it. The oats which Kalina Ivanovich had sowed in the shifting sands, without any manure, had yielded hardly any crop, and not even an appreciable quantity of straw. We still had no fields of our own. By January we found ourselves without fodder. At first we made shift somehow, begging for fodder now in the town, now from the neighbours, but people soon stopped giving us any. Kalina Ivanovich and I haunted the thresholds of offices to no avail.

At last real catastrophe came. Bratchenko, with tears in his eyes, told me that the horses had not been fed for two days. I was silent. Swearing and sobbing, Anton went on cleaning out the stables; but there was nothing more for him to do. The horses were lying on the ground, and Anton drew my special attention to this circumstance.

Next day Kalina Ivanovich returned from town in the worst of tempers.

"What's to be done? They won't give us anything. What is to be done?"

Anton stood in the door silent.

Kalina Ivanovich flung out his arms and glanced at Bratchenko:

"Are we to go out and steal – or what? What can one do? Poor dumb creatures!"

Pushing the door open, Anton flung himself out of the room. An hour later I was told that he had left the colony.

"Where's he gone to?" I asked.

"How do I know? He didn't say a word to anyone."

Next day he returned, accompanied byia villager and a cart leaded with straw. The villager was wearing a new coat and a fine sheepskin cap. The cart rumbled rhythmically into the yard – it had well-fitting plugs and the coats of the horses gleamed. The villager immediately recognized in Kalina Ivanovich an authority:

"A lad told me in the road, that the tax in kind is received here."

"What lad?"

"He was here just now... He came with me...."

Anton was peeping out of the stable trying to convey something to me by means of mysterious gestures.

Kalina Ivanovich, smiling into his pipe, drew me aside:

"What's to be done? Let's take this load from him and then we'll see!"

By now I understood what it was all about.

"How much is there here?" I asked the villager.

"There should be about twenty poods. I didn't weigh it."

Anton appeared on the scene.

"You told me yourself, on the way, that there were only seventeen," he objected. "And now you say twenty! Seventeen poods!"

"Unload it. And then come to the office and I'll give you a receipt."

In the office, or rather the tiny room which I had at last managed to screen off on the premises of the colony, I wrote down, with my own guilty hand on one of our forms, that I had received seventeen poods of oaten straw from Citizen Onufri Vats, as payment of tax in kind.

Vats bowed low, thanking me for he knew not what, and took his departure.

Bratchenko, so happy that he even sang, was busy with all his henchmen in the stable. Kalina Ivanovich, laughing uneasily, was rubbing his hands.

"Confound it! We shall get into trouble over this business!" he said. "But what were we to do? We couldn't let the animals starve! They're state property too, after all!"

"What was that muzhik so jolly about, when he went, I wonder?" I asked.

"Why shouldn't he be? He thought he would have to go to town, to climb the hill, and to stand in line when he got there. And here be said seventeen poods, the parasite, and nobody checked him, perhaps there are only fifteen!"

Two days later a cart loaded with hay was led into our yard.

"Payment of taxation in kind. Vats paid his here."

"And what's your name?"

"I'm one of the Vatses, too. Vats, Stepan Vats."

"Just a minute!" I went to look for Kalina Ivanovich, and hold a hurried consultation with him. In the doorway I met Anton.

"Well, you've shown them where to come to pay their taxes in kind, and now...."

"Take it, Anton Semyonovich – we'll explain somehow!"

It was impossible to take it, and equally impossible to refuse it. Why, it would be asked, should we take it from one Vats, and refuse it from another?

"Go and unload the hay, and I'll write you out a receipt."

We accepted two more cartloads of baled straw and forty poods of oats.

Shaking in my shoes, I awaited retribution. Anton would cast a thoughtful glance at me now and again, smiling almost imperceptibly out of the side of his mouth. But he no longer fought with all who came to him demanding horses, and, cheerfully carrying out all orders for the transport of freight, worked in the stables like a Hercules.

At last I received the brief but expressive inquiry:

"You are requested to inform us immediately on what authority the colony is accepting payment of taxation in kind.

"District Commissar for Supplies Ageyev."

I did not even tell Kalina Ivanovich about this inquiry. And I did not reply to it. What answer had I?

In April a pair of black horses harnessed to a tacharzka [Ukrainian cart – *Tr.*] flew into the yard of the colony, and the terrified Bratchenko flew into my office.

"They've come!" he gasped.

"Who's come?"

"Perhaps it's about the straw! He looks awfully angry."

He seated himself behind the corner of the stove, and fell silent.

The District Commissar for Supplies was true to type – clad in a leather jacket, armed with a revolver, young, spruce.

"Are you the director?" he asked.

"Yes."

"Did you get my inquiry?"

"I got it."

"Why didn't you answer? What's the meaning of this – am I supposed to come myself? Who gave you permission to accept payment of taxation in kind?"

"We accepted payment of taxation in kind without permission."

The District Commissar for Supplies jumped out of his chair, shouting: "What d'you mean – without permission? Do you realize what this implies? You will be arrested for this, do you know that?"

I knew that.

"Do your stuff," said I in hollow tones to the District Commissar for Supplies. "I'm not attempting to defend myself, or get out of it. And please don't shout! Do what you think necessary!"

He strode obliquely from corner to corner of my tiny office.

"This is one hell of a business!" he muttered, as if to himself, and then he snorted like a war horse.

Anton came out of his corner from behind the stove, following with his glance the peppery District Commissar for Supplies. Suddenly he exclaimed in a low voice like the hum of a beetle:

"Anyone would stop caring whether it was payment in kind or what it was, if the horses hadn't been fed for four days! If your fine black horses had done nothing but read the newspapers for four days, would you have been able to gallop up to the colony like you did?"

Ageyev came to a halt, astonished.

"And who may you be? What are you doing here?"

"This is our head groom – he's a more or less interested party," I said.

The District Commissar for Supplies resumed his striding across the room, and suddenly came to a stop in front of Anton.

"Did you at least enter it on your books? This is one hell of a business!"

Anton leaped over to my table, and whispered anxiously:

"It is entered, isn't it, Anton Semyonovich?"

Neither Ageyev nor I could help laughing.

"It's entered."

"Where did you get such a fine lad?" asked the District Commissar for Supplies.

"We make them ourselves," I smiled.

Bratchenko raised his eyes to the face of the District Commissar for Supplies and asked with grave friendliness:

"Shall I feed your blacks?"

"Go ahead and feed them!"

13

OSADCHY

The winter and spring of 1922 were marked by terrific explosions in the Gorky Colony. They came one after another with hardly a breathing space, and they are now fused in my memory in a sort of tangled mass of misfortunes.

And yet, despite so much that was tragic in those days, they were days of growth, both material and moral. How it was that these two phenomena – tragedy and growth – could logically exist side by side, I should at present have some trouble in explaining. But they did. The usual day in the colony was, even then, a wonderful day, filled with toil, mutual confidence, and feelings of human fellowship; in addition to all this, there were always laughter, jokes, enthusiasm, and a fine cheerful spirit. And yet scarcely a week passed in which some incredible occurrence did not plunge us into the abyss, involving us in a chain of events so fatal, that we almost lost our normal outlook, and became like sick persons, reacting to the outward world with lacerated nerves.

Quite unexpectedly anti-Semitism cropped up in our midst. Up to then there had been no Jews in the colony. In the autumn the first one came, and after this, one at a time, several more. One of them had worked in some capacity in the Gubernia Criminal Investigation Department, and he was the first to receive the full impact of the wild rage of our original inmates.

At first I was unable to make out who were the major, and who the minor offenders. Later arrivals at the colony were anti-Semitic simply because they had found a convenient outlet for their hoodlum instincts, while the older ones had had more frequent opportunities to insult and bully the Jewish boys.

The name of our first Jewish member was Ostromukhov. He was beaten up in season and out of season.

To be beaten up, to be continually mocked at, to have a decent belt or a sound pair of boots substituted by worn-out articles, to be cheated out of their food, or have it befouled, to be incessantly teased, to be called all manner of insulting names, and, worst of all, to be kept in a state of continual terror and humiliation – such was the fate in the colony, not of Ostromukhov alone, but also of Schneider, Gleiser, and Krainik. It was a matter of excruciating difficulty for us to struggle against all this. Everything was carried out in the utmost secrecy, with extreme caution, and almost without risk, since the Jewish boys were terrified out of their wits from the very beginning, and afraid to complain. It was only possible to build up surmises on indirect signs, such as a dejected appearance, silent and timid behaviour, or through vague rumours arising from friendly chats between the teachers and the more impressionable of the younger boys.

It was, however, impossible entirely to conceal from the pedagogical staff the systematic persecution of a whole group of their charges, and the time came when the raging of anti-Semitism in the colony was a secret from no one. It even became possible to establish the names of the worst bullies. They were all our old friends – Burun, Mityagin, Volokhov, Prikhodko. But the dominant roles belonged to two boys – Osadchy and Taranets.

His liveliness, wit, and organizing ability had long placed Taranets in the first ranks among the boys of the colony. But the arrival of older boys somewhat restricted the field of his activities. His power complex now found an outlet in intimidating and persecuting the Jewish boys. Osadchy, who was sixteen years old, was sullen, stubborn, strong, and thoroughly demoralized. He was proud of his part, and this, not because he found any nostalgic beauty in it, but out of pure obstinacy, because it was *his* past, and his life was nobody's business but his own.

Osadchy knew how to savour life, and always took good care that his days should not pass without some sort of enjoyment. He was not very fastidious in his ideas of enjoyment, usually contenting himself with ia visit to Pirogovka, a village on the near side of the town, whose inhabitants were a mixture of kulaks and small traders. At that time Pirogovka was noted for its abundance of pretty girls, and samogon, and it was these attractions which constituted Osadchy's principal enjoyment. His inseparable companion was the colony's most notorious loafer and glutton, Galatenko.

Osadchy sported a magnificent forelock, which prevented him from seeing the world around him, but was undoubtedly an enormous asset when laying siege to the affections of the maidens of Pirogovka. Whenever I had occasion to interfere with his private life, Osadchy would cast glances at me from beneath this forelock, full of ill-humour, and as I thought, dislike. I would not allow him to go to Pirogovka, insistently demanding a greater share of his interests for the colony.

Osadchy became the chief inquisitor of the Jewish boys. He could hardly, however, be called an anti-Semite. It was simply that the defencelessness of the Jewish boys, and the impunity with which they could be persecuted, afforded him opportunities to shine in the colony in all his native wit and bravado.

We had to think twice before embarking upon a straightforward, open campaign against our Jew-baiters, since any such campaign might have been fraught with the direst consequences for the Jewish boys themselves. Such types as Osadchy would not scruple, at a pinch, to use their knives. It would be necessary, therefore, either to go gradually, to work below the surface, taking every precaution, or to put an end to it all with a single explosion.

I began by trying the first method. My idea was to isolate Osadchy and Taranets. Karabanov, Mityagin, Prikhodko and Burun were all my friends, and I counted on their support. But the most I could achieve here was their promise to leave the Jewish boys alone.

"Who are we to protect them from – the whole colony?"

"None of that, Semyon," I said. "You know quite well who I mean!"

"Well, and if I do? Supposing I do stick up for them, I can't tie Ostromukhov to me, can I? They'll catch him, all the same, and beat him up worse than ever!"

Mityagin frankly told me:

"I can't do anything about it – it's not in my line – but I won't hurt them. What do I want with them?"

Zadorov sympathized with my attitude more than any of them, but he could not declare open warfare against boys like Osadchy.

"Something very drastic will have to be done," he said, "but what, I don't know. They keep all that from me, same as they do from you. They never touch anyone in front of me."

In the meantime the situation with regard to the Jews was going from bad to worse. The Jewish boys bore bruises on their persons every day now, but when questioned, refused to name their tormentors. Osadchy strutted about the colony, looking defiantly at me and the teachers from beneath his magnificent forelock.

Deciding to take the bull by the horns, I summoned him to my office. He flatly denied everything, but his whole appearance showed that he was only doing so for convention's sake, and that in reality he did not give a rap what I thought of him.

"You beat them up every day!"

"Nothing of the sort!" he said indifferently.

I threatened to send him away from the colony.

"All right, do!"

He knew very well what a long and agonizing business it was to expel anyone from the colony. Endless applications would have to be made to the Commission, all sorts of forms and reports handed in, and Osadchy himself, not to mention a host of witnesses, sent over and over again for interrogation.

Besides it was not Osadchy in himself who interested me just now. The whole colony looked on at his exploits, and many regarded him with approval and admiration. To expel him from the colony would have been to perpetuate this feeling in the form of a permanent reminder of the martyred hero Osadchy, who had feared nothing, obeyed no one, beaten up the Jews, and for this had been expelled. Moreover, Osadchy was not the only one who persecuted the Jewish boys. Taranets, less violent than Osadchy, was infinitely more inventive and subtle. He never beat them up, and in front of others was almost affectionate to the Jewish boys; but at night he would stick pieces of paper between the toes of one or other of them, set light to the paper, and get back to bed, feigning sleep. Or, getting hold of a pair of clippers, would persuade some hulking fellow such as Fedorenko to clip Schneider's hair to the very roots on one side of his head, and then go through the motions of discovering that the clippers had suddenly got out of order, and jeer at the poor boy, who followed him about in tears, imploring him to finish what he had begun.

The delivery from all these misfortunes came about in the most unexpected manner, and one not very creditable to the colony.

One evening the door of my office opened, and Ivan Ivanovich ushered in Ostromukhov and Schneider, both of them bleeding profusely and spitting blood, but not even crying, so accustomed had they become to violence.

"Osadchy?" I asked.

The teacher on duty related that Osadchy had pestered Schneider, who was on dining room duty, all through suppertime – making him take back the platefuls he was handing round, change the bread, and so on. Finally, just because Schneider, accidentally tipping up a plate, dipped his thumb into the soup he was serving, Osadchy rose from his place, and, in front of the teacher on duty, and the whole colony, struck Schneider in the face. Schneider himself might have kept silent, but the teacher on duty was no coward, and there had never before been a fight in front of a member of the teaching staff. Ivan Ivanovich ordered Osadchy to leave the dining room and go and report himself to me. Osadchy moved towards the dining room door, but stopped in the doorway, exclaiming:

"I'll go to the director, but first I'll make that Ikey sing!"

And here, a minor miracle took place. Ostromukhov, always the meekest of the Jewish boys, suddenly jumped from the table, and threw himself upon Osadchy.

"I'm not going to let you beat him up!" he cried.

It all ended in Osadchy beating up Ostromukhov right there in the dining room; and on the way out, observing Schneider cowering in the covered entrance, he struck him a blow so violent that one of his teeth came out. Osadchy refused to go to me.

In my office, Ostromukhov and Schneider were smearing the blood over their faces with their grimy sleeves, but did not cry, having evidently given themselves up for lost. I was myself convinced that if I did not once for all relieve the tension, the Jewish boys would have to save themselves by precipitate flight, or be prepared for a veritable martyrdom. What chiefly oppressed me, and made my blood run cold, was the indifference shown to the massacre in the dining room by all the other boys – even Zadorov. I felt at this moment as lonely as during the first days of the colony's existence. But in those first days I had looked neither for support nor sympathy from any quarter, it had been a natural loneliness which I had recognized to be inevitable. Now, however, I had become spoiled and was accustomed to the constant co-operation of my charges.

Several other persons were by now in my office, as well as the sufferers.

"Call Osadchy," I said to one of them.

I was almost sure that Osadchy, having taken the bit between his teeth, would refuse to come, and had firmly resolved, if necessary, to fetch him myself, even if I had to take out my revolver.

But Osadchy came, bursting into the office with his jacket thrown over his shoulders, his hands in his trouser pockets, overturning a chair on his way. He was accompanied by Taranets. Taranets tried to look as if all this was extremely amusing, and that he had only come in the hope of an entertaining spectacle.

Osadchy, glancing at me over his shoulder, said:

"Well, I've come.... What is it?"

I pointed to Schneider and Ostromukhov.

"What's the meaning of this?"

"Is that all? What the hell! Two little sheenies! I thought you really had something to show me."

And suddenly the pedagogical soil gave way beneath me with a loud explosion. I felt as if I were in a kind of human void. The heavy abacus lying on my table suddenly flew at the head of Osadchy. I missed my aim, and the frame struck the wall with a clatter and fell to the ground.

Senseless with rage, I felt about on the table for a heavy object, but instead, suddenly picked up a chair and rushed at Osadchy with it. In a panic he stumbled towards the door, but his coat fell off his shoulders on to the floor, entangling his feet, and bringing him down.

My senses returned to me – somebody was taking me by the shoulder. I looked back – Zadorov was smiling at me.

"That swine isn't worth it!"

Osadchy was sitting on the floor, whimpering. Taranets, deathly pale, his lips trembling, was seated perfectly still on the window sill.

"You bullied these kids, too!" I said.

Taranets slipped down from the window sill.

"I give you my word of honour I'll never do it again!"

"Get out of here!"

He went out on tiptoe.

At last Osadchy got up, holding his jacket in one hand, while with the other hand he demolished the last trace of his nervous weakness – a solitary tear slowly crawling down his grimy cheek. He looked at me quietly, gravely.

"You'll spend four days in the cobbler's shop, on bread and water."

"All right – I'll do it."

On the second day of his arrest, he called me to the cobbler's shop, and said:

"I won't do it any more. Will you forgive me?"

"We'll talk about forgiveness when you've finished your term."

At the end of four days he no longer asked for forgiveness, but said sullenly:

"I'm going away."

"Go on, then."
"Give me my papers." "You won't get any papers."
"Goodbye, then!"
"Goodbye."

14

INKPOTS AS GOOD-WILL PROMOTERS

We did not know where Osadchy had gone. Some said he had set out for Tashkent, where everything was cheap, and a gay life could be enjoyed, others, that Osadchy had an uncle in our town, or perhaps it was only a friend who was a drayman.

I did not know how to recover my mental equilibrium after this fresh pedagogical setback. The boys bombarded me with questions – hadn't I heard anything about Osadchy?

"What's Osadchy to you?" I asked. "What makes you worry so?"

"We're not worrying," said Yarabanov, "but it would be better if he were here. It would be better for you."

"I don't understand."

Karabanov turned a Mephistophelian glance upon me.

"Maybe you don't feel so good inside... in your soul?"

"You go to hell, with your talk about souls!" I yelled. "What do you think – am I to give up my soul to you now?"

Karabanov quietly slipped away from me.

In the meanwhile the colony rang with life. All around me was its cheerful music, and I could hear from beneath my window (somehow everyone seemed to gather beneath my window), the sounds of the jokes and pranks with which the daily tasks were interspersed; and there seemed to be no bickering. And one day Ekaterina Grigoryevna said to me, like a nurse trying to humour a very sick patient: "Stop eating your heart out – it'll pass!"

"I'm not worrying! Of course it'll pass! How are things in the colony?"

"I can hardly explain it to myself," she replied. "Things are fine in the colony, quite human, you know. Our Jewish boys are darlings – they're a bit overawed by everything that's happened, but they're working splendidly, if they are a bit shy! Would you believe it – the seniors are simply coddling them! Mityagin fusses round like a nurse – once he actually made Gleiser wash himself, and he cut his hair and even sewed on his buttons for him!"

Everything was going well. Yes, but what of the soul of the pedagogue? It was given up to chaos in which a veritable jumble of thoughts and feelings ran riot. One question especially pursued me – was I never to discover wherein lay the secret? Everything seemed to have been in my hands, I only had to gather it up. There was a new look in the eyes of many of the boys, and then everything had collapsed ignominiously. Could it be that we would have to begin all over again?

I was enraged by the disgracefully low level of pedagogical technique, and my own lack of technical skill. And I pondered with disgust and fury over the science of pedagogics.

"How many thousands of years has it been in existence?" I thought. "What names – what brilliant ideas – Pestalozzi, Rousseau, Natorp, Blonsky! How many volumes, what reams of paper, how many reputations! And at the same time – a void. It all amounts to nothing, and no one can tell me how to deal with one young hooligan! There is no method, no means, no logic-nothing! Nothing but a lot of claptrap!"

Least of all did I worry about Osadchy. I had written him off as a bad debt, entering him on the list of losses and spoilage inevitable in any enterprise. Nor was I much impressed by his melodramatic departure.

Besides, he soon returned.

And then fresh disaster came upon us, on hearing of which I at last realized what was meant by people's hair standing on end.

One still winter night a gang of the Gorky boys, Osadchy among them, got involved in a brawl with the lads of Pirogovka. The brawl developed into a regular fight, our side chiefly using cold steel (Finnish knives), the other side using firearms – sawn-off rifles. The fight ended in a victory for our side. The village lads were driven from their position at the head of the street, whence they fled ignominiously, locking themselves into the building of the Village Soviet. By three o'clock the Village Soviet was taken by storm, in other words, the doors and windows were broken in, and the fight turned into energetic pursuit. The village boys escaped through these doors, and windows, and ran to their homes, the Gorky boys returned in triumph to the colony.

The worst of it was that the premises of the Village Soviet itself were thoroughly smashed up, and the next day it was impossible to work there. In addition to windows and doors, tables and benches had also been rendered useless, papers scattered, and inkpots broken.

The next morning the bandits woke up as innocent as babes, and went about their work. But at noon the chairman of the

Pirogovka Village Soviet came to me with the story of the previous night.

I gazed with astonishment at the skinny, canny little villager. I could not understand how he could go on talking to me, why he did not call the militia, and have all these ruffians, and myself with them, put under arrest.

But the chairman related it all more in sorrow than in anger, his chief anxiety appearing to be that the colony should repair the windows and doors, and have the tables mended. He ended by asking if the colony would let him, the Pirogovka chairman, have a couple of inkpots!

I was simply overwhelmed with astonishment, completely failing to understand the reason for such an indulgent attitude on the part of the authorities. Then I decided that the chairman, like myself, unable to grasp the full horror of the incident, was simply talking because he felt the necessity of reacting somehow or other. I judged him by myself – who could do nothing but mutter trivialities.

"Of course, of course!" I assured him. "We'll repair everything. Inkpots? You can have these!"

The chairman took an inkpot, holding it carefully in his left hand, pressed against his abdomen. It was an ordinary safety inkpot.

"We'll repair everything," I repeated. "I'll send a man at once. The only thing we shall have to put off will be the windowpanes – we shall have to go to town to get glass."

The chairman cast a grateful glance at me.

"Oh, tomorrow will do – when you get the glass – then you can do it all together."

"M'hm. All right, tomorrow then!"

But why doesn't he go then, this remarkably meek chairman?

"Are you going straight home?" I asked him.

"Yes."

The chairman glanced over his shoulder, pulled a yellow handkerchief out of his pocket, and wiped his perfectly clean moustache. Then he moved closer to me.

"It's like this, you see," he said. "Your lads yesterday took.., they're all just young fellows, you know... and my lad was there, too. Well, as I say, they're all quite young, it's all in fun, nothing serious – God forbid! Their chums have them, and he wanted one, too.... It's just as I was saying... in our times, you know... they all carry them...."

"What on earth are you driving at? Forgive me, I don't quite understand...."

"The gun!" blurted out the chairman.

"What gun?"

"The gun!"

"What about it?"

"Well, for God's sake – it's just what I say! They were fooling about... you know, yesterday, I mean. And your lads took one away from mine, and from another of them, or perhaps they lost them – they'd all had a drop too much, you know. Where do they get the stuff from, I'd like to know!"

"Who had a drop too much?"

"Well, for God's sake! Who? Who? How can one know who? I wasn't there, but they all say your chaps were drunk."

"And yours?"

The chairman hesitated.

"I wasn't there, I tell you," he repeated. "Of course yesterday was Sunday. But that's not what I've come about. They're young, your lads, too. I'm not saying anything... there was a scrimmage, nobody was killed, or even wounded. Or perhaps some of your boys *were?*" he concluded nervously.

"I haven't spoken to our boys yet." "I couldn't say – somebody said there were two or three shots. Maybe as they were running away – your lads are very fiery, you know, and our country boys, they're not so quick at the uptake, you know.... Tee-hee!"

The old fellow laughed, screwing up his eyes, ever so loving and friendly.... Such old men are always called "Dad" by everyone. Looking at him, I could not help laughing, too, but within, all was chaos.

"So you think nothing special happened – they fought, and they'll make it up," I suggested.

"That's just it, that's just it – they must make it up. In my young days we fought over girls in real earnest. My brother Yakov was beaten to death by the other lads. You just call your lads and give them a talking, so that they won't do it any more."

I went out on to the porch.

"Call all the boys who were in Pirogovka last night!"

"Where are they?" asked a sharp little chap who happened to he crossing the yard on extremely urgent business of his own.

"Don't you know who was in Pirogovka last night?"

"Aren't you sly? I'd better tell Burun to go to you."

"All right – call Burun!"

Burun appeared on the porch.

"Is Osadchy in the colony?" I asked.

"Yes. He's working in the joiners' shop."

"You tell him this – our boys were on the spree in Pirogovka yesterday, and it's a very serious affair."

"Yes, the fellows were talking about it."

"Very well, then. Just you tell Osadchy that they're all to come to me – the chairman's in my room. And let there be no nonsense, it could end very unpleasantly."

My office filled up with the "heroes" of Pirogovka – Osadchy, Prikhodko, Chobot, Oprishko, Galatenko, Golos, Soroka, and a few others whose names have slipped my memory. Osadchy seemed quite at his ease, as if there had never been anything wrong between us, and I had no wish to rake up old scores in front of outsiders.

"You were in Pirogovka yesterday, you were drunk, there was rough-housing. People tried to stop you, and you beat up the village lads, and smashed up the Village Soviet. Isn't that so?"

"It wasn't quite like you say," volunteered Osadchy. "The fellows were in Pirogovka, that's true, and I was there three days, you know, I... but we weren't drunk, that's not true. Their Panas and our Soroka were at it from the morning, and Soroka was a bit tight... just a little, you know. Golos was treated by friends. But all the rest were as dry as a bone. And we didn't start anything with anybody, we just walked up and down, like everybody else. And then some guy – Kharchenko it was – came up to me and shouted. 'Hands up!' and pointed his gun at me. I did give him a sock in the jaw then, it's true. That's how it all started. They were angry with us because the girls liked going with us best."

"What 'all started'?"

"Oh, nothing, there was just a scrimmage. If they hadn't fired, nothing would have happened. But Panas fired, and Kharchenko too, and so we began to chase them. We didn't want to beat them up – just to take their guns away – and they locked themselves in. Prikhodko – you know what he is! – he up and – "

"Never mind all that! Where are the guns? How many did you get?"

"Two!"

Osadchy turned to Soroka.

"Bring them here!" I commanded.

The guns were produced. I sent the boys back to the workshops. The chairman hovered around the guns.

"So I can take them?"

"Oh, no! Your son has no right to carry a gun. Nor has Kharchenko. And I have no right to give them back to you."

"What do I want them for? Don't you give them up, let them stay here, maybe they'll come in handy in the woods, to frighten off thieves.... I just wanted to ask you not to make too much of the whole business... boys will be boys, you know...."

"You mean you don't want me to report...."

"Why yes, you know...."

I laughed.

"Why should I? We're neighbours, aren't we?"

"That's it!" exclaimed the old man joyfully. "We're neighbours! These things will happen! And if every little thing were to be reported to the authorities...."

The chairman departed, and I breathed freely.

I ought to have made pedagogical capital out of this business. But both the boys and I were so relieved that everything had ended satisfactorily that this time I dispensed with pedagogics. I did not punish anyone, only making them promise never to go to Pirogovka again without my permission, and to try and establish friendly relations with the lads of the village.

15
"OURS IS A BEAUTY!"

By the winter of 1922 the number of our girls was increased to six. Olya Voronova had outgrown her plainness, and become quite a pretty girl. The boys began to take notice of her in good earnest, but Olya was equally good-natured and aloof with them all. Her only friend among them was Burun. Protected by the Herculean form of Burun, Olya feared nobody in the colony, and could even afford to ignore the infatuation of Prikhodko, the strongest, stupidest; and most feckless boy in the colony. Burun was not in love with her; a healthy, youthful friendship existed between him and Olya, greatly adding to the prestige of both in the colony. Despite her beauty, Olya did not make herself conspicuous in any way. She loved the land – work in the fields however heavy had the attraction of music for her, and she would say of herself: "When I'm grownup I'll marry a muzhik – that I will!"

The leading spirit among the girls was Nastya Nochevnaya. She had been sent to the colony with an enormous sheaf of papers, in which all sorts of things were recorded of her – that she was a thief, a receiver of stolen goods, that she had run a den of thieves. We regarded Nastya as something of a marvel, for she was a person of extraordinary charm and integrity. Although barely fifteen, she was distinguished by her stateliness, her fair complexion, the proud carriage of her head, and her firmness of character. She knew how to scold the other girls when necessary, without asperity or shrillness, and could quell a boy with a single glance and a brief, impressive reproof.

"What d'you mean by crumbling your bread and then throwing it away? Have you come into a fortune, or have you taken lessons from the pigs? Pick it up this instant!" she would say, in her deep, throaty voice, with its undertones of restrained force.

Nastya made friends with the women teachers, read a great deal, and advanced undeviatingly towards the goal she had set herself – the Rabfak. But for Nastya, as for all the others who shared her ambition – Yarabanov, Vershnev, Zadorov, Vetkovsky – the Rabfak was still a great way off. Our fledglings were as yet very backward, and found the greatest difficulty in mastering the intricacies of arithmetic and politgramota [rudimentary politico-civic studies – *Tr.*]. The most advanced of them was Raissa Sokolova, whom we had sent to the Kiev Rabfak in the autumn of 1921.

We knew in our hearts that this was a hopeless undertaking, but our women teachers did so want to have a student of the Rabfak in the colony. The aspiration was a laudable one, but Raissa was not a particularly suitable object for so sacred a cause. She prepared for her Rabfak entrance examination almost the whole summer, but had to be driven by main force to her books, for Raissa herself by no means aspired to education of any sort.

Zadorov, Vershnev, Rarabanov, who were all endowed with a taste for study, were extremely displeased that Raissa was going to be promoted to the status of a student. Vershnev, remarkable for his ability to read day and night, and even while working the bellows in the smithy, was a lover of righteousness, and a searcher after truth; he could not mention without indignation Raissa's brilliant future.

"C-c-an't you see," he stammered, "Raissa will end up in jail, anyhow?"

Karabanov was still more definite in his expressions.

"I never thought you would have done anything so rash!"

Ziadorov, no whit abashed by Raissa's presence, smiled disdainfully, saying, with a scornful gesture:

"Rabfak student! You might as well try to make a silk purse out of a sow's ear." Raissa replied to all these sarcasms with her languid simpering smile; she did not in the least desire to get into the Rabfak, but she was gratified, and the idea of going to Kiev pleased her.

I agreed with the lads. Indeed, what sort of a student would Raissa make? Even now, while studying for the Rabfak, she used to receive mysterious notes from the town, and leave the colony on the sly every now and then. With equal secrecy she was visited by Korneyev, a boy who had only stayed in the colony three weeks, during which time he had robbed us deliberately and systematically, and had then become involved in a robbery in the town – a wanderer from one criminal investigation department to another, a thoroughly depraved and loathsome individual, one of the few people whom I had recognized, at first sight, as incorrigible.

Raissa did pass the entrance examination for the Rabfak. But a week after we received this inspiring news we learned from some source or other that Korneyev also had left for Kiev.

"Now she'll really learn something!" said Zadorov.

The winter passed. Raissa wrote every now and then, but little could be made of her letters. Now it seemed as if everything was going splendidly, now she seemed to be finding her studies extremely difficult, and always she was in need of money, although she received a stipend. Every month we sent her twenty or thirty rubles. Zadorov declared that Korneyev fared sumptuously on this money, and this was probably not far from the truth. The women teachers, who had been the initiators of the Kiev scheme, were mercilessly held up to scorn:

"Anyone could see it was no good – only you couldn't! How is it that we could see it, and you couldn't?"

In January Raissa unexpectedly turned up al the colony, with all her hampers, saying that she had been allowed to come home for the holidays. But she had no papers in confirmation of this, and her behaviour clearly showed that she had not the slightest intention of returning to Kiev. The Kiev Rabfak, in reply to my inquiries, informed me that Raissa Sokolova had stopped attending the institute, and had left its hostel for an unknown destination.

Everything was now clear. To do the boys justice, they did not tease Raissa or taunt her with her failure, they seemed to have dismissed the whole adventure from their minds. During the first few days after her arrival, they made endless fun of Ekaterina Grigoryevna, who was crestfallen enough as it was, but on the whole they seemed to think that what had happened was nothing out of the ordinary, and had been foreseen by them all along.

In March, Natalya Markovna Osipova communicated to me her disquieting suspicion that Raissa displayed certain symptoms of pregnancy.

My blood ran cold. A girl member of a juvenile colony discovered to be pregnant! I was well aware of the existence in the vicinity of our colony – in the town and the Department of Public Education – of numbers of those virtuous prudes who are always awaiting the opportunity to raise a hue and cry: sexual immorality in a juvenile colony! Boys living with girls! I was alarmed both by the atmosphere in the colony, and the situation of Raissa, as one of my charges. I asked Natalya Markovna to have a "heart-to-heart talk" with Raissa.

Raissa flatly denied that she was pregnant, even professing indignation.

"Nothing of the sort!" she cried. "Who thought up such beastliness? And since when have the teachers begun spreading gossip?" Poor Natalya Markovna really felt that she had done wrong. Raissa was very fat, and the apparent pregnancy might be explained by unhealthy obesity, the more so as there were really no definite external signs. We decided to believe Raissa.

But a week later, Zadorov called me into the yard, one evening, for a private talk

"Did you know Raissa was pregnant?'"

"And how do you know?" "You're a funny chap! D'you mean to say you can't see it? Everyone knows, and I thought you did too."

"Well, supposing she is pregnant, what then?"

"Nothing! But why does she pretend not to be? Since she is pregnant, why does she try and behave as if nothing has happened? Look – here's a letter from Korneyev! See here – 'My dear wifie.' We knew about it long ago."

The teachers also displayed increasing signs of anxiety. I began to be irritated by the whole business.

"What's all the fuss about? If she's pregnant, then she'll give birth to a child. You can conceal pregnancy, but not a birth. It's not such a catastrophe – there'll be a child born, that's all!"

Summoning Raissa to my room, I asked her:

"Tell me the truth, Raissa! Are you pregnant?"

"Why is everybody pestering me? It's a disgrace – sticking to me like burrs! Pregnant! Pregnant! Once and For all, I tell you I'm not!"

Raissa burst into tears.

"Look here, Raissa," I said. "If you're pregnant, there's no need to try and conceal it. We'll help you to get some work, maybe right here, in the colony, and we'll help with money, too. Everything will have to be prepared for the child, baby clothes made, and all that...."

"Nothing of the sort! I don't want any work – leave me alone!"

"All right – you can go!"

We in the colony could learn nothing definite. She might have been sent to a doctor for examination, but on this point the opinion of the staff was divided. Some were urging for the immediate elucidation of the affair, others agreed with me that such an examination would be extremely unpleasant and offensive for a young girl, and that, after all, there was no necessity for it, sooner or later the whole truth would be known, and there was no hurry. If Raissa was pregnant, she could not be much past the fifth month. Let her calm down, and get accustomed to the idea, by which time it would be difficult to conceal anything. Raissa was left to herself.

On the 15th of April there was a big congress of teachers in the town theatre, at the opening meeting of which I gave a lecture on discipline. I finished my lecture at the first session, but my statements aroused such impassioned debate that the discussion of the lecture had to be put off till the next day. Almost our entire teaching staff and several of the older pupils attended the meeting, and we had to spend the night in town.

By then, interest in our colony was being shown beyond the limits of our district, and the next day the theatre was as full as it could hold. Among other points raised was that of coeducation. At that time coeducation was forbidden by law in colonies for juvenile delinquents, and ours was the only one in the whole country in which the experiment was being made.

While answering this question, the thought of Raissa just passed through my mind, but whether she was or was not pregnant seemed to me to have no bearing on the question of coeducation. I assured the meeting that in this respect all was well in our colony.

During the interval I was called into the vestibule. There I ran into the panting Bratchenko – he had ridden in extreme haste into town, and refused to tell any of the teachers what had happened.

"There's trouble in the colony, Anton Semyonovich," he said. "A dead baby has been found in the girls' dormitory."

"A dead baby!"

"Dead! Quite dead! In Raissa's hamper. Lenka was washing the floor, and happened to look into the hamper – perhaps she meant to take something. And there she saw a dead baby."

"What are you talking about?"

Our feelings were indescribable. Never before had I experienced such horror. The women teachers, pale and weeping, got out of the theatre somehow, and returned in a droshky to the colony. I was unable to leave, still having to counter the attacks which my lecture had provoked.

"Where's the baby now?" I asked Anton.

"Ivan Ivanovich locked it in the dormitory. It's there, in the dormitory."

"And Raissa?" "Raissa's sitting in the office, the fellows are guarding her."

I sent Anton to the militia with a declaration as to the discovery, remaining behind myself, to continue the discussion on discipline.

I only got back to the colony in the evening. Raissa was sitting on the wooden bench in my office, dishevelled, and wearing the apron in which she had been working in the laundry. She did not look at me when I came in, only let her head sink still lower. Beside her on a bench was Vershnev, surrounded with books – he was obviously looking for some reference, for he rapidly turned the leaves of volume after volume, and paid no attention to anyone.

I gave the order to unlock the door of the dormitory, and remove the hamper with the corpse to the linen room. Quite late in the evening, when everyone had gone to bed. I asked Raissa:

"Why did you do it?"

Raissa raised her head, gave me a blank, scarcely human look, and smoothed the apron over her knees.

"I did it, and that's all about it!"

"Why didn't you do what I told you?"

Suddenly she began to cry quietly.

"I don't know!" I left her to spend the night in the office under the guard of Vershnev, whose passion for reading was the best guarantee that he would stay awake. We were all afraid that Raissa would make some attempt on her own life.

The next morning an investigator arrived, but his investigations did not take long – there was hardly anyone to interrogate. Raissa related the details of her crime with terse precision. She had given birth to the child in the night, right there in the dormitory, where there were five other girls sleeping. Not one of them had waked up. Raissa's explanation of this was of the simplest: "I tried not to moan."

Immediately after the birth she had strangled the baby with her shawl. She denied having premeditated the murder.

"I didn't mean to, but it cried."

She had hidden the corpse in the hamper she had taken with her to the Rabfak, meaning to take it out the next night and leave it in the woods. She thought the foxes would eat it, and nobody would be any the wiser. The next morning she had gone to work in the laundry, where the other girls were washing their linen. She had had breakfast and dinner with all the rest, as usual – only some of the boys noticed that she was very glum.

The investigator took Raissa away, and ordered the corpse to be sent to the mortuary at one of the hospitals for a post mortem.

The teaching staff was completely demoralized by the whole affair. They thought the last days of the colony had arrived.

The boys were in a somewhat excited state. The girls were afraid of the dark and of their own dormitory, where they would not for the world stay without the boys. For several nights Zadorov and Karabanov hung about the dormitory. It all ended in neither the girls nor the boys sleeping, or as much as undressing. During these days the favourite occupation of the boys was frightening the girls – suddenly appearing beneath their windows draped in sheets, getting up appalling concerts in the vents of the stoves, or hiding under Raissa's bed, in order, when night fell, to imitate, at the top of their voices, the crying of a baby.

The murder itself was regarded by the boys as a perfectly simple phenomenon At the same time they disagreed with the teachers as to Raissa's motive. The teachers were convinced that Raissa had strangled her baby in an access of maidenly modesty – her overwrought state, the sleeping girls, the sudden cry of the child... her terror that it would wake her companions.

Zadorov almost split his sides with laughing when he heard the explanations of the ultrapsychologically-minded teachers.

"Drop that nonsense!" he exclaimed. "Maidenly modesty, indeed! She planned it all out beforehand and that's why she wouldn't admit she was going to have a baby soon! It was all planned out beforehand with Korneyev... to hide it in the hamper, and take it into the woods. If she had done it out of modesty, would she have gone so calmly to work the next morning? If I had my way, I would shoot that Raissa tomorrow! She's a worm, and a worm she will remain! And you go on about maidenly modesty – she never had any in her life!"

"Very well, then, what *was* her idea? Why did she do it?" asked the teachers in desperation.

"Her idea was very simple! What does she want with a baby? You have to look after a baby, feed it, and all that! A fat lot they wanted a child – especially Korneyev!"

"Oh, it couldn't be that!"

"Couldn't it? What a set of suckers! Of course Raissa will never admit it, but I'm quite sure if she was properly managed all sorts of things would come out...."

The other boys agreed wholeheartedly with Zadorov. Karabanov was perfectly convinced that it was not the first time Raissa had played "this trick," that probably something of the sort had occurred even before she came to the colony.

On the third day after the murder, Karabanov took the corpse of the child to the hospital. He returned very much elated.

"Oh, the sights I've seen! They've got all sorts of kids there in jars – twenty... thirty.... Some of them are ghastly – such heads! And one had its legs doubled up under it – you couldn't tell if it was a human being or a frog. Ours isn't like that! Ours is a beauty next to those!"

Ekaterina Grigoryevna shook her head reproachfully, but even she could hardly repress a smile.

"How can you, Semyon! You ought to be ashamed of yourself!"

The boys stood round laughing. They were sick of the dejected, sour countenances of the teachers.

Three months later Raissa was called to trial. The whole Pedagogical Council of the Gorky Colony was summoned to the court. "Psychology" and the theory of maidenly modesty prevailed in the courtroom. The judge reproached us for having failed to foster the right atmosphere and the right attitude. We had nothing to say for ourselves, of course. I was called privately to the judge and asked if I was ready to take Raissa back to the colony. I replied that I was.

Raissa received a sentence of eight years on probation, and was immediately handed over to be kept under supervision at the colony.

She returned to us just as if nothing had happened, bringing with her a pair of magnificent brown boots, attired in which at our evening parties she shone in the whirl of the waltz, evoking excruciating envy in the breasts of our laundresses and the Pirogovka girls.

"You'd better send Raissa out of the colony, Nastya Nochevnaya advised me, "or we'll do it ourselves! It's disgusting to have to share a room with her!"

I hastened to get her a job in the knitting mills.

I came across her in the town every now and then. Visiting the town much later, in 1928, I was surprised to recognize Raissa behind the counter in an eating house – she was much fatter than she had been, but at the same time she was more muscular, and the lines of her figure had greatly improved.

"How are you getting on?" I asked her.
"All right! I'm working at the counter. I have two kids, and a decent husband."
"Korneyev?"
"Oh, no!" she smiled. "That's all over! He was knifed in a street fight long ago. And, Anton Semyonovich–"
"Well, what is it?"
"Thanks for not letting me sink. Ever since I began to work at the mills I left my past behind me."

16
GABER SOUP

In the spring a fresh disaster came upon us – spotted typhus. The first to sicken was Kostya Vetkovsky.

Ekaterina Grigoryevna, who had once studied at a medical institute, attended us on those rare occasions when we could neither dispense with a doctor nor quite make up our minds to call one in. She had become the colony's specialist on the itch, and was skilled at first aid in cases of cuts, burns and bruises, and, during the winter, owing to the imperfections of our footwear, frostbitten toes. It seemed as if these were the only ills our inmates condescended to indulge in – they showed not the slightest inclination to have dealings with doctors and their remedies.

I always felt the greatest respect for my charges for this very aversion to medicine, and learned a great deal from them in this regard myself. It became quite a natural thing with us to take no notice of a temperature of 100, and we paraded our powers of endurance in front of one another. As a matter of fact this attitude was more or less forced upon us, since doctors visited us with extreme reluctance.

And so when Kostya fell ill, and his temperature went up to almost 102, it was regarded as something new in the experience of the colony. Kostya was put to bed, and we did all we could for him. In the evenings his friends gathered round his bed, and since he was popular a regular crowd surrounded him every evening. Not wishing to deprive Kostya of company or upset the boys, we also spent the evening hours at the patient's bedside.

Three days later Ekaterina Grigoryevna, in great alarm, communicated her suspicions to me – it looked very like spotted typhus. I forbade the other boys to go near his bed, but it would have been quite impossible to isolate him in any effective fashion – we had nowhere else but the dormitories to work and sit in of an evening.

When, in another day or two, Kostya got worse, he was wrapped in the wadded quilt which served him as a blanket, and placed in the phaeton. I drove into town with him.

About forty persons were walking about, lying down, and groaning in the hospital waiting room. The doctor was long in coming. It was obvious that the hospital staff was in a chronic state of exhaustion, and that very little good was to be expected from placing a patient in the hospital. At last the doctor came. He raised our Kostya's shirt with a weary gesture, saying wearily, with much senile grunting, to the feldsher [Medical assistant – *Tr.*] waiting with uplifted pencil: "Spotted fever. Send him to the fever huts."

In a field just outside the town stood about a score of wooden huts, left over from the war. I wandered long among nurses, patients, and attendants, the latter bearing stretchers covered with sheets. The patient was supposed to be received by the feldsher on duty, but no one knew where he was, or wanted to look for him. At last, losing patience, I fastened upon the nearest nurse and made free with the words "a disgrace" "inhuman!", "outrageous!" My fury was not without effect – Kostya was undressed, and led away.

On my return to the colony I learned that Zadorov, Osadchy, and Belukhin all had high temperatures. Zadorov, it is true, was still up and about, and I came upon him at the moment when he was arguing with Ekaterina Grigoryevna, who was trying to persuade him to go to bed.

"How funny you are!" he was saying. "Why should I go to bed? I'll just go to the smithy – Sofron will cure me in a moment."

"How will Sofron cure you? Why do you talk such nonsense?"

"The way he cures himself – vodka, pepper, salt, naphtol, and a dash of cart grease."

Zadorov burst out into his usual expressive, frank laughter.

"See how you've spoilt them, Anton Semyonovich!" said Ekaterina Grigoryevna. "He'll let Sofron cure him! Get along with you, and go to bed!"

Zadorov fairly exuded heat, and it was obvious that he could hardly stand. I took him by the elbow and silently piloted him to the dormitory. In the dormitory Osadchy and Belukhin were already in bed. Osadchy suffered, and made a great fuss about himself. I had long noted that such "dare-devil" lads always bore sickness very badly. Belukhin, on the other hand, was in his usual high spirits.

Belukhin was the jolliest, happiest boy in the whole colony. He came of a long line of working-class forbears, in Nizhni Tagil; he had left home in search of flour during the famine, and had been retained in Moscow after a raid by the militia, and put into a children's home, from which he had run away to the streets. Caught once again, he had again run away. An enterprising individual, he preferred speculation to stealing, but afterwards was the first to recount his exploits with good-natured guffaws – so bold, original, and unsuccessful had they been. At last Belukhin had realized that he would never make a speculator, and decided to go to the Ukraine.

At one time or another Belukhin, a bright and knowing lad, had been to school. He knew a little about everything, but for all that, was crassly, astoundingly ignorant. There are such lads: they seem to have been through the grammar, they know fractions, they even have a dim conception of simple interest, but all this is so clumsily applied, that the effect is ludicrous. Belukhin's very manner of speaking was clumsy, but it was at the same time intelligent and spirited.

Laid low by the typhus, he was inexhaustibly garrulous, and his wit, as ever, was amazing in its perfectly fortuitous combination of words:

"Typhus – that's medical intellectuality – why should it attack a dyed-in-the-wool worker? When Socialism is born, we won't let that bacillus cross the threshold, and if it comes on urgent business – for ration tickets, or something, because, after all, it's got to live too – we'll refer it to the secretary. And we'll make Kolya Vershnev secretary, because he sticks to books like fleas do to dogs. Kolya will deal with this medical intellectual – fleas and bacillus are all the same to him, and all equal under a democracy."

"I'll be the secretary, and what will you b-b-be under Socialism?" stammered Kolya Vershnev.

Kolya was sitting at the foot of Belukhin's bed, with a book as usual, and, also as usual, dishevelled and tattered.

"I'll write the laws, for you to go about dressed like a human being, and not like ia tramp, so that even Toska Solovyov can't stand it. How can you be such a reader, and look like a monkey? I don't suppose even an organ-grinder would have such a black monkey. Would he, Toska?"

The lads laughed at Vershnev. Vershnev did not take offence, but only looked affectionately at Belukhin out of his good-natured grey eyes. They were great friends, had come to the colony at the same time, and worked side by side in the smithy but while Belukhin was already working at the anvils, Kolya preferred to remain at the bellows, because there he could keep one hand free to hold a book.

Toska Solovyov, more often called Anton Semyonovich (he and I had the same name and patronymic), was only ten years old.

He had been found in our woods by Belukhin, unconscious, and in the last stages of starvation. He had come to the Ukraine from the Samara region with his parents, but had lost his mother on the way, and could not remember anything after that. Toska had a frank, pretty, childish face, which was almost always turned upon Belukhin. Toska had evidently seen very little in the course of his short life, and this gay, confident mocker, Belukhin, who did not know the meaning of fear and was such a thorough man of the world, had captured his imagination, and bound him to himself.

Toska was standing at the head of Belukhin's bed, his eyes blazing with love and admiration. His childish treble rang out in peals of laughter:

"Black monkey!"

"Toska here will be a fine fellow one day," said Belukhin, dragging him towards himself over the head of the bed.

Toska bent in confusion over Belukhin's quilted blanket.

"Listen, Toska, don't you go reading books like Kolya – look at him, he's gone and addled his own brains!"

"He doesn't read books – the books read him!" said Zadorov from the next bed.

I was sitting nearby, playing chess with Karabanov, and thinking to myself: they seem to have forgotten they have typhus.

"Call Ekaterina Grigoryevna, one of you,", I said.

Ekaterina Grigoryevna entered like an angel of wrath.

"What's all this sentimentality? Why is Toska hanging about here? What are you thinking about? It's preposterous!"

Toska nervously jumped off the bed, and retreated. Karabanov clutched his arm, crouched down, and started back towards the corner, in pretended panic.

"I'm afraid too!" he said.

"Toska!" croaked Zadorov, "take Anton Semyonovich's hand, too! How could you desert him?"

Ekaterina Grigoryevna looked helplessly from side to side amidst the joyous crowd.

"Just like Zulus!" she exclaimed.

"Zulus – those are the ones who go about without trousers, and use their friends for provisions," said Belukhin gravely. "One of them goes up to a young lady, and says: 'Allow me to accompany you!', and she, of course, is delighted. 'Please don't trouble! I can accompany myself,' she says. 'Oh, no! That won't do!' says he,

'You can't accompany yourself.' Then he takes her to the corner, and gobbles her up, without even mustard."

From the distant corner came Toska's shrill laughter. Even Ekaterina Grigoryevna had to smile.

"Zulus may eat young ladies, but you let little children go near typhus patients. It's just as bad!"

Vershnev seized the opportunity to avenge himself on Belukhin.

"Zulus d-d-don't eat young ladies," he stuttered, "and they're ever so much more c-c-cultured than you! You'll infect Toska!"

"And you, Vershnev," said Ekaterina Grigoryevna. "Why are you sitting on that bed? Go away this minute!"

Vershnev, somewhat confused, began gathering up the books he had scattered all over Belukhin's bed.

Zadorov stuck up for him.

"He's not a young lady! Belukhin won't eat him!"

Toska, already at Ekaterina Grigoryevna's side, said meditatively:

"Matvei wouldn't eat a black monkey!"

Vershnev held a regular pile of books under one arm, while under the other Toska suddenly appeared, kicking and laughing. Then the whole group flung itself on to Vershnev's bed, in the remotest corner of the room.

The next morning the deep hearse-like farm cart, built according to the design of Kalina Ivanovich, was filled to overflowing. On the floor of it, wrapped in quilts, sat our typhus patients. Across the top of it was a plank, on which Bratchenko and I perched. My heart was heavy, foreseeing a repetition of the trouble I had encountered when accompanying Vetkovsky. Besides, I was by no means certain that it was to their recovery the boys were really travelling.

Osadchy lay in the bottom of the cart, feverishly drawing the quilt over his shoulders. Dingy, grey wadding protruded through the quilt, and at my feet I could see Osadchy's boots, rough and worn. Belukhin pulled the quilt over his head, rolling it into the form of a tube.

"People will think we're a lot of priests," he said. "They'll wonder where on earth all these priests are going in a farm cart!"

Zadorov smiled in reply, his very smile showing how sick he felt.

At the fever huts everything was the same. I found a nurse who worked in the ward where Kostya was lying. She pulled herself up with difficulty in her headlong career along the corridor.

"Vetkovsky? In there, I think."

"How is he?"

"Nothing is known as yet."

Behind her back Anton made a slashing gesture with his whip.

"Nothing is known! I like that! What does it mean – nothing is known?"

"Is that boy with you?" asked the nurse, glancing with distaste at the damp Anton, who smelled of the stables, and to whose trousers were sticking bits of straw.

"We're from the Gorky Colony," I began cautiously. "One of our boys – Vetkovsky – is here. And I've brought three more – also typhus cases I think."

"You'll have to go to the waiting room.

"But there's such a crowd there. Besides, I should like the boys to be together."

"We can't give in to everyone's whims."

And on she pressed.

But Anton barred her way.

"What's the matter with you? You might at least speak to a fellow!"

"Go to the waiting room, comrades, it's no use standing here, talking!"

The nurse was angry with Anton, and so was I.

"Get out of here!" I cried. "Who asked you to interfere?"

Anton, however, remained where he was, gazing in astonishment from me to the nurse, and I continued speaking to the latter in the same irritated tone:

"Kindly let me say a word. I want my boys to recover. For every one of them who recovers I'm ready to give two poods of wheat flour. But I desire to deal with one person. Vetkovsky's in your ward. See that the others are taken there, too."

The nurse seemed to be taken aback – no doubt insulted.

"What d'you mean 'wheat flour'?" she tasked. "What's this – a bribe? I don't understand!"

"It's not a bribe, it's a bonus, see? If you don't understand, I'll find another nurse. This is no bribe: we are asking for a little extra care for our patients, a little extra work, perhaps. The point is, they're undernourished, and they haven't any relatives, you see."

"I'll take them in my ward without any wheat flour. How many are there of them?"

"I've just brought three more, but I'll probably be bringing some more along in a little while."

"All right – come with me!"

Anton and I followed the nurse. Anton winked significantly, nodding towards the nurse, but it was obvious that he, too, was amazed at the turn affairs had taken. He meekly accepted my refusal to take any notice of his grimaces.

The nurse led us to a room at the remotest corner of the hospital, and I sent Anton for our patients.

Of course they all had typhus. The feldsher on duty looked rather surprised at our quilts, but the nurse said in resolute tones:

"They're from the Gorky Colony. Send them to my ward."

"But have you any room?"

"We'll manage. Two are leaving today, and we'll find somewhere to put another bed."

Belukhin parted with us gaily.

"Bring some more," he said. "It'll be all the warmer!"

We were able to fulfil his request in two days, when we brought in Golos and Schneider, and, a week later, three others.

And this, fortunately, was all.

Anton visited the hospital several times to ask the nurse how our patients were getting on. The typhus did not do our boys much harm.

We were just beginning to think about going to town to fetch some of them, when suddenly, an one of the first days of spring, a ghostly figure wrapped in a wadded quilt emerged from the woods into the noon sunlight. The ghost approached the smithy, and squeaked: "Well, my brave smiths! How are you getting along here? Still reading? Take care you don't wear your brains out!"

The boys were delighted. Belukhin, though wasted and sallow-faced, was as jolly and fearless as ever.

Ekaterina Grigoryevna fell upon him – what did he mean by coming on foot? Why hadn't he waited to be sent for?

"You see, Ekaterina Grigoryevna, I would have waited," he explained. "But I did so long for some honest grub! Whenever I thought to myself: They're eating our rye bread there, and kondyor, and whole basins of porridge – such a longing spread over my whole psychology... I simply couldn't bear to look at that gaber soup of theirs. Oh, my! Oh, my!"

He could hardly speak for laughing. "What gaber soup?"

"You know – Gogol wrote about it, and he made it sound awfully good. And they were fond of serving that gaber soup in the hospital, but every time I looked at it, I had to laugh. I simply couldn't adapt myself. Oh, my! Oh, my! All could do was laugh! And the nurse would scold me, and that made me laugh still more, and I just laughed and laughed. Whenever I remembered the word gaber soup I simply couldn't eat. The moment I took up my spoon I began to die of laughter. So I just went away. Have you had dinner here? I suppose it's porridge today, eh?"

Ekaterina Grigoryevna got some milk for him from somewhere or other. A sick person mustn't eat porridge right away.

Belukhin thanked her joyfully:

"Thank you! Thank you for humouring my dying wishes!"

But nevertheless he poured the milk on to the mush. Ekaterina Grigoryevna gave him up as a bad job.

The rest came back soon after.

Anton took a sack of wheat flour to the home of the nurse.

17
SHARIN ON THE WARPATH

Raissa's baby, the typhus epidemic, the winter with its frozen toes, its felling of trees, and other hardships, were gradually forgotten, but in the Department of Public Education they could not forgive me for what they called my barrack discipline.

"We'll finish off that police regime of yours!" they told me. "We need to build up social education, not to establish a torture chamber."

In my lecture on discipline I had ventured to question the correctness of the generally accepted theory of those days, that punishment of any sort is degrading, that it is essential to give the fullest possible scope to the sacred creative impulses of the child, and that the great thing is to rely solely upon self-organization and self-discipline. I had also ventured to advance the theory, to me incontrovertible, that, so long as the collective, and the organs of the collective, bad not been created, so long as no traditions existed, and no elementary labour and cultural habits had been formed, the teacher was entitled – nay, was bound! – to use compulsion. I also maintained that it was impossible to base the whole of education on the child's interests, that the cultivation of the sense of duty frequently runs counter to them, especially as these present themselves to the child itself. I called for the education of a strong, toughened individual, capable of performing work that may be both unpleasant and tedious, should the interests of the collective require it.

Summing up, I insisted upon the necessity of the creation of a strong, enthusiastic – if necessary an austere – collective, and of placing all hopes on the collective alone. My opponents could only fling their pedagogical axioms in my face, starting over and over again from the words "the child."

I was quite prepared for the colony to be "finished off," but our urgent daily problems – the sowing campaign, and the endless repairs to the new colony – prevented me from worrying about my persecution by the Department of Public Education. Someone there must have stuck up for me, for it was long before I was "finished off." Otherwise, what could have been simpler than to remove me from my post?

I avoided visiting the Department, however, for they spoke to me there in a manner which was far from cordial, if not actually contemptuous. One of my chief molesters was a certain Sharin, a handsome, gallant individual – dark, wavy-haired, a provincial lady-killer. He bad thick, red, moist lips, and strongly-marked, arched eyebrows. Who knows what he had been before 1917, but now he was a great expert on – of all things! – social education. He had acquired with ease the fashionable phraseology, and had the gift of warbling windy linguistic trills which, he was convinced, were fraught with pedagogical and revolutionary values.

He had adopted an attitude of supercilious hostility towards me ever since, on one occasion, I bad been unable to restrain my uncontrollable laughter.

One day he came to the colony, where, in my office, his eyes fell upon a barometer on the table.

"What's that thing?" he asked. "A barometer."

"What d'you mean – a barometer?"

"Just a barometer," I replied, astonished. "It tells us what the weather's going to be."

"Tells you what the weather's going to be?" he repeated. "How can it do that, lying here on your table. The weather isn't in here, it's out-of- doors."

It was then that I gave way to outrageous, uncontrollable laughter. I might have been able to restrain myself if Sharin had not looked so learned, if he had not had such an imposing head of hair, such an air of erudite assurance.

This moved him to ire.

"Why do you laugh?"' he asked. "And you call yourself a pedagogue! Is that the way you're bringing up your charges? You should explain, if you see I don't understand, not laugh."

But I was incapable of such magnanimity, and could only go on laughing. I had once heard a story which was almost the exact replica of my conversation with Sharin about the barometer, and I found it infinitely amusing that such silly stories should actually find their illustration in real life, and that an inspector from the Gubernia Department of Public Education should furnish material for one.

Sharin went off in a huff.

During the debate on my lecture on discipline, he criticized me ruthlessly.

"The localized system of medico-pedagogical influence on the personality of the child," quoth he, "inasmuch as it is differentiated in the organization of social education, should predominate to the extent that it is in accord with the natural demands of the child, and to the extent that it opens creative possibilities in the development of the given structure – biological, social, or economic. From the aforesaid it follows...."

For two whole hours, hardly pausing to take breath, his eyes half-closed, he flooded the audience with the viscous stream of his erudition, ending up with the touching sentiment: "Life is joy."

And it was this same Sharin who smote me hip and thigh in the spring of 1922.

The Special Department of the First Reserve Army sent a boy to the colony, with the express order that he should be admitted. The Special Department and the Cheka had sent us boys before. We took this one in. Two days later Sharin summoned me:

"Did you accept Evgenyev?"

"Yes, I did."

"What right have you to accept anyone without our permission?"

"He was sent by the Special Department of the First Reserve Army."

"What's the Special Department to do with me? You have no right to accept anyone without our permission."

"I can't refuse the Special Department. And if you consider they have no right to send boys to me, then settle that point with them. It's not for me to be an arbiter between you and the Special Department."

"Send Evgenyev back at once!"

"Only on your written instructions."

"My oral instructions ought to be enough for you."

"Let me have them in writing.

"I'm your superior, and I could arrest you on the spot, and give you a week's detention for nonfulfilment of my oral instructions."

"All right – do!"

I saw the man was longing to use his right to have me imprisoned for a week. Why go on looking for a pretext, when here is one ready to hand?

"You don't mean to send the boy back?" he asked.

"I'm not going to send him back without written instructions. I would much prefer, you see, to be arrested by Comrade Sharin than by the Special Department."

"Why would you prefer to be arrested by Sharin?" asked the inspector, obviously intrigued.

"It would be nicer, somehow. After all, it would be in the pedagogical line."

"In thiat case you are under arrest."

He picked up the receiver of the telephone.

"The militia? Send a militiaman immediately for the director of the Gorky Colony – I've put him under arrest for a week. Sharin."

"What am I to do? Wait in your office?"

"Yes, you will remain here!"

"Perhaps you'll let me out on parole. While the militiaman is on his way I could get something from the stores, and send the cart black to the colony."

"You will stay where you are."

Sharin seized his velour hat from the hat-stand – it went very well with his black hair – and rushed out of the office. Then I took up the receiver, and asked for the chairman of the Gubernia Executive Committee. He heard me out patiently.

"Look here, old chap," he said. "Don't let yourself get upset, but just go quietly home. Or perhaps it would be better to wait for the militiaman and tell him to call me up."

The militiaman arrived.

"Are you the director of the colony?"

"Yes."

"Come along with me, then."

"The chairman of the Gubernia Executive Committee has given me instructions to go home. He asked you to ring him up."

"I'm not going to ring anybody up. The chief can ring up from headquarters. Come on!"

In the street Anton stared with astonishment to see me under the escort of the militiaman.

"Wait for me here," I told him.

"Will they let you go soon?"

"What do *you* know about it?"

"That dark chap just came by and said: 'You can go home. Your director isn't coming.' And some women in hats came out and they said: 'Your director is arrested.' "

"You wait. I'll soon be back."

At headquarters I had to wait for the chief. It was four o'clock before he released me.

Our cart was piled high with sacks and boxes. Anton and I jogged peacefully along the Kharkov highroad, each thinking of his own affairs – he, probably, of fodder and pastures, I of the vicissitudes of fate, which seemed to have been specially made for the directors of colonies. We drew up every now and then to adjust the slipping sacks, perched ourselves upon them again, and proceeded on our way.

Anton was just tugging at the left rein preparatory to taking the turning to the colony, when Laddie suddenly shied, jerked up his head, and attempted to rear. From the direction of the colony a motorcar as bearing down on us, making for the town with a terrific hooting, clattering and snorting. A green velour hat flashed by, and Sharin cast a frightened glance at me. Beside him, his coat collar turned up, sat the moustached Chernenko, chairman of the Workers and Peasants' Inspection.

Anton had no time to wonder over the unexpected onrush of the motorcar, for Laddie had tangled something up in the complicated and unreliable system of harness. Nor had I any time for wondering, for a pair of colony horses, harnessed to a clattering farm car and filled to bursting point with boys, was racing up to us at full gallop. In front stood Karabanov, driving the horses, his head lowered, fiercely following the vanishing car with his gleaming gipsy eyes. The cart was going too fast to stop at once, the boys, shouting something, leaped to the ground, laughing and trying to hold Kararbanov back. At last Karabanov came to himself and realized what was going on. The crossroads took on the aspect of a fair.

The boys surrounded me. Karabanov was obviously dissatisfied that everything had ended up so prosaically. He did not even get down from the cart, but turned the horses' heads angrily, swearing at them.

"Turn round, you devils! Fine horses we've got ourselves!"

At last, with a final outburst of rage he managed to get the right-hand horse turned, and galloped off to the colony, still standing, bobbing up and down morosely over the bumps in the road.

"What's up with you all? What's the fire brigade out for?" I asked.

"Are you all crazy?" asked Anton.

Jostling and interrupting one another, the boys told me what had happened. They had an extremely vague conception of the whole affair, although they had all witnessed it. They had only the vaguest idea where they were off to in their carriage-and-pair, and what they intended to do in town, and were even astonished to be questioned about it.

"As if we knew! We'd have seen when we got there."

Zadorov was the only one capable of giving a coherent account of what had passed.

"It all happened so suddenly, you see," he explained. "Like a bolt from the blue. They came in a car, and hardly anyone noticed them. We were all working. They went into your office, and did something or other there... one of our kids found out and he told us they were rummaging in the drawer. What could it be? The kids all ran to your porch, just as they were coming out. We heard them say to Ivan Ivanovich: 'Take over the directorship.' Then wasn't there a row! It was impossible to make anything out – someone was yelling, someone was taking the strangers by the coat lapels, Burun was shouting all over the colony: 'What have you done with Anton?' A regular riot! If it hadn't been for me and Ivan Ivanovich, it would have come to fisticuffs. I even had my buttons torn off. The dark chap was frightened out of his wits and made for the motorcar, which as standing waiting. They were off in no time, and the boys after them, yelling, shaking their fists, you never saw anything like it! And just then Semyon drove up from the other colony with an empty cart."

We turned into the colony yard. Karabanov, now quieted down, was in the stable, unharnessing the horses, defending himself against Anton's reproaches.

"You treat horses as if they were automobiles. Look – you've driven them into a sweat!" exclaimed Anton.

"Don't you see, Anton, we couldn't think about the horses just then! Can't you understand?" replied Karabanov, his eyes and teeth gleaming.

"I understood before you did – in town," said Anton. "You've all had dinner, and we've been dragged about to the militia."

I found my colleagues in a state of mortal fear. Ivan Ivanovich was only fit to be put to bed.

"Only think, Anton Semyonovich, how it might have ended?" he gasped. "Their faces were all so ferocious – I was sure it would come to knives in a minute. Zadorov saved the situation – he was the only one who kept his head. We tried to pull them back, but they were just like hounds, furious, yelling... ugh!"

I did not question the boys, and tried to behave as if nothing special had happened. They, for their part, showed little curiosity. They were probably no longer interested – the members of the Gorky Colony were first and foremost realists, and could only be held by what was of practical application.

I was not summoned to the Department of Public Education, and I did not go there on my own initiative. But a week later I had business in the Gubernia Workers' and Peasants' Inspection. I was sent for by the chairman in his office. Chernenko received me like a brother.

"Sit down, old chap, sit down!" he said, pumping away at my hand, and regarding me with a joyous beam. "What fine fellows those of yours are! You know, after what Sharin told me, I expected to see wretched, unhappy beings, pitiful creatures, you know... and those sons-of-bitches, how they swarmed round us – devils, regular devils! And the way they ran after us – I never saw anything like it, damn me, if I did! Sharin sat there muttering: 'I don't think they'll catch us up!' And I said: 'So long as the car doesn't break down!' It was priceless! I haven't had such fun for ages! When I tell people about it they split their sides with laughter, they almost fall off their chairs...."

My friendship with Chernenko dated from that moment.

18

A LINK-UP WITH THE VILLAGE

The repairing of the Trepke estate turned out to be an extremely complicated and difficult business. There were numbers of houses, all of which required, not so much repairs, as practically rebuilding. Money was tight all the time. The aid rendered by local government departments manifested itself chiefly in all sorts of orders for building materials, which had to be taken to other towns – Kiev, Kharkov.... And there our orders were regarded with contempt, only about ten per cent of the materials was issued, and sometimes none at all. The half truckload of glass which, after several journeys to Kharkov, we managed to obtain, was taken from us on the rails, just outside our town, by some organization infinitely more influential than our colony.

Our lack of money made it extremely difficult to hire labour, and we had to do almost everything ourselves, though we did manage to get some carpentry done through an cartel.

But we were not long in finding financial resources, for the new colony abounded in ancient, broken-down sheds and stables. The Trepke brothers had run a stud farm, and the breeding of pedigree horses had not so far been included in our plans – the restoration of these stables would have been beyond our means, anyhow. "Not for the likes of us," as Kalina Ivanovich said.

We began to take down these buildings and sell the bricks to the villagers. There were plenty of purchasers – every self-respecting householder needs to make himself a stove or make a cellar, while the representatives of the kulak tribe, with the avidity which is their characteristic, simply bought bricks to keep in reserve.

The work of breaking up the stables was done by our boys. Picks were fabricated in the smithy from all sorts of odd scraps and the work went with a swing.

Since the boys worked half the day and spent the other half at their lessons, they went to the new colony in two shifts. These groups made their way between the two colonies with the most businesslike air, which, however, did not prevent them from occasionally deviating from their path to give chase to some hen which had imprudently strayed from its yard for a change of air. The capturing of this hen, and still more the complete assimilation of all the calories contlained in it, were complicated operations demanding energy, prudence, coolness, and enthusiasm. These operations were still further complicated by the fact thiat the members of the colony were, when all is said and done, to a certain extent involved in the history of civiliation, and thus could not dispense with fire.

Altogether the journeys to work in the new colony enabled the members of the original colony to get into closer contact with the peasant world, while, in full accordance with the theories of historical materialism, it was the economic base of peasant life which interested the boys first and foremost, and to which, in the period under consideration, they came the closest. Without entering very deeply into a discussion of the various superstructures, my charges made straight for larder and cellar, disposing, to the best of their ability, of the riches contained therein. Justly anticipating resistance to their activities on the part of the population, with its petty proprietary instincts, the boys endeavoured to pursue the history of culture during the hours when such instincts slumber – that is, at night. And, in full accordance with scientific principles, the boys, for a certain period, employed themselves solely on the satisfaction of the elementary demand of mankind – the demand for food. Milk, smetana, lard, pies – such was the brief nomenclature drawn up by the Gorky Colony for use in their contacts with the village.

So long as this matter, so scientifically established, was in the hands of boys like Karabanov, Taranets, Volokhov, Osadchy, and Mityagin, I could sleep peacefully, for they were all distinguished by complete mastery of their subject, and by thoroughness. Of a morning, the villagers, after making a brief inventory of their property, would draw the conclusion that two jugs of milk were missing, while the two jugs standing there empty corroborated the findings of the inventory. But the padlock of the cellar door was always found to be unbroken, and the door fastened, and the roof intact, while the dog had not once barked in the night, and all objects, animate and inanimate, regarded the world around them with open, trusting eyes.

It was quite another state of affairs when the younger generation took up the study of primordial culture. Then it was that the padlock met its master's eyes with features petrified with horror, its very life having, truth to say, been undermined by clumsy treatment with a master key, if not with a crowbar originally intended for the task of restoring the former Trepke estate. The dog, as its master now recalled, had not merely barked in the night, but bad almost barked its head off, and nothing but the master's reluctance to leave his bed had deprived the dog of immediate reinforcements. The unskilled, rough-and-ready work of the younger members soon led to their experiencing in their own persons the horrors of pursuit by an irate householder, raised from his bed by the aforesaid dog, or even having lain in wait for the uninvited guests since the evening hours. Ad this it was that constituted the elements of my anxiety. The unsuccessful juniors made off with all haste for the colony – a thing their elders would never have done. The householder did the same, waking me up, and demanding that the offender be given up. But the offender was already in bed, so that I felt emboldened to put the guileless question: "Would you be able to identify the boy?"

"How could I identify him? I only saw him run back here."

"Perhaps it wasn't one of our lads," I suggested, becoming more and more guileless.

"Not one of yours? Before you came there were never any such goings on here!" The victim began to check off on his fingers the facts at his disposal:

"Last night Miroshnichenko had his milk stolen, the night before, Stepan Verkhola had his lock broken, last Saturday two chickens disappeared from the yard of Grechany, Petro; and the day before that, Stovbin's widow – you know who I mean! – had two tubs of smetana ready for the market, and when the poor woman went into her cellar, she found everything turned upside down, and the smetana all gone. And Vassili Moshchenko, Yakov Verkhola, and that hunchhack – what's his name? – Nechipor Moshchenko, all had their...."

"But where are your proofs?"

"Proofs, you say! I came out, and I saw them run back here, I tell you! Besides, who else could it be? Your chaps nose out everything on their way to Trepke."

By that time I was no longer so indulgent in my attitude to these occurrences. I pitied the villagers, and it was infuriating and alarming to have to acknowledge to myself my own utter powerlessness. It was particularly embarrassing for me that I did not even know about everything that went on, so that there could be no limits to my suspicions. And my nerves, due to the events of the winter, were now in a somewhat shaken state.

On the surface, everything seemed to be all right in the colony. In the daytime all the boys worked and studied, in the evening they joked and disported themselves, at night they went to bed, to wake up jolly and contented the next morning. And it was in the night that the sallies to the village took place. The elder boys received my indignant remonstances in meek silence. For a time the complaints of the peasants quieted down, but very soon their hostility to the colony would break out anew.

Our situation was rendered the more difficult in that robberies on the highroad were still going on. They had now assumed a somewhat altered character, the robbers taking from the villagers not so much money as provisions, and moreover in the very smallest quantities. At first I thought this was not the work of our hands, but the villagers, in private conversation, asserted:

"Oh, no! It must have been your boys. When we catch them and give them a beating, then you'll see!"

The boys reassured me eagerly:

"They're lying – the kulaks! Maybe one of our chaps sometimes goes to their cellars. That does happen. But robbing on the highroad – never!"

I could see that the boys were sincerely convinced that none of our lot went in for highway robbery, and I could see, too, that such robbery would be considered indefensible by the older boys. My nervous tension was somewhat relaxed by this knowledge, only however to be increased by the next rumour, the next encounter with the village spokesmen.

And then, quite suddenly, one evening, a platoon of mounted militiamen swooped down upon the colony. Sentries were posted at all the exits from our dormitories, and a thorough search was begun. I also was arrested in my own office, and it was precisely this which ruined the whole thing for the militia. The boys met the militiamen with doubled fists; they leaped through windows; brickbats were already beginning to be hurled about in the darkness, and hand-to-hand fights were going on in the corners of the yard. A regular crowd fell upon the horses drawn up in front of the stable, causing them to gallop wildly off into the forest. After loud altercations and a tremendous scuffle, Karabanov burst into my office, shouting:

"Come as quick as you can – there'll be an awful disaster!"

I rushed out into the yard, to be immediately surrounded by an infuriated crowd of boys, seething with rage. Zadorov was in hysterics.

"Will there ever be an end to all this?" he yelled. "Let them send me to prison, I'm sick of everything! Am I a prisoner, or am I not? A prisoner? Why? What's the search about? Poking their noses into everything...."

The terrified platoon commander endeavoured, nevertheless, to keep up his authority.

"Tell your pupils to go to the dormitories this minute and stand beside their beds!"

"On what grounds are you making a search?" I asked him.

"That's not your business. I have my orders."

"Leave the colony at once." "What d'you mean by that?"

"Without the permission of the Chief of the Gubernia Department of Public Education I shall not allow a search to be made. Understand that – I won't have it! And I shall use force to prevent it."

"Take care we don't search *you!*" shouted one of the boys, but I thundered at him: "Silence!"

"Very well," said the platoon commander threateningly, "you'll have to change your tone...."

He gathered his men around him, and with the help of the boys, who were beginning to cheer up – they found their horses, and departed, pursued by ironic injunctions.

In the town I procured an admonition for someone in the militia, but after this raid, events began to develop with extraordinary rapidity. The villagers came to me in indignation, threatening, shouting:

"Yesterday your boys took butter and lard from Yavtukh's wife on the highroad."

"That's a lie!" retorted one of the boys.

"Yes, they did! And pulled their caps over their eyes, so as nobody should recognize them."

"How many of them were there?" I asked.

"There was one, the woman says. One of your boys he was. He had on a coat like they wear."

"It's a pack of lies! Our fellows don't go in for that!"

The villagers went away, we maintained a dejected silence, and Karabanov suddenly burst out:

"It's a lie, I tell you – a lie! We'd know about it...."

The boys had long begun to share my anxiety, and even the assaults upon the cellars seemed to have ceased. With the approach of dusk, the colony seemed as if paralyzed in anticipation of something unforeseen, new, grievous and insulting. Karabanov, Zadorov, Burun, went from dormitory to dormitory, searched the darkest corners of the yard, ransacked the woods. Never in my life have my nerves been in such a bad state as they were at that time.

And then....

One evening the door of my office burst open, and a crowd of lads hustled Prikhodko into the room. Karabanov, holding Prikhodko by the collar, pushed him violently towards my table.

"There!"

"Using the knife again?" I asked wearily.

"Knife – nothing! He's been robbing on the highroad."

The world seemed to be tumbling in ruins over my shoulders. Mechanically I tasked the silent, trembling Prikhodko:

"Is it true?"

"Yes," he whispered, almost inaudibly, his eyes on the ground.

Catastrophe arrived in the fraction of a second. A revolver suddenly appeared in my hand.

"Hell!" I exclaimed. "I'm through with you!..."

But before I could raise the revolver to my temple a crowd of yelling and weeping lads was upon me.

I came to my senses in the presence of Ekaterina Grigoryevna, Zadorov, and Burun. I was lying on the floor between the table and the wall, with water streaming all over me. Zadorov, who was holding my head, lifted his eyes to Ekaterina Grigoryevna, saying:

"Go over there – the boys... they might kill Prikhodko...."

In a moment I was out in the yard. I got Prikhodko away in an unconscious condition, covered with blood.

19

A GAME OF FORFEITS

This was in the beginning of the summer of 1922. Nobody in the colony ever mentioned Prikhodko's crime. He was severely beaten up by the other boys and had to keep his bed for a long time, and we did not pester him with any questions whatever. I gathered that there had been nothing special in what he had done. No arms were found on him.

But Prikhodko was for all that a real bandit. The near-catastrophe in my office, and his misfortune made no impression on him. And in the future he continued to cause the colony much unpleasantness. At the same time he was loyal in his own way, and would have broken the skull of any enemy of the colony with crowbar or with axe. He was an extremely limited individual, always under the power of the latest impression, swayed by every idea that entered his dull brain. But there was no better worker than Prikhodko. The hardest tasks could not subdue his spirit, and he was a mighty wielder of axe or hammer, even when these were used for purposes other than breaking his neighbour's skull.

After the unfortunate experiences already described, the members of the colony harboured violent wrath against the peasants. The lads could not forgive them for having been the cause of our troubles. I could see that if they refrained from outrages against the peasants, it was only out of pity for me.

My talks, and the talks of my colleagues about the peasantry and their work, and about the necessity of respecting this work, were never received by the boys as the talk of people who were better informed, or wiser than themselves. They considered that we knew very little about such things – in their eyes we were town intellectuals, incapable of understanding how profoundly unpleasant the peasants were.

"You don't know them. We know what they're like, to our own cost. They're ready to cut a man's throat for half a pound of bread, and just try to get something out of them.... They wouldn't give a crust to a starving man, they'd rather their grain rotted in their barns."

"We're bandits – all right, we are! Still we know we did wrong, and we've been – er – forgiven. We know that. But they – they care for no one. According to them the tsar was bad, and so is the Soviet government. The only people they consider any good are those who ask nothing themselves, and give them everything gratis. Muzhiks – that's what they are!"

"Oh, I can't bear those muzhiks! I can't bear the sight of them – I'd shoot the lot!" said Burun, an inveterate townsman.

Burun's favourite amusement at the market was to go up to some villager, standing beside his cart, eyeing with distaste the town miscreants milling around him, and to ask him:

"Are you a crook?"

The villager would forget his cautiousness in his indignation.

"Eh?"

"Oh, you're a muzhik!" Burun would exclaim, laughing, unexpectedly moving with the rapidity of lightning towards the sack on the cart. "Look out, Pop!"

The villager would respond with a string of oaths, which was just what Burun wanted – he enjoyed it as the amateur of music enjoys a symphony concert.

Burun made no bones about telling me:

"If it weren't for you, they'd have a hard time of it!"

One of the main causes of our unfriendly relations with the peasantry was the fact that the colony was surrounded entirely by kulak farmsteads. Goncharovka, where most of the inhabitants were real working peasants, as as yet far away from our daily life. Our nearest neighbours, all those Moussi Karpoviches and Yefrem Sidoroviches, were snugly ensconced in neatly-roofed, whitewashed huts, surrounded not by wattle hurdles, but by real fences, and were careful not to let anyone into their yards. When they came to the colony they wearied us with incessant complaints about taxation, prophesying that the Soviet government would never last with such a policy. And at the same time they drove fine stallions, while on holidays samogon ran in rivers, and their wives smelt of new print dresses, smetana and cheesecakes. And their sons were unrivalled suitors and dazzling cavaliers; no one else had such well-tailored coats, such new dark-green peaked caps, such highly polished boots, adorned winter and summer with magnificent shining galoshes.

The colonists well knew the economic position of each of our neighbours, they even knew the state of an individual seed-drill or harvester, for they were always fixing and repairing these implements in our smithy. They knew, also, the melancholy lot of the numerous shepherds and workers whom the kulaks so frequently turned ruthlessly from their doors, without even playing them their wages.

To tell the truth I myself became infected by my charges with dislike for this kulak world nestling behind its gates and fences.

For all that, these continual quarrels made me uneasy. And to this must be added our hostile relations with the village authorities. Luka Semyonovich, while surrendering the Trepke field to us, never lost hope of getting us turned out of the new colony. He made strenuous efforts to have the mill and the whole Trepke estate handed over to the Village Soviet, ostensibly for the organization of a school. He managed, with the help of relatives and cronies in the town to purchase one of the annexes in the new colony for transference to the village. We beat off this attack with fists and palings, but I had the utmost difficulty in getting the sale cancelled, and in proving, in the town, that the annex was simply being purchased for firewood for Luka Semyonovich and his relatives.

Luka Semyonovich and his henchmen wrote and dispatched to the town endless complaints of the colony, reviling us in various government departments; it had been on their insistence that the raid had been made on us by the militia.

As far back as the winter Luka Semyonovich had burst into my office one evening, demanding imperatively:

"You show me the registers where you enter the money you get from the village for your work in the smithy."

"Get out!" I replied.

"What's that?"

"Get out of here!"

No doubt my looks gave little promise of success in the elucidation of the fate of the money, and Luka Semyonovich made himself scarce without a murmur. After this, however, he became the sworn enemy of myself and our whole organization. The members of the colony, in their turn, detested Luka with all the ardour of youth.

One hot noonday in June a regular procession appeared against the horizon on the opposite bank of the bake. When it drew nearer to the colony we were able to distinguish its astounding details – two muzhiks were leading Oprishko and Soroka, whose arms were bound to their sides.

Oprishko was in every respect a dashing personality, fearing nobody in the colony but Anton Bratchenko, under whom he worked, and who chastised him whenever he thought fit. Oprishko was much bigger and stronger than Anton, but the totally inexplicable adoration he bore for the head groom and the fascination of the latter's triumphant disposition prevented him from ever using these advantages. Oprishko carried himself with the utmost dignity in regard to the rest of the boys, never allowing them to impose upon him. His excellent temper was in his favour, for he was always jolly and cared for nothing hut jolly society, so that he was only to be found tin those parts of the colony where there was never a hangdog look or a sour countenance. At first he had utterly refused to leave the collector [Temporary home for waifs – Tr.] for the colony, and I had had to go and fetch him myself. He received me lying on his bed, with a scornful glance.

"To hell with you," he said. "I'm not going anywhere!"

I had been told of his heroic qualities, so that from the first I adopted the proper tone in addressing him.

"I'm extremely sorry to disturb you, Sir," I said, "but duty compels me to beg you to take your place in the carriage prepared for you."

Oprishko was at first astonished by my "gallant address," and even made as if to get off the bed, but then his former whim got the upper hand and he once more let his head sink on to the pillow.

"I told you I wasn't going...."

"In that case, honoured sir, I shall be compelled, to my profound regret, to convey you by force."

Oprishko raised his curly head from the pillow and looked at me with unfeigned astonishment.

"For God's sake, where did you spring from?" he exclaimed. "D'you think it'll be so easy to take me by force?"

"Bear in mind...."

I made my voice menacing, letting a shade of irony creep into it.

"...dear Oprishko...."

And here I suddenly roared at him: "Get up, you! What the hell are you lying there for? Get up, I tell you!"

He leaped from the bed and rushed to the window.

"I'll jump out of the window, so help me, I will!" he cried

"Either you jump out of the window minute," I said contemptuously, "or get into the cart – I have no time to play about with you!"

We were on the third floor, so Oprishko laughed gaily, and frankly. "There's no getting away from you!" he said. "What's to be done? Are you the director of the Gorky Colony?"

"Yes, I am."

"Why didn't you say so at once? I'd have gone with you long ago."

He started making energetic preparations for the way.

In the colony he took part in every single enterprise of the other boys, never, however, playing first fiddle, apparently seeking entertainment rather than profit.

Soroka was younger than Oprishko. He had a round, comely face, was thoroughly stupid, incoherent and extraordinarily unlucky. Whatever he undertook he came to grief. So when the boys saw that it was he who was tied up beside Oprishko, they were displeased.

"What on earth does Dmitri want to get mixed up with Soroka for?" they muttered.

The convoy consisted in the chairman of the Village Soviet and our old friend Moussi Karpovich.

Moussi Karpovich was the picture of injured innocence. Luka Semyonovich was as sober as a judge and bore himself with official aloofness. His red beard was neatly combed, an embroidered shirt of dazzling whiteness showed beneath his jacket, it was obvious that he had just come from church.

The chairman began.

"A fine way you're bringing up your lads," he said.

"What's that to do with you?" I retorted.

"I'll tell you what – people have no peace from them – robbing on the highway, stealing everything."

"Hey, Pop – what right have you to tie them up?" came a voice from the crowd of colony boys.

"He thinks this is the old regime."

"He ought to be taken in hand!"

"You be quiet!" I adjured them. "Tell me what is the matter," I said, turning to the men.

Now Moussi Karpovich took up the tale.

"My old woman hung a petticoat and a blanket on the fence, and these two passed by, and next thing I know the things are gone. I run after them, and they take to their heels. Now I can't run as fast as they do, you know! Fortunately Luka Semyonovich was just coming out of church, and we got hold of them...."

"Why did you tie them up?" came from the crowd again.

"So's they shouldn't run away. That's why...."

"We don't have to discuss that here," put in the chairman. "Let's go and draw up a statement."

"We can get on without a statement. Did they return the things?"

"What if they did? There's got to be a statement."

The chairman had made up his mind to humiliate us, and the occasion favoured him – for the first time boys from the colony had been caught red-handed.

Such a situation was extremely unpleasant for us. A deposition spelt inevitable jailing – for the lads, and for the colony an irreparable disgrace.

"These boys have been caught for the first time," I said. "All sorts of things are apt to happen between neighbours. The first time should be forgiven."

"No," said the red-haired one. "No forgiving! Come on to the office and take a deposition!"

Moussi Karpovich remembered old scores.

"You remember how you took me, one night? You still have my axe – and look what a fine I had to pay!"

I had no reply to this.

Yes, there was no way out. The kulaks had us floored. I directed the conquerors to the office, calling out to the boys in my rage:

"Now you've gone and done it, confound you! This time it is petticoats! We shall never get over the disgrace! I shall have to start thrashing the rotters! And those fools will be jailed!"

The boys held their silence. They bad indeed "gone and done it." With these ultra-pedagogical utterances, I, too, went towards the office.

For two hours I begged and implored the chairman, promising that such a thing would never happen again, agreeing to make a new pair of wheels together with axle for the Village Soviet at cost price. At last the chairman presented his final terms:

"Let all the lads ask me themselves!"

During these two hours I contracted a lifelong hatred for the chairman. While the conversation was going on the bloodthirsty thought kept passing through my mind – perhaps one day the chairman will get caught in a dark place, and if he gets beaten up, I won't be the one to save him.

Do as I would, there was no other way out. I told the boys to line up at the porch, and the authorities came out to the steps. With my hand at the peak of my cap, I said, on behalf of the colony, that we deeply regretted the error of our comrades, requested forgiveness for them, and promised that in future such occurrences would not be repeated. Luka Semyonovich uttered the following speech:

"Undoubtedly such things should be punished with the utmost severity of the law, for the villagers are undoubtedly toilers. Therefore, if a villager hangs up a skirt, and you take it, you are enemies of the people, of the proletariat. I who have been authorized by the Soviet government cannot allow unlawfulness, according to which any bandit and criminal can take what he likes. And your asking me and promising and that – God knows what'll come of it. If you ask me bowing low, and your director promises to bring you up honest citizens, and not bandits... then I'll forgive you unconditionally."

I was trembling with humiliation and rage. Oprishko and Soroka, pale as death, stood in the ranks of the colonists.

The chairman and Moussi Karpovich shook hands with me, said a few magniloquently magnanimous words, which, however, I did not even hear.

"Break up!"

Over the colony the burning sun shone out and became a fixed glare. The smell of mint hovered over the earth. The motionless air hung over the forest like a rigid blue screen.

I looked around me.... The same colony, the same rectangular buildings, the same boys, and tomorrow everything would begin all over again – petticoats, the chairman, Moussi Karpovich, journeys to the dreary, flyblown town.... Right in front of me was the door of my room, with its camp beds and unpainted table, and on the table a packet of shag.

"What's to be done? What am I to do? What am I to do?" I turned towards the forest.

There is no shade in a pine forest at noon, but everything is always clean and tidy, one can see a long way, and the slender pines range themselves beneath the sky in splendid order, like a neatly set stage.

Although we lived in the forest I scarcely ever found myself in its depths. Human affairs held me ruthlessly down to tables, lathes, sheds and dormitories. The quiet and purity of the pine forest, the air saturated with the smell of resin, had a magnetism all its own. One felt as if one would like never to leave it, as if one would like oneself to become a slender, wise, fragrant tree, and to take up one's stand beneath the sky in such refined, elegant society.

A branch snapped behind me. I glanced round – the whole forest seemed to be filled with colonists. They moved cautiously along the aisles formed by the tree trunks, advancing towards me at a run only by the very furthest glades. I halted in amazement. They, too, froze in their places, shooting at me penetrating glances, filled with a sort of motionless, terrified anticipation.

"What are you doing here? What are you following me about for?"

Zadorov, who happened to be nearest to me, stepped out from behind a tree and said almost gruffly:

"Come black to the colony!"

My heart seemed to miss a beat.

"What's happened in the colony?"

"Nothing whatever. Let's go back!"

"Say what you mean, confound you!"

I stepped rapidly towards him. Two or three of the others approached, the rest held aloof. Zadorov said in a whisper:

"We'll go, only do us a favour."

"What on earth do you want?"

"Hand over your revolver!"

"My revolver?"

All of a sudden I guessed what he meant, and burst out laughing. "Oh, my revolver! With pleasure! You're a funny lot! I could just as well hang myself, or throw myself into the lake."

Zadorov suddenly broke out into resounding laughter.

"All right, then, keep it! We got it into our heads that.... You're just having a walk? Go on, then. Back, fellows!"

What had happened?

When I had turned into the forest, Soroka had rushed to the dormitory.

"Oh, lads! Oh, fellows! Oh, come quick to the forest Anton Semyonovich is going to shoot himself!"

Without waiting for him to finish speaking they all rushed out of the dormitory.

In the evening everyone seemed extraordinarily embarrassed – Karabanov alone playing the fool, and twisting about between the beds like one possessed. Zadorov grinned disarmingly, and for some reason kept pressing the small blooming face of Shelaputin to himself. Burun would not leave my side, maintaining a resolutely mysterious silence. Oprishko had given himself up to hysterics, lying on the bed in Kozyr's room, and weeping into the dirty pillow. Soroka had hidden himself somewhere to get away from the jeers of the boys.

Zadorov said:

"Let's play forfeits!"

And we actually played forfeits. Pedagogics sometimes assumes queer forms – forty lads, all half-ragged and half-hungry, playing forfeits as merrily as possible in the light of an oil lamp.... Only the traditional kisses were missing.

20

A HORSE FOR A HARVESTER

Festival of the First Sheaf (1925)

In the spring the question of horses had us almost stumped. Laddie and Bandit were simply no good any more, it was impossible to work with them. Every day, from the early morning, Kalina Ivanovich uttered counter-revolutionary speeches in the stable, reproaching the Soviet government with mismanagement and cruelty to animals.

"If you want to run a farm," he would say, "then you've got to provide horses, and not torment dumb animals. Theoretically that's a horse, of course, but actually it just falls down all the time, and it's pitiful to look at it, let alone make it work."

The attitude of Bratchenko was extremely simple. He loved horses simply because they were horses, and any extra work imposed upon his favourites infuriated and grieved him. By way of answer to all entreaties and reproaches he kept in reserve the unanswerable argument:

"Now would *you* like to draw a plough? I'd like to see the fuss you'd make...."

He interpreted Kalina Ivanovich's utterances as instructions not to let the horses do any work whatever. And he did not like to press him too far. In the new colony the stables had already been repaired, and two horses would have to he transferred to them in the early spring for ploughing and sowing. But there were no horses to transfer.

One day, while talking to Chernenko, I touched upon our difficulties – we could manage somehow or other with the implements we had, anyhow for this spring, but what are we to do for horses? Sixty desyatins, after all! And if we didn't plough and plant, wouldn't the villagers crow over us?

Chernenko thought for a moment, and suddenly leaped up joyfully.

"Half a mo! Haven't I got an Economic Department here? We don't require so many horses in the spring. I'll give you three, temporarily, we'll save on their feed, and you can return them in about six weeks. You can have a talk with our manager of supplies."

The supply manager of the Workers' and Peasants' Inspection was a severe and practical individual. He demanded stiff payment for the hire of the horses – five poods of wheat for each month, and wheels for their gig.

"You have a wheelwright's shop, haven't you?" he said.

"Do you want to flay us alive? Do you know who we are?"

"I'm the supply manager, and not a dispenser of charities. And you should just see our horses! I wouldn't let you have them for anything in the world, myself – you'll ruin them, overwork them, I know you. It took me two years to find those horses. They're not just horses, they're simply beauties!"

But I was ready to promise him a hundred poods of wheat a month and wheels for all the carriages in town. We had to have the horses.

The supply manager made out an agreement in duplicate in which everything was set down most impressively, in detail:

"...hereinafter to be referred to as the Colony... the said wheels to be considered as handed over to the Economic Department of the Gubernia Workers' and Peasants' Inspection after their acceptance by a special commission, and the drawing up of a corresponding deed... for every day beyond that fixed for the return of the horses, the Colony agrees to pay the Economic Department of the Gubernia WPI ten pounds of wheat per horse.... In the event of the Colony failing to fulfil the terms of this agreement, the Colony is to pay a forfeit amounting to five times the value of the losses entailed...."

The next day Kalina Ivanovich and Anton drove into the colony in great triumph. Our junior boys had been looking out for them since the morning; the whole colony, teachers included, was tense with expectation. Shelaputin and Toska were the luckiest of all – they met the procession on the highroad and immediately clambered up on to the horses. Kalina Ivanovich could neither smile nor speak, so completely was his whole being filled with importance and grandeur. Anton did not so much as turn his head in our direction – all living creatures except the three black horses tied to the tail of our cart had lost significance for him.

Kalina Ivanovich clambered out of the cart, shook the straw off his jacket and said to Anton:

"You look after them, settle them in properly. These are not ordinary horses – like Bandit."

Anton, throwing out abrupt orders to his assistants, thrust the former favourites into the furthest and least convenient stalls, threatening with the saddle girth any of the curious who happened to peep into the stable, and replied to Kalina Ivanovich in a voice of gruff familiarity:

"Get us some proper harness now, Kalina Ivanovich, this rubbish won't do!"

The horses were all black, tall and well-nourished. In the eyes of the boys their very names had a certain aristocratic flavour. They were called Lion, Falcon, and Mary.

Lion turned out a disappointment. He was a handsome stallion, but not adapted to farm work, tiring quickly, and short-winded. Falcon and Mary, however, were in every way suitable – strong, quiet, good-looking. It is true that Anton's dream that the horses would be trotters enabling us to eclipse all the town drivers with our turnout, was not fulfilled, but they were splendid at the plough and the seed-drill, and Kalina Ivanovich could only grunt out his satisfaction in his evening reports of the amount of land ploughed and sown. The only thing which caused him anxiety was the exalted position of the horses' owners.

"Everything is fine," he would say, "only it's too bad to be mixed up with the Workers' and Peasants' Inspection. They can do whatever they like. And where could one complain? To the Workers' and Peasants' Inspection?"

Life began to stir in the new colony. One of the houses was ready, and six colonists were in stalled in it. They lived there alone, without adult surveillance and with nobody to cook for them, providing themselves with what they could get from our storerooms and cooking their food to the best of their abilities on a small stove in the orchard. Their duties included the guarding of the orchard and the building work, duty at the Kolomak ferry, and work in the stables, in which two horses were kept, under the care of Oprishko, as Bratchenko's emissary. Anton himself decided to stay in the original colony, where there were more people, and where it was consequently livelier. He made daily visits of inspection to the new colony, visits which were feared not only by Oprishko and his assistants, but by all the colonists.

Terrific work was going on in the fields of the new colony. The sixty desyatins had all been sown, without, it is true, any particular agronomical skill, or correct planning of the fields, but nevertheless spring wheat, winter wheat, rye and oats were all sown. And a few desyatins were planted with potatoes and beets. Weeding and earthing were required here, and we had to make the most strenuous efforts to keep up with all this work. By now we had sixty colonists altogether.

There was a constant coming and going between the two colonies throughout the day, and far into the night: groups of boys were daily going out to work, other groups returning; our own carts went out with grain fodder, and provisions for the colonists; hired carts came from the village with building material, Kalina Ivanovich jolted in an ancient cabriolet he had wangled somewhere or other, Anton galloping by on Lion, sitting his horse with wonderful grace.

On Sundays almost the whole colony – teach- ers and all – went to bathe in the Kolomak, and the neighbouring youths and maidens, Komsomols from Pirogovka and Goncharovka, and the offspring of our kulak farmsteads, gradually got in the habit of gathering with us on the bank of that delightful stream. Our carpenters made a little jetty on the other side of the Kolomak, and we hoisted over it a flag bearing the letters "G.C." A green boat bearing a similar flag ferried all day between this jetty and our side of the river, with Mitka Zhevely and Vitka Bogoyavlensky plying the oars. Our girls, thoroughly alive to the importance of our position on the Kolomak, made sailor jumpers for Mitka and Vitka, using all sorts of remnants of girls' clothes; and many a little chap, both in our colony and for mile around, nourished in their bosoms a furious envy for these happiest of mortals. The banks of the Kolomak became our central club.

The colony itself was alive and resounding with the sustained intensity of work, the inevitable cares arising from this work, the arrival of village customers, Anton's grumblings, Kalina Ivanovich's harangues, the endless laughter and tricks of Karabanov, Zadorov and Belukhin, the mishaps of Soroka and Galatenko, the harp-like music of the pine trees, sunshine, and youth.

By now we had forgotten the very existence of dirt, lice and the itch.... The colony shone with cleanliness and brand-new patches, neatly added wherever there was a sign of weakness – in trousers, a fence, the wall of a shed, or the old porch. The same old camp beds still stood in the dormitories, but it was forbidden to sit on them during the day, unpainted-benches of pine wood being provided for that purpose. In the dining room similar unpainted tables were daily scraped with knives especially made in the smithy.

By this time, important changes had taken place in the smithy. Kalina Ivanovich's diabolical plan had been accomplished in its entirety, Golovan having been dismissed for drunkenness and counter-revolutionary conversation with customers. He had not even attempted to get the smithy equipment back, knowing the hopelessness of such an undertaking. On leaving, he only shook his head reproachfully and ironically, exclaiming:

"You're like all masters! Just because you're the masters, you think you have a right to rob a fellow!"

Belukhin was not to be confounded by such utterances; not for nothing had he read books, and lived in the world. He smiled cheerfully into Golovan's face, saying:

"What an ignorant citizen you are, Sofron! You've worked with us for more than a year, and still don't understand! Why, all this is the means of production!"

"That's just what I say!"

"– and the means of production, you see, according to science, belong to the proletariat. And there it is, the proletariat – d'you see?" And he pointed to the real, live representatives of the glorious, proletarian class – Zadorov, Vershnev, and Kuzma Leshy.

At the head of the smithy was put Semyon Bogdanenko, a hereditary blacksmith, from a family renowned of old in the engine shops of railway yards. Semyon maintained military discipline and cleanliness in the smithy; shoeing irons and hammers, great and small, looked out demurely each from its appointed place, the earthen floor was swept as in the hut of a notable housewife, not a particle of coal was to be seen on the top of the forge, and dealings with customers were brief and concise.

"This isn't a church – no bargaining!" they were told.

Semyon Bogdanenko could read and write, was clean-shaven, and never used bad language.

There was work and to spare in the smithy, both on our own and village inventory. At this time the other shops had almost stopped working, with the exception of the wheelwright's shed, in which Kozyr and two of the boys busied themselves, there being no falling-off in the demand for wheels.

The Economic Department of the Workers' and Peasants' Inspection wanted special wheels, suitable for fitting with rubber tires, and Kozyr had never made such wheels. He was extremely taken aback by this freak of civilization, and every evening after work would grumble mournfully:

"We never had any rubber tires. Our Lord, Jesus Christ, and his apostles went on foot... and now people can't drive with iron rims...."

Kalina Ivanovich would expostulate severely with Kozyr:

"And what about the railway? And automobiles? What have you to say to that? What if your Lord Jesus did go on foot? He must have been ignorant, or just a countryman, like yourself. Perhaps he went on foot because he was a tramp, and if anyone had given him a lift in a car, maybe he would have had nothing against it. On foot! An old man like you ought to be ashamed to talk like that!"

Kozyr would smile timidly, whispering to himself distractedly:

"If I only could see a wheel with rubber tires, maybe, with the Lord's help, we could make them. We don't even know how many spokes they need!"

"Why don't you go to the Workers' and Peasants' Inspection and have a look? You could count them."

"God forbid – how's an old man like me to find the place?"

One day in the middle of July Chernenko took it into his head to give our lads a treat.

"I've been talking to someone," he said, "and some ballerinas are going to visit you – let the boys see them! You know, we've got some splendid ballerinas in our theatre. You can send for them one evening."

"That would be fine!" "Only, take care, they're dainty things – don't let your bandits frighten them. What will you fetch them in?"

"We have a carriage."

"I've seen it. It won't do. Just send horses, and let them use my carriage – they can be harnessed here, and sent for the ballerinas. And set a guard along the road, or someone might try and get hold of them – they're seductive creatures!"

The ballerinas arrived late one evening, trembling the whole way, to the amusement of Anton, who kept reassuring them:

"What are you afraid of?" he asked. "You have nothing to be stolen. It isn't winter – in the winter they'd take your coats off you."

Our guard, suddenly popping out of the woods, reduced the ballerinas to such a state that they had to be given heart-drops the moment they arrived at the colony.

They danced with extreme reluctance, and our kids took a violent dislike to them. One of them was quite young, and the possessor of a beautiful, expressive back, by means of which, throughout the evening, she showed her supercilious and fastidious indifference to the whole colony. Another, somewhat older, gazed at us with unconcealed terror. Anton was extremely irritated by this one.

"I ask you – was it worth driving two horses to town and back twice over? I can bring any amount of that sort from town on foot."

"Only yours wouldn't dance," laughed Zadorov.

"Oh, wouldn't they just!"

Ekaterina Grigoryevna took her place at the piano which had long ago been an ornament of our dormitories. She was not much of a performer, and her music was not adapted to ballet dancing, while the ballerinas were by no means tactful enough to disregard a mistake of two or three bars. They were exasperated by the outrageous mistakes and pauses. Besides, they were in a great hurry to get to some very interesting engagement that evening.

While the horses were being harnessed in front of the stables, in the light of lanterns and to the accompaniment of Anton's hissing profanities, the ballerinas were in a great state of anxiety – they were sure they would be late for their engagement. So great was their nervousness and their contempt for this colony in the wilds, for these silent boys, for the utterly alien surroundings, that they could not even speak, and could only moan softly and huddle up to one another. Soroka, seated on the coachman's box, was fussing about with the harness, and saying he would not drive. Anton, unchecked by the presence of guests, answered him: "Who do you think you are – a driver, or a ballerina? What are you dancing about on the box for? What d'you mean, you won't go? Get up there!"

At last Soroka gave a jerk to the reins. The ballerinas fell silent, regarding in mortal fear the gun slung over Soroka's shoulder. But the carriage really did make a start. And then, suddenly again a cry from Bratchenko:

"What have you done, you ass! Have you gone mad to harness the horses like that? Look where you've put Red, just look! Reharness them! Falcon must always be on your right – how many times have I told you?"

Soroka unhitched his gun with leisurely movements, and laid it across the feet of the ballerinas. Faint sounds of restrained sobbing issued from the carriage.

At my back Karabanov was saying:

"So they *have* turned on the waterworks!" I was afraid they wouldn't! Nice work, lads!"

Five minutes later the carriage made a fresh start. We raised our hands to the peaks of our caps with the utmost reserve, and without the faintest hope of receiving any response. The rubber tires had begun to bounce over the stones, when a clumsy shape, waving its arms and shouting, flew past us in pursuit of the carriage.

"Stop Stop, for Christ's sake! Do stop, dear friends!"

Soroka pulled at the reins in perplexity; one of the ballerinas was thrown out of her seat.

"Oh, I almost forgot, may the Lord forgive me! Just let me count the spokes!"

Kozyr bent over a wheel, the sound of sobbing from the carriage grew louder, and a pleasant contralto was added to it:

"No, now!" it admonished.

Karabanov pushed Kozyr away from the wheel.

"You, Pop, go to – "

Unable to contain himself, Karabanov plunged, snorting, behind a tree. I could not bear it any longer.

"Go on, Soroka!" I cried. "Enough of this dawdling! "What d'you think you're here for?"

Soroka dealt Falcon a flick with a wide sweep of the whip. The boys gave way to unrestrained laughter, Karabanov groaning beneath a bush, even Anton laughing.

"Wouldn't it be a joke if they were stopped by bandits? Then they really *would* be late for their engagement!"

Kozyr stood about in the crowd looking perplexed, quite unable to understand what could have happened to prevent him from counting the spokes.

We had so much to think about that we did not notice that six weeks had elapsed. The supply manager of the Workers' and Peasants' Inspection came punctual to the moment.

"Well, what about our horses?"

"They're all alive."

"When are you going to send them back?"

Anton turned pale.

"What d'you mean 'send them back'? And who's going to do the work?"

"Contract, comrades," said the manager of supplies in his dry voice. "Contract. And when can we have the wheat?"

"The wheat? First it must be harvested and threshed. The wheat is still in the fields."

"And the wheels?"

"Well, you see, our wheelwright didn't count the spokes – he doesn't know how many spokes go to a wheel. And the dimensions...."

The manager of supplies considered himself a great man in the colony. Supply manager to the Workers' and Peasants Inspection, you know!

"You'll have to pay forfeits under the contract. According to the terms of the contract. From today, you know, ten pounds a day, ten pounds of wheat. Take it or leave it."

The supply manager took his departure. Bratchenko, following his droshky with angry eyes, said 'briefly: "The swine!"

We were greatly upset. We needed the horses desperately, but we couldn't give him our whole harvest!

Kalina Ivanovich grumbled:

"I'm not going to give them any wheat, the parasites! Fifteen poods a month and now another ten pounds a day! They write everything by theory there, but we have to work for our bread. And then give up our bread to them, and give them back the horses! Get it where you can, but don't think I'm going to give you any wheat."

The boys were up in arms against the contract.

"Rather than give them up our wheat, let it dry on the stalks! Let them harvest the wheat, and leave us the horses!"

Bratchenko settled the question in a spirit of compromise.

"You can give up the wheat, and the rye, and the potatoes, but you can say what you like – they won't get the horses."

July came. The boys were mowing the grass, and Kalina Ivanovich was not easy in his mind.

"The boys mow badly, they don't know how. And this is only the hay, how it'll be when it comes to the rye, I don't know. There are seven desyatins of rye, eight of wheat, and then there's the spring corn and oats. What's to be done? We shall have to buy a reaper."

"How can we, Kalina Ivanovich? Where are we to find the money for a harvester?" "Well then – a reaper. They used to cost n hundred and fifty rubles, or two hundred."

In the evening he brought me a handful of grain:

"Look, we shall have to reap – in two days, not a minute later!"

Preparations were made to reap with scythes. It was decided to celebrate the harvest, to celebrate the festival of the first sheaf. On the warm sands of our colony the rye ripened early, and this was convenient for the organization of a holiday, for which we prepared as for a great festival. Many guests nere invited, a splendid dinner was prepared, a beautiful and significant ritual was thought out for the solemn commencement of our harvest. But the field was already adorned with arches and flags, new costumes had been made for the boys, and Kalina Ivanovich still seemed deeply perturbed.

"The harvest is ruined by the time it's reaped, the grain will have begun to scatter. We've been working for the crows."

But in the sheds the boys nere sharpening their scythes, and making rakes to fix on them, consoling Kalina Ivanovich:

"Nothing will be lost, Kalina Ivanovich – we'll do it no worse than the real muzhiks do."

Eight reapers were appointed.

On the very day of the celebrations Anton waked me in the early morning.

"Some old mnan has brought us a harvester."

"A harvester!"

"A sort of machine. A great big one with sails – a harvester. He wants to know if we'll buy it."

"Tell him to go away. How can we pay for it? You know yourself how things are."

"He says we can have it in exchange. He wants to exchange it for a horse."

I dressed and went to the stables. In the middle of the yard stood a harvesting machine, still fairly new, obviously specially repainted for sale. It nas surrounded by a crowd of our boys, and there was Kalina Ivanovich glancing fiercely now at the harvester, now at its owner, now at me.

"Has he come to make fun of us? Who brought him here?"

The owner was unharnessing his horses. He was a respectable-looking individual with a venerable grey beard.

"Why do you want to sell it?" inquired Burun.

The owner looked up.

I've got to marry off my son. And I *have* a harvester, another one. One is enough for us, but I've got to give my son a horse."

Karabanov whispered into my ear

: "He's lying I know him...."

"Aren't you from Storozhevoye?" he asked, turning to the old man.

"That's right – from Storozhevoye. And who may you be? Aren't you Semyon Karaban? Panas' son?"

"Of course I am" replied Semyon joyfully.

"Then you must be Omelchenko! I suppose you're afraid they'll confiscate it? Isn't that it?"

"They might confiscate it, for one thing, and then I'm marrying off my son...."

"I thought your son was with the atamans."

"Oh, no God forbid!"

Semyon took upon himself the conduct of the whole operation. He talked long with the owner, standing close to the horses' heads; the two nodded to one another, pounding one another on back and shoulder. Semyon bore himself like a real farmer, and it was obvious that Omelchenko regarded him as a knowledgeable person.

Half an hour later Semyon held a secret consultation on Kalina Ivanovich's doorstep. This meeting was attended by myself, Kalina Ivanovich, Karabanov, Burun, Zadorov, Bratchenko, and two or three more of the older boys. The rest stood round the harvester, silently marvelling that there were people on the earth who possessed such a model of mechanical perfection.

Semyon esplained that the old man wanted a horse for his harvester, that there was going to be a stocktaking of machinery in Storozhevoye and that the owner of the harvester was afraid it would be confiscated without reimbursement, whereas a horse would not be confiscated, for he was marrying off his son.

"It may or may not he true," said Zadorov. "It's not our business, but we must have the harvester. We could take it out into the fields today."

"But what horse would you give away?" asked Anton. "Laddie and Bandit are no good. Would you give Red away?"

"And why not Red?" said Zadorov. "After all, it's a harvester!"

"Red? Why you..."

Karabanov interrupted the hotheaded Anton.

"Of course we can't give Red away," he agreed. "He's the only real horse in the colony. Why Red? Let's give him Lion! He's a splendid-looking horse and still fit for stud."

Semyon looked slyly at Kalina Ivanovich.

Kalina Ivanovich did not even reply to Semyon. Knocking out his pipe against the doorstep, he got on to his feet saying: "I have no time for such nonsense."

And turned back to his room.

Semyon winked at his departing back, whispering:

"Really, Anton Semyonovich, let's! It'll all come right in the end. And we shall have a harvester."

"They'll jail us."

"Who? You? Not on your life! A harvester is worth more than a horse. Let the Workers' and Peasants' Inspection take the harvester instead of Lion. What difference does it make to them? No loss, and we shall be reap in our grain. Lion's no good anyhow."

Zadorov laughed infectiously.

"What a story! After all, why not?"

Burun said nothing, merely smiling and jerking the ear of rye between his teeth up and down. Anton laughed with sparkling eyes.

"That would be a joke," he said, "for the Workers' and Peasants' Inspection to harness a harvester to it phaeton, instead of Lion."

The boys looked at me with glowing eyes.

"Say yes, Anton Semyonovich, do say yes! What's the harm? Even if they jail you, it won't be for more than a week!" Burun became serious at last, and said:

"There's no getting round it – we shall have to give the stallion away. If we don't, everyone will call us fools. The WPI, too!"

I looked at Burun and said simply:

"You are right! Go and fetch the stallion, Anton."

They all rushed headlong for the stable.

The owner of the harvester was pleased with Lion. Kalina Ivanovich pulled at my sleeve and whispered:

"Are you mad? Are you tired of life, or what? To hell with the colony, and the rye! Why should you risk your neck?"

"Stop that, Kalina! What the hell! We'll have a harvester."

An hour later the old man left, taking Lion. And two hours after that, Chernenko, arriving at the colony for our holiday, saw the harvester in the yard.

"Oh, you fine fellows! Wherever did you get that beauty?"

The boys fell suddenly silent, with the silence that precedes a storm. I regarded Chernenko with a sinking heart, and replied:

"Quite by chance."

Anton clapped his hands and leaped up and down.

"Right or wrong, Comrade Chernenko, but the harvester's ours. Would you like to do a little work today?"

"On the harvester?"

"That's right!"

"All right, it'll bring back the old days. Come on, then! Let's try it!"

Chernenko and the boys busied themselves with the harvester right up to the time for the celebrations, oiling, polishing, adjusting, testing.

The moment the opening ceremonies were over, Chernenko climbed up on the harvester, and clattered over the field. Karabanov, almost choking with laughter, cried out at the top of his voice:

"Oh, oh! There goes the true master!

The supply manager of the Workers' and Peasants' Inspection walked about the field, asking everyone he met: "How is it Lion isn't anywhere to be seen? Where's Lion?"

Anton pointed with his whip to the east.

"Lion's in the new colony. We'll be reaping there tomorrow, let him have a rest!" Tables were set out in the woods. The boys sealed Chernenko at the festive board, plied him with pie and borshch, and held him in talk.

"That was a good idea of yours, to get a harvester," he said.

"It was, wasn't it?"

"Very good, very good!"

"Which is better, Comrade Chernenko, a horse or a harvester?" asked Bratchenko, his eyes blazing.

"Well, that depends.... It depends what kind of a horse...."

"Let's say a horse like Lion!"

The WPI manager of supplies put down his spoon, his very ears twitching in alarm. Karahanov suddenly burst out laughing and hid his head beneath the table. Following his lead all the other lads started shaking in paroxysms of laughter. The supply manager leaped up and looked round wildly at the trees, as if seeking for help. And Chernenko was completely mystified. "Why – is there anything wrong with Lion?"

"We exchanged Lion for a harvester, we exchanged him today," I said, without the slightest inclination to laugh.

The supply manager collapsed on to the bench, and Chernenko stared open-mouthed. Everyone fell silent.

"Exchanged him for a harvester!" muttered Chernenko, glancing at the supply manager.

The affronted supply manager rose in his seat.

"It's nothing but schoolboy impertinence!" he exclaimed. "Hooliganism, obstinacy...."

Suddenly Chernenko broke into a joyful smile.

"Oh, sons-of-bitches! Did you really? What shall we do with a harvester?"

"Well, we have our contract – five times the amount of losses," cut in the supply manager harshly.

"None of that!" said Chernenko with distaste. *"You* couldn't do a thing like that!"

"I couldn't?"

"That's just it, you couldn't, and therefore shut up! And *they* could! They've got to reap, and they know their grain is worth more than your 'five times,' you see! And it's fine, too, that they're not afraid of you and me. In a word, we're going to present them with the harvester today."

Working havoc with the festive tables and the soul of the supply manager of the WPI, the boys tossed Chernenko skywards. When the latter, shaking himself and laughing, at last stood on his own feet, Anton came to him, saying:

"And what about Mary and Falcon?"

"Well, what about them?"

"Must we give them back?"

Anton inclined his head in the direction of the supply manager.

"Of course you must!"

"I'm not going to," said Anton.

"Yes you are – you've got the harvester," said Chernenko angrily.

But Anton, too, could be angry.

"Take your harvester!" he cried. "To hell with your harvester! Can we harness Karabano to it?" Anton retired to the stable.

"Why, the son-of-a-bitch" exclaimed Chernenko in perplexity. Around, all was silence. Chernenko glanced at the manager of supplies.

"You and I have got ourselves into a mess," he said. "You'll have to sell the horses to them on some sort of an instalment plan, the devils! Fine boys, even if they are bandits! Come on, let's find that raging devil of ours!"

Anton was lying on a heap of hay in the stable.

"All right, Anton," said Chernenko, "I've sold you the horses."

Anton raised his head.

"Not too dear?"

"You'll pay somehow or other."

"That's something like" said Anton. "You're a clever guy!"

"I think so, too," smiled Chernenko.

"Cleverer than your supply manager."

21

Horrid Old Men

Summer evenings in the colony were delicious. The tender, limpid sky made a vast background, the outskirts of the forest were hushed in the twilight, the sunflowers edging the truck garden had gathered in a single silhouette, and seemed to be resting after the day's heat, the steep, chilly slope to the lake was merged in the falling dusk. There would be people sitting on a porch somewhere, their muffled talk faintly audible; but one could never make out who they were, and how many there were of them.

While it is still almost light, there comes an hour when it is difficult to recognize objects, or distinguish them from one another. At that hour the colony always seemed to be deserted. Where could all the boys be? one asked oneself. A stroll through the colony would enable you to see them all. In the stable a group of five are discussing something beneath a horse collar on the wall; there is quite a gathering in the bakery, for the loaves will be ready in half an hour, and all who are in any way involved in this event – those on supper duty, and those on general duty – are seated on benches in the swept and garnished bakery, in peaceful conversation. Around the well the company bears a casual nature – one has come for a pail of water, another was just passing, yet another was detained there because someone bad been looking for him since the morning – all have forgotten about the water, and remembered something else, something, perhaps, of no particular importance – but what can be unimportant on a sweet summer evening?

At the far end of the yard, just where the slope towards the lake begins, a flock of little chaps are perched upon a fallen willow, which has long ago lost its bark, and Mityagin is spinning one of his inimitable yarns:

"....and so, in the morning, when the people came to the church, they looked round – not a single priest to be seen! What could have happened? Where had all the priests gone to? And the watchman said: 'You know what? The devil has probably carried off our priests to the marsh. We have four priests! "Four?" Yes, that must be it – four priests have been carried off to the marsh in the night.' "

The boys were listening in rapt silence, their eyes glowing, the silence only broken by an occasional joyful squeak from Toska. It was not so much the devil who amused him, as the stupid watchman who had been on duty all night and could not make out whether it was his own or strange priests whom the devil had taken to the marsh. A picture was conjured up of fat priests, all alike, with no names of their own, of the whole fussy, difficult undertaking. Just fancy! To carry them one by one on his shoulders to the marsh!

From among the bushes, where there had once been a garden, comes the explosive laughter of Olya Voronona, followed by the teasing baritone voice of Burun, again laughter, this time not from Olya alone, but from a whole chorus of girls, and Burun springs into the glade, holding his crumpled cap on his bead, and pursued by a gay, motley throng. Shelaputin lingers in the glade, unable to make up his mind whether to laugh or run away, for the girls have accounts to square with him too.

But these peaceful, meditative, poetical evenings did not always correspond to our moods. The storerooms of the colony, the cellars of the villagers, even the rooms of the teaching staff, had not ceased to be the objects of nefarious activities, though not on such a scale as had marked our colony in the first year. Missing articles had become a rarity. If a new specialist in this art did make his appearance amongst us, he quickly realized that he would have to deal not with the director, but with the majority of the collective itself, and the collective could be extremely cruel in its reactions. Earlier in the summer I had had difficulty in getting a new boy out of the grip of the other members of the colony, who had caught him trying to get into Ekaterina Grigoryevna's room through the window. They beat him up with the blind fury and ruthlessness of which the mob alone is capable. When I made my appearance in their midst, I was just as furiously pushed aside, and somebody called out passionately: "Make Anton get the hell out of here!"

That summer Kuzma Leshy was sent by the Commission to the colony. He must have been of partly gipsy descent. His huge black eyes were well placed on his dusky countenance, and supplied with an excellent rotatory apparatus, and nature had imposed a definite assignment upon these same eyes – to miss nothing which lay handy and could be stolen. The other members of Leshy's body blindly carried out the orders of those gipsy eyes: Leshy's feet carried him to the place where the handy article lay, his hands reached out for it obediently, his black bowed obediently to take advantage of any natural means of shelter, his ears were ever on the alert for suspicious rustlings or other warning sounds. What part Leshy's head took in all this it would be hard to say. Later in the history of the colony Leshy's head was appreciated at its worth, but at first it seemed to everyone the most unnecessary part of his body.

This Leshy caused us both grief and entertainment. There was not a day when he did not get into trouble. Once it was for sneaking a lump of lard from the cart, only just arrived from town, another time for stealing a handful of sugar from the storeroom under the storekeeper's very nose, he would pinch shag from his comrades' pockets, eat up half the bread on the way from the bakery to the kitchen, or pick up a table knife during a business talk in the room of one of the teachers. Leshy never worked to a plan of the slightest intricacy, or used any instrument, however primitive. He was so made as to regard his hands as his best instrument. The lads tried beating him up, but Leshy merely grinned:

"What's the good of beating me? I don't know myself how it happened. I'd like to see what you would have done!"

Kuzma was a cheerful lad. In the course of his sixteen years he had accumulated such experience, travelled much, seen a lot, put in time in the prisons of many gubernias, could read and write, was witty, remarkably agile and fearless in his movements, could dance the hopak beautifully, and did not know the meaning of shyness.

For these qualities the other boys forgave him much, but his thievish tendencies soon began to get on everyone's nerves. At last he got himself into a very ugly mess, which kept him on his back for a long time after. He broke into the bakery one night and was severely beaten up with a log. Our baker, Kostya Vetkovsky, had long suffered from continual shortage of bread, only coming to light during delivery, and then there was a chronic diminution in surplus weight after baking, and chronic scoldings from Kalina Ivanovich. Kostya laid a trap which was successful beyond expectation, and Leshy walked straight into it, one night. The next morning Leshy went to Ekaterina Grigoryevna, asking for help. He had been climbing up a tree to get some mulberries, he said, and got scratched. Ekaterina Grigoryevna was extremely surprised at such a sanguinary result of a mere fall from a tree, but it was none of her business – she bandaged Leshy's countenance and helped him to the dormitory – for Leshy could not have got so far alone. Until the right moment came Kostya confided to no one the details of that night in the bakery, but he spent all his spare time at Kuzma's bedside, reading him *The Adventures of Tom Sawyer*.

When Leshy recovered he himself told the whole story, and was the first to laugh at his own misfortune.

"Listen, Kuzma," said Karabanov, "If I always had such bad luck, I would long ago have given up stealing. You'll get yourself killed one of these days."

"I keep wondering myself," mused Kuzma, "how it is I'm always so unlucky. It's probably because I'm not a real thief. I'll have to try again a few times, and if nothing comes of it, I shall have to give it up. That's right, isn't it, Anton Semyonovich?"

"A few times?" I repeated. "In that case don't put it off, try today, nothing will come of it, anyhow. You're no good at such things."

"No good?" "None at all. But Semyon Petrovich told me you'd make a splendid smith."

"Did he?"

"Yes, he did. But he said, too, that you had sneaked w new taps from the smithy – they're probably in your pockets this very minute."

Leshy came as close to blushing as his dusky countenance permitted. Karabanov seized Leshy's pocket, guffawing as only Karabanov could guffaw.

"Of course they are! Here's your first time, and you muffed it!"

"Oh, hell!" said Leshy, emptying his pockets.

Within the colony it was only cases of this sort which arose. Things were much worse in respect to the so-called environments. The village cellars continued to enjoy the sympathy of the colonists, but this matter was now perfectly regulated, and reduced to a highly-organized system. Only seniors took part in cellar operations, juniors mere excluded, and at the slightest attempt on their part to go underground, these seniors ruthlessly and in all good faith pressed criminal charges against them. The seniors arrived at such extraordinary skill that even the tongues of the kulaks did not venture to lay this dirty business to the door of the colony. Moreover, I had every reason to believe that the executive leadership in all cellar operations was in the hands of no less an expert than Mityagin.

Mityagin had been born a thief from his childhood. If he did not steal in the colony, it was because he respected its inmates, and thoroughly understood that to steal in the colony as to injure his comrades. But nothing was sacred to Mityagin at the town markets or on the premises of the villagers. He often absented himself from the colony in the night, and the next morning it would be difficult to get him up for breakfast. He always asked for leave on Sundays, returning late at night, sometimes in a new cap or muffler, and always with gifts which he distributed among the younger boys. The little ones adored Mityagin, who, somehow or other, managed to conceal from them his frankly predatory philosophy.

Mityagin still retained his affection for me, but the subject of stealing was never broached between us. I knew that he was not to be helped by talking.

And yet Mityagin caused me great anxiety. He was on of the most intelligent and gifted of the boys, and therefore enjoyed universal respect. He knew how to display his thievish nature in the most attractive light. Me was always surrounded by a suite of older boys, and this suite behaved with the tact of Mityagin himself, with Mityagin's own respect for the colony and the teachers. It was difficult to ascertain what this company occupied itself with in the mysterious hours of dark. To do this it would have been necessary either to spy on them, or to interrogate a few of the boys, and it seemed to me that either of these systems would disturb the tone which had been so laboriously created.

Whenever I happened to learn of one of Mityagin's escapades, I would openly haul him over the coals at a meeting, sometimes inflict a penalty on him, or call him into my office to reprove him in private. Mityagin usually maintained silence with a perfectly calm demeanour, smiling with the utmost cordiality and good humour, and when leaving, invariably calling out in affectionate, grave tones:

"Good night, Anton Semyonovich!"

He was a frank supporter of the colony's good name, and was extremely indignant when anyone got caught.

"I don't understand where these asses spring from? Always biting off more than they can chew!"

I foresaw that we should have to part with Mityagin. It was annoying to have to acknowledge my powerlessness, and I was sorry for Mityagin. He himself probably realized there was no good in his staying in the colony, but he did not want to leave a place in which he had made so many friends, and where the little ones were drawn to him as flies are drawn to sugar.

Worst of all was the fact that even boys who seemed to be reliable members of the collective – Karabanov, Vershnev, Volokhov –

began to be infected by the Mityagin philosophy. The only one to show real, open opposition to Mityagin was Belukhin. It is noteworthy that the enmity between Mityagin and Belukhin never assumed the form of a brawl, or came to fighting or even quarrelling. Belukhin openly announced in the dormitory that so long as Mityagin was there, there would always be thieves in the colony. Mityagin heard him with a smile on his face, and replied without the slightest rancour:

"We can't fall be honest folk, Matvei. What the hell would your honesty be worth if there were no thieves? You get all the credit through me."

"I get credit through you! Why d' you talk such nonsense?"

"Just like that! I steal, and you don't steal, and so you gain glory. And if nobody stole, everyone mould be the same. I consider Anton Semyonovich ought purposely to take in chaps like me. Otherwise there'd be no way for chaps like you to make good."

"What rubbish!" said Belukhin. "There are countries where there aren't any thieves. There's Denmark, and Sweden, and Switzerland. I've read there aren't any thieves there."

"That's ia lie!" stammered Vershnev. "They steal there, too. And what's the good of not having thieves? Look how insignificant they are – Den-denmark and Switzerland!"

"And what about us?"

"Us? Just look at us, just see how we've shown ourselves – look at the Revolution, just look at it!"

"People like you are the first to oppose a revolution, so there!" shouted Belukhin.

Utterances like these would especially infuriate Karabanov. He would leap out of bed, shaking his fists, and darting ferocious glances from his black eyes at the good-natured face of Belukhin.

"What are you making all this fuss about?" he would cry. "What if Mityagin and I eat an extra roll, is that going to harm the Revolution? You measure everything in rolls."

"Stop hurling your rolls at me! It's not the roll, it's that you're a swine, going about digging into the earth with your snout!"

By the end of the summer the activities of Mityagin and his companions assumed colossal dimensions on the neighbouring melon beds. In our parts watermelons and muskmelons had been abundantly sown this year, some of the more prosperous farmers having planted several desyatins with them.

The stealing of melons began with an occasional raid on the melon beds. Stealing from melon beds has never been accounted a criminal offence in the Ukraine, and village boys have always gone in for minor raids on them. The owners maintained a more or less good-natured attitude to such raids – twenty thousand melons were sometimes gathered on a single desyatin, and if a hundred or so disappeared during the summer, the loss was scarcely felt. For all that, a hut was always erected in the middle of the melon field, in which there lived some old man who did not so much protect the melons as keep a record of uninvited guests.

Every now and then one of these old men would come to me with his complaints: "Your lads were in the melon field yesterday. Tell them it's not right to do that. Let them come straight to the hut, there's always enough to treat a fellow. Just tell me – I'll choose you the best watermelon in the field myself."

I transmitted the old man's request to the boys. They gratified it that very evening, merely introducing a slight amendment to the system proposed by the old man: while the very best melon chosen by the old man was being eaten, to the accompaniment of friendly conversation about the quality of the melons last year as compared to the crop the year of the Japanese war, uninvited guests were roving over the melon field, filling the turned-up hems of their shirts, pillowcases, and sacks with melons, while quite dispensing with conversation of any sort. That first evening, taking advantage of the old man's kind invitation, Vershnev suggested that Belukhin should visit him. The others raised no objections to this preferential treatment. Matvei returned from the melon field content.

"It was ever so nice, upon my word, it was! We had a talk, and made a guy happy...."

Vershnev sat on a bench smiling calmly. Karabanov burst into the room.

"Well, Matvei, did you have a good time?"

"You see, Semyon, me can be good neighbours, too."

"All very well for you! You've had your fill of melon, but what about us?"

"You're a funny guy! You can go to him yourself!"

"I like that! You ought to be ashamed of yourself! A man invites us, and are we all to go? That would be beastly cheek – there's sixty of us!"

The next day Vershnev again proposed that Belukhin should go to see the old man. Belukhin magnanimously refused the offer – let someone else go!

"How am I to find anyone else? Come on! You needn't eat any melon. You can just sit and talk."

Belukhin decided that Vershnev was right. He even liked the idea of going to see the old man and showing that the colonists didn't only go to him for the sake of watermelons.

But the old man received his guest extremely coldly, and Belukhin had no chance of displaying his disinterestedness. On the contrary the old man showed him his gun and said:

"Your felons carried off half the melons while you were sitting here talking, yesterday. How can you? I see I shall have to treat you differently. I shall shoot, that I will!"

Belukhin, covered with confusion, returned to the colony and, once in the dormitory, began to shout out his indignation. The boys all laughed, and Mityagin said:

"What's the matter with you – has the old man hired you as his lawyer? Yesterday you gobbled up the best melon, while keeping well within the law – what more do you want? And perhaps we never saw a single one. What proof has the old man?"

The old man did not come to me any more. But it was clear by many signs and tokens that an orgy of stealing was going on.

One morning, glancing into the dormitory, I noted that the whole floor was strewn with melon rind. I gave the monitor a rowing, punished someone or other, and demanded that this should not happen again. And for the next few days the dormitories were as clean as usual.

The mild, exquisite summer evenings, filled with the murmur of conversation, with an atmosphere of affection, with unexpected bursts of resonant laughter, melted into solemn, crystalline nights.

Dreams, the fragrance of pine and mint, the rustlings of birds and the echo of the barking of dogs in some distant village, hovered over the sleeping colony. I went out on to my porch. From round the corner appeared the monitor on night duty, and asked me the time. Bouquet, the spotted dog, followed him through the evening coolness on noiseless paws. I could sleep in peace.

But this peace covered extremely complicated and disquieting events.

Ivan Ivanovich happened to ask me:

"Is it by your order that the horses roam about the yard all night long? They might be stolen...."

Bratchenko fired up.

"Aren't the horses to be allowed a breath of air, then?" he asked.

The next day Kalina Ivanovich asked:

"What makes those horses look into the dormitory windows?"

"What on earth do you mean?"

"Go and see for yourself! The moment day breaks they stand under the windows. What makes them do it?"

I verified this statement: it was quite true – in the early morning all our horses, and the bullock Gavryushka, presented to us on account of his age and uselessness by the economic section of the Department of Public Education, ranged themselves beneath the windows among the lilacs and the bird-cherry trees, standing there motionless for hours, apparently in anticipation of something pleasant.

In the dormitory I questioned the boys:

"What makes the horses look into your windows?"

Oprishko sat up in bed, glanced towards the window, smiled, and shouted to someone:

"Servozha – go and ask those idiots what they're standing under the windows for?"

Giggles came from beneath blankets. Mityagin, stretching, said in his bass voice:

"We shouldn't have taken such inquisitive beasts into the colony – it's just another worry for you."

I attacked Anton.

"What's all this mystery about? What makes the horses hang about here every morning? What do you tempt them with?"

Belukhin pushed Anton aside.

"Don't you worry, Anton Semyonovich," he said. "No harm will come to the horses. Anton gets them here on purpose, so they must expect something nice."

"That's enough of your chatter!" said Karabanov.

"I'll tell you. You forbade us to throw melon rind on the floor, and there's always someone among us who happens to have a melon...."

"What d' you mean 'happens to have'?"

"Why, of course! Sometimes the old man treats us, sometimes they bring them from the village...."

"The old man treats you?" I repeated reproachfully.

"Well, he, or somebody else. And where are we to throw the rinds? So Anton lets the horses out. And the fellows treat them."

I left the dormitory.

After dinner Mityagin staggered into my office bearing an enormous melon.

"For you to try, Anton Semyonovich."

"Where did you get it from? Get out of here with your melon! I mean to take you all in hand, in good earnest."

"The melon is perfectly legitimate, and was specially chosen for you. The old man has been paid real money for that melon. And of course it's high time you did take us in hand, we won't be offended if you do."

"You get out of here with your melon and your talk!"

Ten minutes later, a regular deputation entered, bearing the melon referred to. To my astonishment, the spokesman was Belukhin, who could hardly speak for laughing.

"These swine, Anton Semyonovich, if you only knew how many melons they eat every night! What's the use of concealing it? Volokhov alone... but of course that's not the point.... How they get them – let that lie on their consciences but there's no getting away from it, they treat me, the bounders. They've found out the weak place in my youthful heart, you know – I simply adore melons. Even the girls get their share, and Toska gets treated, too. It has to be admitted that they're not quite without generous feelings. Well, and we know you don't get any melon, all you get is unpleasantnesses on account of these accursed melons. Therefore we beg you to accept our humble offering. I'm an honest person, not one of your Vershnevs, you can believe me, the old man has been plaid for this melon, more, perhaps, than the value of the human toil invested in it, as it says in economic politics."

Thus concluding, Belukhin suddenly fell serious, placed the melon on my table, and moved modestly aside.

Vershnev, disheveled and tattered as ever, peeped from behind Mityagin.

"P-p-political ec-c-conomy, not economic p-p-politics," he amended.

"It's all the same."

"How did you pay the old man?" I asked.

Karabanov began checking off on his fingers:

"Versnnev soldered a handle on his mug: Gud put a patch on his boot, and I kept watch for him half the night."

"I can just imagine how many melons you added to this one during the night."

"Quite true!" said Belukhin. "I can answer for that! We keep in touch with that old man now. But there's a melon field just outside the forest, where the watchman's a spiteful guy – always ready to shoot."

"What – and have you begun going to the melon fields?"

"No – I don't go myself, but I hear the shots – you know, one sometimes happens to be passing by...."

I thanked the boys for the magnificent melon.

A few days later I saw the "spiteful guy." He came to me, utterly disheartened.

"How's all this going to end?" he exclaimed. "They used to go out stealing mostly in the night, and now there's no escape from them even in the daytime – they come at dinnertime in bands. It's enough to make one cry – you go after on, and the others run over the whole field."

I warned the boys that I should go myself and help to guard the melon field, or that I would hire a watchman at the expense of the colony.

"Don't you believe that muzhik,' said Mityagin. "It's not a matter of melons – he won't let anyone pass by the melon fields."

"And why should you? What takes you there?"

"What's it to do with him where we go? Why should he fire?" Another day Belukhin warned me:

"This is going to end badly. The chaps are simply furious. The old man's afraid of sitting in the hut now, he's got two others watching with him, and they've all got guns. And the chaps won't stand for that!"

The same night the boys from the colony advanced in skirmish array towards the melon field. The military drill to which I had subjected them was of use here. By midnight, half the colony was lying beside the boundary of the melon field, after having sent out patrols and scouts. When the watchmen raised the alarm the boys shouted "Hurrah!" and rushed to the attack. The watchmen retreated into the woods, in their panic leaving their guns in the hut. Some of the boys occupied themselves with plucking the fruits of conquest, rolling the melons down the slope towards the boundary of the field, the others embarked upon reprisals by setting fire to the big hut.

One of the watchmen rushed to the colony and waked me up. We hastened to the field of battle.

The hut on its mound was enveloped in flames, and giving off a glow as if a whole village was on fire. As we ran up to the melon field a few shots rang out. I could see the boys, lying in regular squads among the melon beds. Every now and then these squads rose to their feet and ran towards the burning hut. Somewhere on the right flank Mityagin was giving out orders.

"Don't go straight, go round!"

"Who's that shooting?" I asked the old man.

"How do I know? There's nobody there. Maybe somebody left a gun there, maybe the gun's going off by itself."

Everything was, as a matter of fact, over. On my appearance the boys seemed to vanish into thin air. The old man sighed and went home. I went lack to the colony. Utter silence reigned in the dormitories. Everyone was not only asleep, but snoring. I never heard such snoring in my life. I said softly:

"Stop that fooling and get up!"

The snoring ceased, but everyone continued stubbornly to sleep. "Get up, I tell you!"

Tousled heads were raised from pillows. Mityagin looked at me with unseeing eyes:

"What's the matter?"

But Karabanov could not keep it up any longer.

"That'll do, Mityaya, what's the good...."

They all surrounded me and began to narrate with enthusiasm the details of the glorious night. Taranets suddenly jumped as if stung.

"There were guns in the hut!" he exclaimed. "Well, they're burnt now!"

"The wood has burned, but the rest could be used."

And he plunged out of the dormitory.

"This may he all great fun," I said. "But just the same it's real banditry. I can't stand it any more. If you intend going on like this we shall have to part company. It's a disgrace – no peace in the colony, or in the whole district, either by day or by night!"

Karabano seized me by the arm.

"It shan't happen again! We see for ourselves that it's gone far enough. Don't we, fellows?"

The fellows gave a buzz of confirmation.

"That's all nothing but words," I told them. "I give you fair warning, if this banditry goes on, I'll expel somebody from the colony. Mind, this is the last time I shall warn you!"

The next day carts visited the melon field, gathered up all that remained, and departed.

On my table lay the muzzles and smaller parts of the burned guns.

22

AMPUTATION

The boys did not keep their promise. Neither Karabanov, nor Mityagin, nor any of the other members of the group discontinued the raids on the melon fields, or the attacks on the village larders and cellars. At last they organized a fresh, extremely complicated undertaking, which brought about a series of events both pleasant and unpleasant.

One night they stole into Luka Semyonovich's garden, and carried off two hives together with the honey and the bees. They brought the hives into the colony in the night, and deposited them in the cobbler's shop, which was not working just then. In their joy they got up a feast in which many of the boys took part. In the morning a complete list of the participants could have been drawn up, for they all went about with red, swollen faces. Leshy even had to ask for the ministrations of Ekaterina Grigoryevna.

Called to the office, Mityagin immediately acknowledged that the whole adventure had been his doing, refused to name his confederates, and actually expressed astonishment:

"There's nothing in it! We didn't take the beehives for ourselves, we brought them to the colony. If you consider bees shouldn't be kept in the colony, I can take them back."

"What will you take back? The honey's been eaten, and the bees have flown away."

"Just as you like. I meant it for the best."

"No, Mityagin, the best will be for you to leave us in peace! You're already a grownup man, you and I will never agree, we'd better part!"

"I think so too."

It was essential to get rid of Mityagin as soon as possible. It was now clear to me that I had unpardonably postponed the fulfilment of this decision, and had been shutting my eyes to the gradual process of rot which had begun in our midst. There may have been nothing particularly vicious about the adventures in the melon fields, or the raiding of the hives, but the continual interest of the boys in these affairs, days and nights filled with the same everlasting preoccupations and strivings, implied the complete abandonment of the development of our moral tone, and consequently – stagnation. And on the surface of this stagnation extremely unpleasant contours could already be traced by a seeing eye – the offhand manners of the boys themselves, a specific vulgarity in the attitude both to the colony itself and to work of all kinds, a tiresome vacuous facetiousness, the elements of what was undoubtedly cynicism. I could see that even boys like Belukhin and Zadorov, while themselves taking no part in anything criminal, had begun to lose their former radiance of personality and to acquire as it were a scaly surface. Our plans, an interesting book, political questions, were being relegated to the background, while cheap, sporadic adventures and their endless discussion, occupied the centre of attention. All this reacted unfavourably both upon the outward appearance of the boys themselves, and upon the colony as a whole – slack movements, superficial and dubious challenges to witticisms, clothes carelessly thrown on, and dirt swept into corners.

I made out a discharge paper for Mityagin, gave him five rubles for the way – he said he was going to Odessa – and wished him luck.

"May I say goodbye to the fellows?"

"Certainly."

I don't know how they parted. Mityagin left towards evening, seen off by almost the entire colony.

That night everyone went about looking dejected, the younger boys were dull, their habitual unflagging energy slowed down. Karabanov slumped down on an overturned packing case just outside the storeroom, and stayed there till bedtime.

Leshy came into my office. "How we miss Mityagin!" he said.

He waited long for my reply, but I did not answer, and he went away as he had come.

I worked late that night. At about two, leaving the office, I noticed a light in the stable loft. I waked Anton and asked him:

"Who's in the loft?"

Anton shrugged a shoulder indifferently, and said reluctantly:

"Mityagin's there."

"Why is he there?"

"How do I know?"

I climbed up to the loft. Several persons were grouped around a stable lamp – Karabanov, Volokhov, Leshy, Prikhodko and Osadchy. They regarded me in silence. Mityagin was busy in a corner of the loft, I could hardly make him out in the darkness.

"Come to the office, all of you," I said.

While I was unlocking the door of my office, Karabanov gave the order:

"No point in everyone coming. Mityagin and will do."

I raised no objection.

We went into the office. Karabanov flopped down on to the couch, Mityagin standing in the corner by the door.

"What did you come back to the colony for?"

"There was some business to be settled."

"What business?"

"Just a thing we had to do."

Karabanov was looking iat me with a burning, steady gaze. Suddenly he gathered himself together, and, with a snake-like movement, landed at my table, over which he bent, bringing his burning eyes close to my glasses:

"D' you know what, Anton Semyonovich!" he said. "D' you know what? I'll go with Mityagin too!"

"What were you up to in the loft?"

"Nothing special, really. But just the same, not the thing for the colony. And I'll go with Mityagin. Since we don't suit you – very well – we'll go out and seek our fortunes. Perhaps you'll find some better members for the colony."

He had always been something of a play actor, and now he acted the injured party, no doubt hoping that I would be ashamed of my own cruelty, and leave Mityagin in the colony.

I looked Karabanov in the eyes and once more asked:

"What did you all get together about?"

For all reply Karabanov looked questioningly at Mityagin.

I rose from behind the table and said to Karabanov:

"Have you a revolver on you?"

"No," he replied firmly.

"Turn out your pockets!"

"Surely you're not going to search me, Anton Semyonovich!"

"Turn out your pockets!"

"There you are – look!" cried Karabanov almost hysterically, turning out all his pockets, both in his trousers and his jacket, scattering on the floor shag and crumbs of rye bread.

I went up to Mityagin.

"Turn out your pockets!"

Mityagin fumbled clumsily in his pockets. He brought out a purse, a bunch of keys and a master key, smiled shamefacedly and said:

"That's all!"

I thrust my hand into his trouser belt and brought out a middle-sized Browning. There were three cartridges in the clip.

"Whose is it?"

"It's my revolver." said Karabanov.

"Why did you lie to me, and say you had none? All right! Get the hell out of the colony, and be quick about it! Now, get out and stay out! D' you understand?"

I sat down to the table again, and made out a discharge paper for Karabanov. He took the paper in silence, looked contemptuously at the five rubles which I extended to him, and said:

"We can dispense with that! Goodbye!"

He stretched out his hands towards me, squeezing my fingers in a painful grip, made as if to say something, but instead rushed suddenly to the open door and melted into its dark aperture. Mityagin did not put out his hand, and said no word of farewell. He wrapped the folds of his jacket around him with a sweeping gesture, and slunk after Karabanov with the inaudible footsteps of a thief.

I went out to the doorstep. A crowd of boys had collected in front of the porch. Leshy started after the departing figures at a run, but only got as far as the outskirts of the forest and came hack. Anton was standing on the top step, murmuring something. Belukhin suddenly shattered the silence.

"That's that! Well – I admit the justice of it!"

"It may bb-be just," stammered Vershnev, 'b-b-but I c-c-can't help feeling sorry!"

"Who for?" I asked.

'For Semyon and Mityaga. Aren't you?"

"I'm sorry for you, Kolka."

I turned into my office and heard Belukhin adjuring Vershnev.

"You're a fool, you don't understand a thing – books haven't done anything for you."

For two days nothing was heard of those who had gone. I did not worry much about Karabanov – his father lived in Storozhevoye He would go about the town for a week and then he would go to his father. I had no doubt as to the fate of Mityagin. He would rove the streets for a year, serve a few terms in prison, get into some serious trouble, be sent to another town, and in five or six years would either be knifed by his own gang, or sentenced to be shot. There was no other course open to him. Perhaps he would drag Karabanov down with him. It had happened once – after all Karabanov did go robbing, armed with a revolver.

Two days later whispers circulated in the colony.

"They say Semyon and Mityaga are robbing people on the highroad. Last night they rohbed some butchers from Reshetilovka."

"Who says so?"

"The Osipovs' milkwoman came, and she says it was Semyon and Mityagin."

The boys whispered in corners, stopping when anyone came near them. The seniors went about with scowling countenances, would neither read, nor talk, gathering by twos and threes in the evening, exchanging few and inaudible words.

The teachers tried not to mention the boys who had left us in my presence. Once, however, Lydochka said:

"After all, one can't help being sorry for the lads."

"Let's come to an agreement, Lydochka," I said. "You pity them to your heart's content, and leave me out of it."

"Oh, very well!" said Lydia Petrovna huffily.

About five days later, I was returning from town in the cabriolet. Red, who had grown fat on the summer's bounty, was trotting cheerfully home. Next to me sat Anton, with his head bent low on his chest, absorbed in his thoughts. We were quite used to our deserted road, and anticipated nothing of interest on the way.

Suddenly Anton said:

"Look – aren't these our fellows? Well! If it isn't Semyon and Mityagin!"

Ahead of us two figures loomed up in the empty road. Only the keen sight of Anton could have made out with such certainty that these were Mityagin and his comrade. Red carried us rapidly towards them. Anton began to show signs of uneasiness, and glanced at my holster.

"You'd better put your gun in your pocket, where it'll be handier."

"Don't talk nonsense!"

"Have it your own way, then!"

Anton pulled at the reins.

"What a good thing we came across you!" said Semyon. "We didn't part quite good friends, then, you know!"

Mityagin smiled, as ever, cordially.

"What are you doing here?"

"We were hoping to come across you. You said we weren't to show ourselves in the colony, so we didn't go there."

"Why didn't you go to Odessa?"

"It's all right here, so far. In the winter I'll go to Odessa."

"Aren't you going to work?"

"We'll see how things pan out," said Mityagin. "We're not offended with you, Anton Semyonovich, don't think we are! Every one has his own path laid out for him."

Semyon beamed with frank joyfulness.

"Will you stay with Mityagin?" I asked him.

"I don't know. I'm trying to get him to come along with me to my old man, my father, but he keeps making difficulties."

"His father's a muzhik," said Mityagin, "I've had enough of them."

They went with me as far as the turning towards the colony.

"Think kindly of us!" said Semyon, when it came to parting. "Come on, let's have a farewell kiss!" Mityagin laughed.

"You are a sentimental guy, Semyon," he said. "You'll never amount to anything."

"Are you any better yourself?" retorted Semyon.

Their combined laughter resounded throughout the woods, they waved their caps, and we parted.

23

SELECTED SEED

By the end of autumn an extremely gloomy period had begun in the colony – the gloomiest in our whole history. The expulsion of Karabanov and Mityagin had been a most painful operation. The fact that "the very smartest of the fellows" had been expelled, boys who up till then had enjoyed the greatest influence in the colony, left the others rudderless.

Both Karabanov and Mityagin had been excellent workers. Karabanov knew how to throw himself into his work wholeheartedly and exuberantly; he found joy in his work, and infected others with it. Sparks of energy and inspiration had, as it were, flown from his hands. He did not often growl at the lazy or the languid, but when he did he shamed the most inveterate shirker. Mityagin was a splendid complement to Karabanov while at work. His movements, as befitted a true burglar, were distinguished by gentleness and suavity, but everything he did turned out well, all was good luck and good nature. And they were both sensitively responsive to the life of the colony, reacting energetically to the slightest irritation, to all the occurrences of the day.

With their departure, everything suddenly seemed dull and dreary. Vershnev buried himself still deeper in his books, Belukhin's witticisms became excessively earnest and sarcastic, boys like Volokhov, Prikhodko, and Osadchy, turned remarkably serious and polite, the little ones seemed bored and reserved, the whole collective suddenly acquired the outward manifestations of adult society. It had become difficult to collect a jolly company of an evening – everyone seemed to have business of his own to attend to. Zadorov alone maintained his cheerfulness and smiled his charming frank smile, but there was no one to share his liveliness, and he smiled in solitude, sitting over his book, or the model of a steam engine which he had begun to make in the spring.

Certain failures in our farming contributed to the general depression. Kalina Ivanovich was but a poor agronomist, having the wildest notions as to rotation of crops and the technique of sowing, while we had taken over the fields from the villagers in a weed-choked and exhausted condition. And so, despite the superhuman work done by the boys in the summer, our harvest was reckoned in pitiful figures. More weeds than wheat were grown on the winter fields, the spring corn looked wretched, and matters were still worse with the beet and potatoes.

Depression prevailed in the apartments of the teaching staff, too.

Perhaps we were simply tired – none of us had had leave since the opening of the colony. But the teachers made no complaints of fatigue. The old talk about the hopelessness of our work, the impossibility of practising social education on "such lads" was revived, the old theory advanced that all this was a futile waste of soul and energy.

"It'll all have to be given up," Ivan Ivanovich would say. "Look at Karabanov, whom we were all so proud of – he had to be expelled! It's not much good placing special hopes upon Volokhov, Vershnev, Osadchy, Taranets, and a whole lot of others. Is it worth running a colony for Belukhin alone?"

Even Ekaterina Grigoryevna was untrue to our spirit of optimism, which had formerly made her my foremost assistant and friend. She frowned in deep thought, and the results of her reflections were strange and unexpected.

"Listen!" she said. "Supposing we are making a terrible mistake! Supposing there isn't any collective, any collective at all, you know, and we keep on talking about the collective, simply hypnotizing ourselves with our own dreams of a collective."

"Wait a minute!" I said, checking her flow of speech. "What d' you mean 'there isn't any collective'? What about the sixty members of the colony, their work, their life, their friendship?"

"D' you know what all that is? It's a game, an interesting, perhaps an ingenious game. We were carried away by it, and the lads were carried away by our enthusiasm, but it was all temporary. And now it seems we're tired of the game, everyone's bored with it, soon they'll give it up altogether, and everything will turn into the usual, uninspired children's home."

"When you get tired of one game, you can begin to play another," said Lydia Petrovna, endeavouring to cheer us up.

We laughed sadly, but I had not the slightest intention of giving in.

"It's the usual spineless intellectualism that's got you, Ekaterina Grigoryevna," I told her. "The usual whining. It's no good trying to draw any conclusions from your moods – they come and they go. You desired intensely that both Mityagin and Karabanov should be conquered by us. Perfectionism, whims, over-eagerness, invariably end in whimpering and despondency."

I spoke thus, suppressing in myself, perhaps, the very same spineless intellectualism. I, too, sometimes harboured sneaking thoughts: better throw the whole thing up, neither Belukhin nor Zadorov was worth the sacrifices continually required by the colony. It came into my head that we were already exhausted, and that success was therefore impossible.

But the old habit of silent patient endeavour had not abandoned me. I tried, in front of the members of the colony and the teaching staff, to be energetic and confident; I would fall upon the fainthearted teachers, trying to convince them that our troubles were temporary, that all would be forgotten. And I take off my hat to the extraordinary endurance and discipline displayed by our teachers at this difficult time.

They were, as ever, punctual to the minute, active and alert to the slightest jarring note in the colony; they went on duty, according to our splendid traditions, in their best clothes, braced up and scrupulously neat.

The colony forged ahead without smiles or joy, but moved with a good unbroken rhythm, like a machine kept in perfect running order. I observed also that there were good results from my reprisals against the two members – the raids on the village ceased altogether, the cellar and melon field operations had become things of the past. I pretended not to notice the low spirits of my charges, and to behave as if the new spirit of discipline and loyalty with regard to the villagers was quite a natural thing, as if everything was going on as formerly and, as formerly going ahead.

Several new and important undertakings presented themselves. We began building a hothouse in the new colony, laying paths and levelling the yards after the clearing up of the Trepke ruins; fences and arches were put up, a bridge was in progress of construction over the Kolomak at its narrowest point, iron bedsteads for the use of the colony were being made in the smithy, our farm implements were put into repair, and the final repairing of the houses in the new colony was going on at a feverish rate. I relentlessly imposed more and more work on the colony, requiring from the whole of our social structure the former precision and accuracy of execution. I do not know myself, how it was that I took up military training with such ardour – it must have been in obedience to some unconscious pedagogical instinct.

I had some time before introduced into the colony gymnastics and military drill. I have never been a gymnastic expert, and we had not the means to call in an instructor. All I knew was military drill and military gymnastics, and everything appertaining to battle order in a company. Without the slightest premeditation, and without a single pedagogical qualm, I began to train the boys in all these useful branches.

The boys themselves took up these subjects gladly. After work the whole colony came every day for an hour or two to exercise on our drill ground – a spacious rectangular yard. Our field of activities increased in proportion to the increase in our experience. By the winter our skirmishing lines were executing extremely interesting and complicated movements all over the territory of our group of farmsteads. With grace and methodical accuracy we carried out assaults on given targets – huts and storerooms – assaults crowned by bayonet attacks and by the panic which seized the impressionable souls of their proprietors and proprietresses. Huddling behind the snow-white walls, the inhabitants would run out into their yards at the sound of our warlike cries, hastily locking storerooms and sheds, and, then, flattened against their doors, would follow with terrified glances the orderly ranks of our boys.

All this was extremely pleasing to the boys, and very soon we had real rifles, for we were joyfully accepted into the ranks of the General Military Training Department, which tactfully ignored our criminal past.

During training I was exacting and inexorable, like a true commander; and the boys thoroughly approved of this. Thus were the foundations of a new game laid, that game which subsequently became one of the main themes of our life.

The first thing I noticed was the good influence of a proper military bearing. The whole outward appearance of the colonist changed – he became slender and graceful, stopped slouching against table or wall, could hold himself erect with ease and freedom, without feeling the need of props of any sort. By now it was easy to distinguish new boys from old-timers. The gait of the boys became more confident and springy, they began to hold their heads higher, they lost the habit of thrusting their hands into their pockets.

In their enthusiasm for military order the boys contributed many inventions of their own, making use of their natural boyish sympathy for naval and military life. It was just at this time that the rule was introduced into the colony: to reply to every order, in token of confirmation and consent, with the words "very good!" accompanying this splendid reply with the flourish of the Pioneer salute. It was at this time, too, that bugles were introduced into the colony.

Hitherto our signals had been given by means of the bell left over from the former colony. Now we bought two bugles, and some of the boys went daily to the town to take lessons from the bandmaster in playing the bugle from notes. Signals for all occasions occurring in colony life were committed to paper, and by the winter we were able to dispense with the bell. The bugler went on to my porch of a morning, now, and flung over the colony the melodious, sonorous sounds of the signal.

In the calm of evening the sound of the bugle floating over the colony, the lake, the roofs of the farmsteads was particularly thrilling. Someone standing at the open window of a dormitory would take up the signal in a youthful, resonant tenor, someone else would suddenly repeat it on the keys of the piano.

When they heard of our military "craze" in the Department of Public Education, the word "barracks" became for long the nickname of our colony. But I had so much to grieve over that I was not inclined to worry about another little pinprick. I simply had no time.

In August I had brought two baby pigs from the breeding station to the colony. They were of a pure English breed, and therefore protested the whole way against compulsory "colonization," and kept falling through a hole they found in the cart. At last they grew hysterical in their indignation, to Anton's fury.

"As if there wasn't trouble enough without taking pigs."

The Britishers were dispatched to the new colony, where more than sufficient numbers of milling tenders were found among the younger boys. At that time over twenty boys were living in the new colony and with them lived one of the teachers, a somewhat ineffective individual by the name of Rodimchik. The big house, which we had denominated Section A, was already finished, and had been assigned to workshops and classrooms, but for the time the boys were living there. Some other houses and wings were also ready. There was still much work to be done in the huge two-storey empire-style mansion, which was intended for dormitories. New planks were daily nailed to sheds, stables and barns; walls were stuccoed, doors hung.

Our farming received powerful reinforcement. We called in an agronomist, and soon Eduard Nikolayevich Sherre, a being completely incomprehensible to the unaccustomed eye of our inmates, was striding over the colony fields.

Unlike Kalina Ivanovich, Sherre was never moved either to indignation or to enthusiasm, was always equably disposed, and a shade jocular. He addressed all members of the colony, even Galatenko, with the formal "you" (instead of "thou"), never raised his voice, and at the same time entered into no friendships. The boys were astounded when, in reply to Prikhodko's rude refusal. "Currant bushes! I don't want to work in the currant bushes!" Sherre merely expressed cheerful, kindly wonder, without the slightest pose or affectation.

"Oh, you don't want to? Just tell me your name, then, so that I shan't assign any work to you by mistake!"

"I'll go anywhere you like, only not to the currant bushes."

"Never mind, I'll get on without you, you know – and you can find yourself work somewhere else."

"Why?"

"Be so kind as to tell me your name, I have no time for superfluous conversation."

Prikhodko's piratical beauty seemed to fade in a moment. He shrugged his shoulders scornfully and made for the currant bushes, which only a moment ago had seemed to be in such flagrant contradiction to his vocation.

Sherre was comparatively young, but nonetheless he flabbergasted the boys with his unbroken self-reliance and superhuman capacity for work. It seemed to the colonists that he never went to bed. The colony would just be rousing itself in the morning, when Eduard Nikolayevich was already pacing the field with his long ungainly legs. The bugle was blown for bedtime, but Sherre would be in the pigsty, talking to the carpenter. In the day he could be seen almost simultaneously in the stable, on the site of the hothouse, on the road to town, and directing the manuring of the fields; at least, everyone had the impression that all this was going on simultaneously, so rapidly did Sherre's remarkable legs carry him from one place to another.

On the second day after his arrival Sherre had a quarrel in the stable with Anton. Anton was unable to understand or appreciate how anyone could adopt such a mathematical attitude as that which Eduard Nikolayevich insistently recommended, towards so sentient and delightful a creature as a horse.

"What's he taken into his head? Weighing? Whoever heard of weighing hay? Here's your ration, he says, and you must use neither more nor less. And such an idiotic ration – a little of everything. If the horses die I shall be answerable. And he says we're to work by the hour. And he's thought up some sort of a notebook – write down how many hours you work in it."

Sherre was not intimidated by Anton when the latter began bawling, as was his custom, that he wasn't going to let him have Falcon, who, according to Anton's reckoning, was to accomplish the day after tomorrow some particular feat. Eduard Nikolayevich went into the stable himself, led out and harnessed Falcon without so much as a glance at Bratchenko, who was petrified by such an outrage. Anton sulked, hurled the whip into a corner of the stable, and went out. When, however, towards evening, he did look into the stable, he saw Orlov and Bublik bossing around. Anton fell into a state of profound mortification and set off to give in his resignation to me. But Sherre rushed up to him in the middle of the yard, with a paper in his hands, and bent over the offended countenance of the head groom as if nothing at all had happened.

"Listen – your name's Bratchenko, isn't it? Here's your schedule for the whole week. Look, everything's put down exactly, what every horse has to do on a given day, when to be taken out, and so on. It's written here, which horse can be driven, and which is resting. Look through it with your comrades, and let me know tomorrow what alterations you think are required."

The astonished Bratchenko took the sheet of paper and went back to the stable.

The next evening Anton's curly head of hair, and the peaked, close-shaven head of Sherre might have been seen bending over my table engaged in most important business. I was working at the draughting table, but every now and then stopped to listen to their conversation.

"You're quite right. Very well, Red and Bandit can work at the plough on Wednesdays."

"Laddie can't eat beetroot, his teeth...."

"Oh, that doesn't matter, it can be minced finer – you try."

"And supposing someone else wants to go to town?"

"They can go on foot. Or let them hire horses in the village. What's it to do with us?"

"Oho!" said Anton. "That's the way!"

It has to be admitted that one horse a day did not go very far in satisfying our demands for transport. But Kalina Ivanovich could do nothing with Sherre, who cut short his inspired economic logic with the imperturbably cool reply:

"I have nothing to do with your need for transport. Take your provisions on anything you like, or buy yourself a horse. I have sixty desyatins. I will thank you not to raise the question again."

Kalina Ivanovich banged with his fist on the table, shouting:

"If I need a horse, I'll harness it myself!" Sherre entered something into his notebook without so much as glancing at the infuriated Kalina Ivanovich. An hour later, leaving the office, he warned me:

"If the schedule of work for the horses is infringed without my consent I will leave the colony immediately."

I sent hastily for Kalina Ivanovich and said to him:

"Leave him alone! You can't do anything with him!"

"But how am I to manage with one horse? We have to go to town, and to fetch water, and carry wood and provisions for the new colony."

"We'll think something up."

And we did.

New faces, new cares, the new colony, the ineffective Rodimchik in the new colony, the figures of the well set-up colonists, our former poverty, our growing prosperity – all this, like a mighty ocean, imperceptibly swallowed up the last traces of depression and grey melancholy. Since those days I only laughed a little less than formerly, and even the inner, living joy was not powerful enough to diminish the outer austerity which the events and emotions of the end of 1922 had imposed upon me like a mask. This mask caused me no discomfort, I hardly noticed it. But the colonists always saw it. They may have known it was only a mask, but for all that their attitude towards me was marked by a tone of exaggerated respect, a shade of stiffness, perhaps by a certain timidity, which I should have difficulty in defining. On the other hand I always noticed how they seemed to blossom out joyfully, coming into particularly close spiritual contact with me, whenever we happened to have fun together, to have games, to play the fool, or simply to pace the corridors arm-in-arm.

In the colony itself all austerity and all unnecessary gravity had disappeared. Nobody could have said when all this changed and settled down. As before, we were surrounded by laughter and jokes, as before, all were bursting with humour and energy; the only difference was that all this was no longer marred by the slightest breaches of discipline, or by haphazard, slovenly movements.

And after all Kalina Ivanovich found a way out of the transport difficulties. A single yoke was made for Gavryushka the bullock, to which Sherre laid no claims – for what was the use of one bullock? – and Gavryushka fetched water and wood, and did all the freight carrying for the colony. And on a certain delicious April day the whole colony rocked with laughter, laughter such as we had not known for ages – Anton drove in the cabriolet for something from town, and Gavryushka was harnessed to the cabriolet.

"You'll be arrested," I told Anton.

"Just let them try," he replied. "We're all equal now. Gavryushka's just as good as a horse, isn't he? He's a toiler, too."

Gavryushka, quite unabashed, drew the cabriolet to town.

24

SEMYON'S WAY OF SORROWS

Sherre set about things energetically. He did the spring sowing on the six-field system, which he managed to make a lively event in the colony. New agricultural methods were organized wherever he was – in the fields, in the stable, the hog house, the dormitories – or simply on the road, at the ferry in my office or in the dining room. The boys did not always accept his orders without argument, and Sherre never refused to listen to a businesslike objection, sometimes, with dry courtesy and in the concisest possible terms, even condescending to expound his views, but always ending with an inexorable: "Do as say!"

As ever, he spent the whole day in intensive work, without the slightest fuss; as ever, it was hard to keep up with him; and yet he was capable of standing patiently at the manger two or three hours running, or walking five hours behind the seed-drill; he would run backwards and forwards to the hog house every ten minutes, pursuing the pig tenders with courteous but insistent questions.

"When did you give the pigs their bran? Did you remember to enter the time? Did you enter it the way I showed you? Have you prepared everything for washing them?"

The members of the colony began to conceive a restrained enthusiasm for Sherre, though they were quite convinced, of course, that "our Sherre" was only such a wonder because he was "ours," that in any other place he would not have been nearly so wonderful. This enthusiasm manifested itself in silent recognition of his authority and endless discussion of his words, his ways, his imperviousness to emotion, and his knowledge.

This feeling caused me no surprise. I already knew that the boys would never confirm the theory that children are only capable of loving people who display affection for them and make much of them. I had long been convinced that the greatest respect and the greatest love was felt by the young – at any rate the lads in our colony – for people of quite another stamp.

It is what we call high qualifications, confident and precise knowledge, ability, skill, deft hands, terseness, abstention from high-flown phraseology, the steady will to work, which, in the highest degree, attract the young.

You can be as dour as you like with them, exacting to stringency, ignore them, even though they hang about you, show indifference to their affection, but if you shine by your work, your knowledge and your successes, you don't have to worry – you will have them all on your side, and they will never let you down. It does not matter how you show your ability, or what you are – joiner, agronomist, smith, or engine-driver.

On the other hand, however kindly you may be, however entertaining your conversation, however good-natured and cordial your approach, however charming your personality in daily life and leisure, if your work is marked by breakdowns and failure, if it is obvious at every step that you don't know your job, if all you do ends in spoilage and muddle, you will never earn anything but scorn, sometimes indulgent and ironical, sometimes furious and crushingly hostile, sometimes vociferously abusive.

It happened that a stove-maker was called in to make a stove in the girls' dormitory. A round, calorific stove had been ordered. The stove-maker dropped in at the colony quite casually, hung about for a whole day, mended a stove in someone's room, repaired the wall in the stable. He was a quaint-looking fellow – rotund, baldish, with saccharine manners. His speech was seasoned with facetious sayings and phrases, and according to him, there was not another such a stove-maker in the world.

The boys followed him about in a crowd, listening to his stories with incredulity, and receiving his information by no means in the spirit he had counted on inspiring.

"The stove-makers there, children, were older than me, of course, but the Count wouldn't have anyone else. 'Call Artemi, friends,' he would say. 'If *he* makes a stove, that'll be a *stove!*' Of course I was just a young stove-maker, and a stove in the Count's house, you understand, yourselves... Sometimes the Count would see me looking at the stove, and say: 'Do your best, Artemi – do your best!'"

"Well, and how did it turn out?" asked the boys.

"All right, of course. The Count always looked...."

He stuck out his chin arrogantly and imitated the Count looking at the stove Artemi had built. The boys could not control themselves, and burst into peals of laughter – Artemi was so very unlike a count.

Artemi embarked upon the building of the stove with solemn and highly professional words, recalling all the calorific stoves he had ever seen – the good ones made by himself, and the worthless ones made by others. At the same time, without the slightest embarrassment, he gave away all the secrets of his art, and recounted all the difficulties of making calorific stoves:

"The great thing," he said, "is to draw the radius properly. Some people simply can't do the radius."

The boys made a pilgrimage to the girls' dormitory and with bated breath watched Artemi draw his radius.

Artemi chattered incessantly while laying the foundations. When he came to the stove itself, a certain lack of assurance showed in his movements, and his tongue stopped wagging.

I went to have a look at Artemi's work. The boys made way for me, glancing at me with curiosity. I shook my head.

"Why have you made it so bulgy?"

"Bulgy?" repeated Artemi. "It isn't bulgy, it just seems to be, because it isn't finished, it'll be all right later on."

Zadorov screwed up his eyes and looked at the stove.

"Did it look bulgy at the Count's," he asked.

But the irony was lost on Artemi.

"Of course! All stoves do till they're finished."

In three days' time Artemi called me to accept the stove. The whole colony had gathered in the dormitory. Artemi stumped around the stove, with his head in the air. It stood in the middle of the room, bulging lopsidedly, when suddenly it collapsed thunderously, filling the room with bouncing bricks amidst a dust which hid us from one another, although the clatter was powerless to drown the storm of laughter, moans and squeals which burst out at the same moment. Many of those present were struck by bricks, but no one was in a state to notice pain. They laughed in the dormitory, and, rushing out of the dormitory, in the corridors, in the yard, they doubled up in paroxysms of laughter. I extricated myself from the debris and encountered Burun in the next room, who had seized Artemi by the collar and was aiming with his closed fist at the latter's tonsure, which was sprinkled with dust and fragments of bricks.

Artemi was driven away, but his name remained for long a synonym for a know-nothing braggart and bungler.

"What sort of a man is he?" someone would ask.

"He's an Artemi, – can't you see that?" In the eyes of the boys there was no one less like an Artemi than Sherre, who therefore enjoyed universal respect in the colony, so that work on the land went on briskly and successfully. Sherre had yet another talent, – he knew how to find unclaimed property, how to handle bills, how to obtain credit, so that new root-cutting machines, seeders, and buckers, and even boars and cows began to put in their appearance at the colony. Three cows – just fancy! It looked as if quite soon there would be milk.

A veritable enthusiasm for agriculture began to show itself in the colony. Only those lads who had acquired some skill in the workshops were not longing to rush out into the fields. Sherre began to dig hotbeds in the space behind the smithy, and the carpenter's shop was making frames for them. In the new colony hotbeds were being prepared on a vast scale.

In the very height of the agricultural fever, early in February, Karabanov walked into the colony. The boys met him with enthusiastic embraces and kisses. He shook them off somehow or other, and burst into my room.

"I've come to see how you're getting on."

Smiling, joyful countenances were peeping into the office – boys, teachers, laundry workers.

"It's Semyon! Just look! Isn't that fine!"

Semyon strolled about the colony till evening, visited "Trepke," and in the evening returned to me, melancholy and taciturn.

"Tell me how you're getting on, Semyon?"

"All right. I've been living with my father."

"And where's Mityagin?"

"To hell with him! I've dropped him. He went to Moscow, I believe."

"How was it at your father's?"

"Oh, well, villagers, just like it always is. My old man's still going strong. My brother's been killed."

"How's that?"

"He was a guerilla fighter – the Petlyuna men killed him in the town, in the street."

"And what do you mean to do – stay with your father?"

"No. I don't want to stay with my father. I don't know...."

He shifted uneasily in his seat and moved his chair nearer to me.

"Look here, Anton Semyonovich!" he brought out abruptly. "Supposing I were to stay in the colony? How about it?"

Semyon shot a rapid glance at me and lowered his head right on to his knees.

"Why not?" I said simply and gaily. "Stay, or course! We'll all be glad."

Semyon leaped from his chair, shaking with suppressed emotion.

"I couldn't stand it!" he cried. "I couldn't! The first days it wasn't so bad, but afterwards – I simply couldn't. I'd be going about, working, sitting down to dinner, and it would all come over me, till I wanted to cry. I'll tell you what – I've got fond of the colony, and I didn't know it myself. I thought it would pass, and then I thought – I'll just go and have a look. And when I came here, and saw how you were getting on – but it's simply wonderful here! And this Sherre of yours...."

"Don't work yourself up," I said. "You should have come right away. Why torture yourself like that?"

"That's what I thought myself, and then I remembered all the goings on, the way we treated you, and I...." He threw out his hands and fell silent.

"All right," I said. "That'll do."

Semyon cautiously raised his head.

"Maybe you think... that I'm putting it on, like you said. No, no! Oh, if you only knew what a lesson I've had! Tell me straight out – do you believe me?"

"I believe you," I said gravely.

"No, but tell me the truth – you believe me?"

"Oh, to hell with you!" I exclaimed laughing. "You don't mean to go back to your old ways. Do you?"

"You see you don't quite trust me!"

"Don't excite yourself so, Semyon! I trust everybody, only some more, some less. Some people I trust an inch or two, some people a foot or two."

"And me?"

"You, I trust a mile."

"And I don't believe you a bit," retorted Semyon.

"Fancy that!"

"Well, never mind! I'll show you yet...."

Semyon went to the dormitory.

From the very first day he became Sherre's right hand. He had a pronounced agricultural vein, he had acquired a lot of knowledge, and he had instinctive knowledge in his blood, from his fathers and his grandfathers, handed down from their experience of life in the steppe. At the same time he eagerly absorbed new agricultural ideas, and the beauty and grace of agronomical technique.

Semyon jealously followed Sherre's every movement with his eyes, and endeavouring to show him that he too was capable of endurance and incessant work. But he was incapable of emulating the calmness of Eduard Nikolayevich, and was in a continual state of excitement and elation, continually bubbling over – now with indignation, now with enthusiasm, now with sheer animal spirits.

Two weeks later I summoned him, and said simply:

"Here's a power of attorney. Go and get five hundred rubles from the Financial Department."

Semyon opened his eyes and his mouth, turned deathly pale, and at last brought out awkwardly:

"Five hundred rubles! And then what?"

"Nothing!" I replied, looking into the drawer of my table. "Just bring it to me."

"Am I to go on horse?"

"Of course! Here's a revolver in case you need it."

I handed Semyon the very revolver which I had taken from Mityagin's belt in the autumn, still with the three cartridges in it. Karabanov took the revolver mechanically, eyed it wildly, thrust it with a rapid movement into his pocket and left the room without a word. Ten minutes later I heard the clatter of hoofs on the stones, and a rider galloped past my window.

Towards evening Semyon entered my office, belted, in his short smith's leather jacket, slender, svelte, but sombre. In silence he laid a bundle of notes and the revolver on the table.

I picked up the notes and asked in the most indifferent and inexpressive tones I could muster:

"Did you count them?"

"Yes."

I threw the whole bundle carelessly into my drawer.

"Thanks! Go and have dinner."

Karabanov shifted the belt confining his jacket from right to left and made a few rapid steps in the room. But he only said quietly:

"All right," and went out.

Two weeks passed. Semyon greeted me somewhat glumly when we chanced to meet, as if he did not feel at ease with me.

He received my new order no less glumly.

"Go and get me two thousand rubles."

He gave me a long, puzzled scrutiny, while thrusting the Browning into his pocket, and said, weighing every syllable:

"Two thousand? And supposing I don't bring it back?"

I leaped from my chair and shouted at him:

"Kindly stop that idiotic talk! You've got your orders, go and do what you're told! Cut out the psychological stuff!"

Karbanov shrugged his shoulders and whispered vaguely:

"well... all right...."

When he brought me the money he would not let me alone.

"Count it!"

"What for?"

"Please count it!"

"But you counted it, didn't you?"

"Count it, I tell you!"

"Leave me alone!"

He clasped his throat as if something was choking him, then tore at his collar and swayed on his feet.

"You're making a fool of me! You couldn't trust me so! It's impossible! Don't you see? It's impossible! You're taking the risk on purpose! I know! On purpose!"

He sank on to a chair, breathless.

"I have to pay heavily for your services." I said.

"Pay? How?" said Semyon, leaning forward abruptly.

"By putting up with your hysterics – that's how!"

Semyon gripped the window sill.

"Anton Semyonovich!" he growled.

"What's the matter with you?" I cried, really a little alarmed by now.

"If you only knew! If you only knew! All the way I was galloping along the road I kept thinking – if only there was a God! If only God would send somebody out of the woods to attack me! If there were ten of them, any number of them.... I would shoot, I'd bite, I'd worry them like a dog, so long as there was life left in me... and you know, I almost cried. I knew quite well you were sitting here thinking, 'Will he bring it, or won't he?' You were taking a risk, weren't you?"

"You're a funny guy, Semyon! There's always a risk with money. You can't bring a bundle of a notes into the colony without risk. But I thought to myself, if you bring the money the risk will be less. You're young, strong, a splendid horse man, you could get away from any bandit, while they'd easily catch me."

Semyon winked joyfully:

"You're an artful chap, Anton Semyonovich."

"What have I got to be artful about?" I said. "You know how to go for money now, and in future you'll get it for me again. There's no special art needed for that. I'm not a bit afraid. I know very well that you're just as honest as I am. I knew it before – couldn't you see that?"

"No, I thought you didn't know that," said Semyon, and he left the office, singing a Ukrainian song at the top of his voice.

25
REGIMIENTAL PEDAGOGICS

The Commanders' Council. At the table is Ekaterina Grigoryevna

The winter of 1923 brought in its train many important organizational discoveries determining, for a long time ahead, the forms of our collective. Of these, the most important were – detachments and commanders.

There are to this day detachments and commanders in the Gorky Colony, the Dzerzhinsky Commune, and other colonies scattered about the Ukraine.

There was, of course, very little in common between the detachments of the Gorky Colony, or those of the Dzerzhinsky Commune in 1927 and 1928, and the first detachments of Zadorov and Burun. But something fundamental was established as early as the winter of 1923. The theoretical significance of our detachments only asserted itself considerably later, when they shook the pedagogical world with the wide sweep of their onset in marching order, and when they had become a target for the wit of a certain section of pedagogical scribblers. At that time it was the thing to refer to all our work as "regimental pedagogics," and it was taken for granted that this combination of words was in itself the severest condemnation.

In 1923 no one guessed that an important institution, around which stormy passions were to rage, was being created in our forest.

It all started with a trifle.

As usual, counting on our resourcefulness, no one gave us any wood for that year. As before, we used dead trees and the yield of our clearing of the forest. The summer accumulations of this not very valuable fuel were all used up by November, and once again we were in for a fuel crisis. To tell the truth we were all heartily sick of collecting dead wood. It was no trouble to fell, but the gathering up of a hundred poods of what it would have been euphemistic to call wood, required the ransacking of acres of forest, the difficult penetration of thick undergrowth, only to carry back to the colony a dubious assortment of twig and brushwood at the cost of a great and useless waste of energy. This work was ruinous to clothes, for which, as it was, we were sufficiently badly off, while in the winter the search for firewood meant frozen toes and frantic squabbling in the stable. Anton would not hear of sending the horses.

"Do it yourselves, the horses aren't going to be used for that. They're to go for fuel, indeed! D' you call that fuel?"

"But Bratchenko, haven't we got to heat?" asked Kalina Ivanovich, thinking he had found an unanswerable argument.

Anton waved aside the question.

"As far as I'm concerned you needn't. Nobody heats the stable, and we're all right."

In our quandary we did however manage, at a general meeting, to persuade Sherre to call a temporary halt to the carting of manure and mobilize the strongest and best-shed of the boys for work in the forest. A group of twenty was formed, which included our most socially active members – Burun, Belukhin, Vershnev, Volokhov, Osadchy, Chobot and others. They stuffed their pockets with bread in the morning, and spent the whole of the day in the forest. By evening our paved roadway would be adorned with piles of brushwood, for which Anton would sally forth on his two-horse sleigh, donning, as it were, a scornful mask for that purpose.

The boys would return famished but lively. Very often they relieved the return journey by a curious game, in which could be traced elements of their bandit reminiscences. While Anton, with the help of a couple of lads, loaded the sleighs with brushwood, the rest chased one another about the woods, and everything ended in a free-for-all and the capture of bandits. The captured forest dwellers were escorted to the colony by a convoy armed with axes and saws. They were pushed, all in fun, into my office, and Osadchy or

Koryto, the latter of whom had at one time served under Makhno and even lost a finger in his service, noisily demanded of me:

"Off with his head, or shoot him! Found in the woods with arms – perhaps there are some more of them there."

An interrogation began. Volokhov would knit his brows and fasten upon Belukhin.

"Out with it – how many machine guns?"

Belukhin, choking with laughter, would ask: "What's a machine gun? Is it good to eat?"

"What? A machine gun? You son-of-a-gun!"

"So it isn't good to eat? In that case I take no interest in machine guns."

Fedorenko, the most inveterate countryman, would suddenly be asked:

"Own up – didn't you serve under Makhno?"

Fedorenko was not slow in making up his mind how to answer without spoiling the game:

"I did."

"And what did you do there?"

While Fedorenko was thinking out his reply, someone from behind him said, sleepily and stupidly, in Fedorenko's voice:

"Took the cows out to pasture."

Fedorenko looked round, but met innocent countenances. A combined roar of laughter broke out. Koryto looked at Fedorenko fiercely, then turned to me and declared in a tense whisper:

"Hang him! He's a terrible fellow – just look at his eyes!"

I would reply in the same tone:

"Yes, he deserves no quarter. Take him to the dining room and give him two helpings."

"Terrible penalty!" said Koryto in tragic tones.

Belukhin broke in at a gabble:

"For that matter I'm a terrible bandit myself. I used to pasture cows for the atamans."

Only then did Fedorenko smile and close his gaping mouth. The lads began to exchange impressions of their work. Burun said:

"Our detachment brought in twelve cartloads today, not less. We told you there'd be a thousand poods by Christmas, and so there will."

The word "detachment" was an expression used in that period when the waves of revolution had not as yet been diverted into the orderly ranks of regiments and divisions. Guerilla warfare, especially in the Ukraine, where it was so long drawn-out, was carried on exclusively by detachments. A detachment might contain several thousand or less than a hundred members – in either case military feats were performed, with the depths of the forest affording shelter.

Our colonists had a special partiality for the military-guerilla romanticism of the revolutionary struggle. And individuals whom the whim of fate had thrown into the camp of hostile class elements, found in it first and foremost this same romanticism. Many of them neither knew nor understood the true meaning of the struggle, or of class contradictions, and hence it was that the Soviet authorities asked very little of them, and sent them to the colony.

The detachment in our forest, even though it was equipped with nothing but axes and saws, revived the familiar, beloved image of that other detachment, of which, if there were no actual memories, there were innumerable tales and legends.

I had no wish to interfere with the half-conscious play of the revolutionary instincts of our colonists. The pedagogical scriveners who criticized so harshly our detachments and our military games were simply incapable of understanding what it all was about. The word detachment held no pleasing associations for those whom detachments had once given short shrift – seizing their apartments and ignoring their psychology, shooting right and left from their three-inch guns, without respect for their science or their thought-wrinkled brows.

But there was no help for it. Ignoring the tastes of our critics, the colony began with a detachment.

Burun always played first fiddle in the woodcutting detachment, and there was none to dispute this honour with him. Following the rules of the same game, the boys began to call him their ataman.

"We can't call anyone ataman," I said. "It was only bandits who had atamans."

"Why only bandits?" clamoured the boys. "The guerillas had atamans too. The Red partisans had plenty."

"They don't say 'ataman' in the Red Army."

"In the Red Army they have commanders. But we're not the Red Army!"

"What if we're not! 'Commander' is much better."

The felling of wood was over: by the first of January we had over a thousand ponds. But we did not disperse Burun's detachment, which was turned over wholesale to the construction of hothouses in the new colony. This detachment went to work every morning, dining away from home, only coming back in the evening.

One day Zadorov addressed me as follows:

"See how things are with us! There's Burun's detachment, but what about the other chaps?"

We did not waste much time thinking about this. At that period orders were issued for each day in the colony, and one was added for the organization of a second detachment under the command of Zadorov.

The whole of this second detachment worked in the shops, and skilled workers like Belukhin and Vershnev left Burun's detachment and joined Zadorov's.

The further development of detachments proceeded apace. In the new colony a third and fourth detachment, each with its own commander, were organized. The girls formed a fifth detachment under the command of Nastya Nochevnaya.

The system of detachments was finally worked out by spring. The detachments became smaller, and were organized on the principle of the distribution of their members among the workshops. The cobblers always had the number one, the smiths – number six, the grooms – number two, the pig keepers – number ten. At first we had no sort of charter, and the commanders were appointed by myself, but by spring I was beginning to call commanders' meetings (which the lads gave the new and more pleasing name of Commanders' Councils) more and more frequently. I soon got used to undertaking nothing of importance without calling a Commanders' Council; and gradually the appointment of commanders themselves was left to the Council, which thus began to be increased by means of cooptation. It was long before commanders were appointed by general election and made accountable to the electors, and I myself never considered, and still do not consider, such free election as an achievement. In the Commanders' Council the election of a new commander was invariably accompanied by extremely close discussion. Thanks to the system of cooptation we always got the most splendid commanders, and at the same time we had a Council which never ceased its activities as a body, and never resigned.

One very important rule, preserved up to the present day, was the absolute prohibition of any privileges whatsoever for commanders, who never got anything in the way of extras, and were never exempted from work.

By the spring of 1923 we had made a great improvement in our detachment system, and one which turned out to be the most important invention of our collective during the thirteen years of its existence. It was this alone which enabled our detachments to be fused into a real, firm, and single collective, with both working and organizational differentiation, the democracy of the general assembly, the order, and the subordination of comrade to comrade.

This invention was – the composite, or "mixed" detachment.

The opponents of our system, attacking so violently "regimental pedagogics," had never seen one of our commanders at work. But this did not matter so much. What mattered much more was that they had never even heard of the mixed detachment, and thus had no idea whatever of the main principle of our system.

The mixed detachment was called into life by the fact that our principal work was agriculture. We had up to seventy desayatins, and in the summer Sherre demanded all hands for the work. At the same time each member of the colony was assigned to one or other of the workshops, and nobody wanted to lose his contacts there, for all regarded farming merely as a means of livelihood and the improvement of our life, and the workshop as a means of gaining skill.

In the winter, when work on the land was almost at a standstill, all the workshops were filled, but by January Sherre began to demand members of the colony for work in the hothouses and for carting manure, and these demands became every day more insistent.

Work on the land was marked by the continual change of its place and nature, and consequently led to all sorts of divisions of the collective for all sorts of tasks. The absolute authority of our commanders during work, and their responsibility from the very first, seemed to us a most important point, and Sherre was the first to insist that one of the members of the colony should be responsible for discipline, for the implements, for the work itself, and for its quality. Not a single rational person would now be found to raise objections to these demands, and even then, I think, it was only the pundits who had any objections.

We hit upon the idea of mixed detachments for the satisfaction of quite natural organizational requirements.

The mixed detachment is a temporary detachment, organized for not more than a week at a time and receiving short, definite tasks, such as weeding potatoes in a particular field, ploughing a particular allotment, sorting a consignment of seeds, carting a certain amount of manure, sowing a definite area, and so on.

Each assignment demanded different numbers of workers – in some mixed detachments, only two persons were required, in others five, eight, or even twenty. The work of the mixed detachments also varied as to the time it required. In the winter, while school was being attended, the boys worked either before or after dinner, in two shifts. When school was out, a six-hour day was introduced, with everyone working simultaneously, but the necessity for exploiting to the full both livestock and inventory led to some boys working from six a.m. to noon, and others from noon to six p.m. Sometimes there was so much to do that working hours had to be increased.

All this variety of work as to type and length of time, caused a great variety in the mixed detachments themselves. Our network of mixed detachments began to look something like a railway schedule.

It was well known throughout the colony that 3-1 Mixed worked from eight a.m. till four p.m., with an interval for dinner, and invariably in the truck garden, that 3-0 worked in the orchard, 3-R worked on repairs, 3-H in the hothouse, that the First Mixed worked from six a.m. till twelve noon, and the Second Mixed from noon till six p.m. The number of mixed detachments soon reached thirteen.

The mixed detachment was always a purely working detachment. As soon as its assignment was completed and the boys had returned to the colony, the mixed detachment ceased to exist.

Each member of the colony belonged to a permanent detachment, with its own permanent commander, its own place in the system of workshops, in the dormitory, and in the dining room. The permanent detachment is a sort of nucleus for the colony, and its commander has to be a member of the Commanders' Council. But from spring on, the nearer we got to summer, the more frequently a member of the colony was assigned to a mixed detachment for a week, with a given function.

Even when there were only two members in a mixed detachment, one of them was appointed commander, and organized and answered for the work. But as soon as working hours were over, the mixed detachment was dispersed. Every mixed detachment was composed for a week, and, consequently, each individual member of the colony usually received an assignment for the next week on new work, under a new commander. The commander of a mixed detachment was also appointed by the Commanders' Council for a week, after which they were, as a rule, no longer commanders in the next mixed detachment, but simply rank-and-file members.

The Commanders' Council endeavoured to make all members of the colony in turn – with the exception of the most glaringly unsuitable-mixed detachment commanders. This was quite fair, since the command of a mixed detachment entailed great responsibility, and a lot of trouble. Thanks to this system, most of the colony members not only took part in work assignments, but also shouldered organizational functions. This was extremely important, and exactly what was required for communist education. And it was thanks to this system that our colony distinguished itself in 1926 by its striking ability to adapt itself to any task, while for the fulfilment of the various tasks there was always an abundance of capable and independent organizers, and proficient managers – persons who could be relied upon.

The post of commander of a permanent detachment was shorn of much of its importance. Permanent commanders hardly ever appointed themselves commanders of mixed detachments, considering that they had enough to do as it was. The commander of a permanent detachment went to work as a rank-and-file member of a mixed detachment, and during work obeyed the orders of the mixed detachment commander, who was, as often as not, a member of the permanent commander's own detachment.

This created an extremely intricate chain of subordination in the colony, in which it was impossible for individual members to become unduly conspicuous, or to predominate in the collective.

The system of mixed detachments with its alternation of working and organizational functions, its practice in command and subordination, in collective and individual activities, keyed up the life of the colony and filled it with interest.

26

THE MONSTERS OF THE NEW COLONY

The repairing of Trepke had been going on for over two years and by the spring of 1923 it appeared, almost to our own surprise, that a great deal had been done, and the new colony began to pray a noticeable part in our life. It was the main sphere of Sherre's activities, for the cowshed, the stables, and the hoghouse were all there. With the onset of the summer season, life did not dwindle to nothing, as it used to, but fairly seethed with activities.

For some time the motive force of this life was still the mixed detachments of the old colony. Throughout the day the almost uninterrupted movements of the mixed detachments could be observed, both in the winding paths and along the boundary lines of the two colonies – some detachments hastening towards the new colony to work, others hurrying back to dinner or supper in the old one.

Ranged in single file, the mixed detachment covered the distance at a rapid pace. Boyish ingenuity and audacity found little difficulty in getting round the rights of property, and ignoring boundaries. At first the owners of farmsteads made feeble attempts to outwit this ingenuity, but soon realized that it was impossible – the boy persistently, and with the utmost sangfroid, carried out revisions of the various communicating paths between the farmsteads, determinedly straightening them in their pursuit of a definite ideal. In those places where the straight line led through a farmyard it became necessary to accomplish this work by other than geometrical means, such obstacles as dogs, hurdles, fences, and gates had also to be overcome.

The easiest of these were the dogs – we had plenty of bread, and even without bread the farmstead dogs had a soft spot for the members of the colony. The uneventful canine life, lacking vivid impressions and healthy laughter, was suddenly brightened up by a host of new and exciting experiences – varied society, interesting conversation, a wrestling match in the nearest heap of straw, and, finally – the acme of bliss – permission to leap alongside the rapidly marching detachment, to snatch a twig from the hand of a little chap and sometimes to be rewarded by a bright ribbon round the neck. Even the chained representatives of the farmsteads' canine police turned traitor, the more so that the main target of aggressive action was missing – from the early spring the boys did not wear trousers – shorts were more hygienic, looked nicer, and cost less.

The disintegration of farmstead society, beginning with the defection of the dogs, went further and further, till all the other obstacles in the way of straightening the line "Colony-Kolomak" became ineffective. First the Andreis, the Nikitas, the Nechipors and the Mikolas, – with an age range of ten to sixteen – came over to our side. It was the romantic aspect of the life and work of the colony which attracted them. They had long been listening to our bugle calls, and feeling the indescribable charm of a big and joyous collective, and now they gaped in admiration iat all these signs of the higher human activities – the "mixed detachment," the "commander," and – grandest of all – the "report." Their seniors were interested by the new methods of agricultural work – the Kherson crop rotation system made not only the boys, but also our fields and our seed-drill more attractive to them. It became a commonplace for every mixed detachment to be joined by a friend from the farmstead, bearing a hoe or spade stealthily extracted from the threshing shed. These lads filled our colony in the evening, too, and became, almost unnoticeably to ourselves, an indispensable part of it. Their eyes showed that to be a member of the colony had become the dream of their lives. Some of them attained this later, when conflicts which had their origin in family and daily life, or in religion, thrust them from their parents' embraces.

And, finally, the disintegration of the farmstead was accomplished by the strongest force in the world – the farmstead girls could not hold out against the charms of the barelegged, spruce, gay and accomplished colony boys. The local representatives of the male sex possessed nothing with which to combat these charms, especially as the colony boys themselves were in no hurry to profit by maidenly accessibility, did not smite the girls between their shoulder blades, seize them by any part of their anatomy, or bully them. Our older generation was by now approaching the Rabfak and the Komsomol, and had begun to feel the charm of refined courtesy and interesting conversation.

The sympathy of the farmstead girls had not as yet taken the form of infatuation. They liked our girls too, for, though intelligent and townbred, they never gave themselves airs. Love affairs came a little later. It was not so much "dates" and nightingale concerts, as social values which the girls sought in our midst. They flocked more and more frequently to the colony. Still afraid to come singly, they would sit in a row on the benches, imbibing in silence all sorts of novel impressions. Could it have been that they were overwhelmed by the prohibition to nibble sunflower seeds, either indoors or out-of-doors?

Wattle fences and gates, thanks to the sympathy felt for our affairs by the younger generation, no longer availed the owners in the old way – that is to say as tokens of the inviolability of private property – and our boys soon became so audacious that in the most difficult places they actually made for themselves a kind of stilemeans of getting over fences not to be met with in other parts of Russia, and consisting in a narrow plank pushed through a wattle fence, and supported by a wooden peg at either end.

The straightening of the Kolomak-Colony line was carried out at the expense of the farmers' crops – this sin must be admitted. And by the spring of 1923, one way or another, this line could have borne comparison with the October railway [the October line runs without a single deviation between Moscow and Leningrad. – *Tr.*], greatly facilitating the work of our mixed detachments.

The mixed detachment was the first to be served at dinner. By twelve-twenty the first mixed detachment had finished its dinner and set off. The teacher on colony duty handed its commander a paper on which all necessary details were entered – the number of the detachment, the list of its members, the name of the commander, the work assigned, and the time for its execution.

Sherre introduced higher mathematics into all this – the task was calculated to the last inch and the last ounce.

The mixed detachment would start out rapidly, and in five or six minutes its column could be made out far into the field. Soon it jumped a hurdle, and disappeared among the huts. Following it, at a distance determined by the length of the talk with the teacher on colony duty, came the second – 3-C or perhaps 3-0. In a very short time the whole field would be cut up by the lines of our detachments. And Toska, perched upon the roof of an icehouse would already be calling out:

"One-P coming back!"

And indeed 1-P can be made out, its column emerging from between the farmstead wattle fences. One-P always works on ploughing and sowing, and in general on work with the horses. It had left home at five-thirty a.m., its commander Belukhin having accompanied it. It was Belukhin whom Toska had been looking out for from the vantage point of the icehouse roof. Another few minutes and 1-P – six members in all – is in the yard of the colony. While the detachment is seating itself at the table in the woods, Belukhin hands in his report to the teacher on colony duty, checked by Rodimchik las to time of arrival and execution of work.

Belukhin is, as ever, in good spirits.

"There was a delay of five minutes, you see. It's the navy's fault. We wanted to go to work, and Mitka was ferrying some speculators across."

"What speculators?" asked the teacher on colony duty, his curiosity aroused.

"Don't you know? They've come to rent the orchard."

"Really?"

"Well, I didn't let them go further than the shore. What d' you think – you're to munch apples and we're just to look on? Row back, citizens, to the point of departure! Hullo, Anton Semyonovich – how's things?"

"Hullo, Matvei!

"Tell me, for God's sake – are you ever going to get rid of that Rodimchik? You know, Anton Semyonovich, it's simply a disgrace! A man like that, you know, going about the colony, and depressing everyone. He even takes away one's desire to work, and then I have to give him the report to sign. Whatever for?"

This Rodimchik was an eyesore to all the members of the colony. By now there were over twenty persons in the new colony, and there was work and to spare. Sherre carried out work with the help of the mixed detachments of the first colony in the fields only. The stables, the cowshed, the ever-expanding hoghouse, were tended by the boys on the spot. An enormous outlay of energy was expended in the new colony on getting the orchard into order. There were four desyatins of the orchard, which was full of fine young trees. Sherre had undertaken work on a huge scale there. The ground in the orchard was ploughed, the trees pruned and freed from excrescences; the great bed of black currants was weeded, paths laid down, and flower beds dug. Our newly-built hothouse had yielded its first products in the spring. A good deal of work was going on on the riverbank, too – the digging of ditches, and clearing away of reeds.

The repairs on the estate were approaching completion. Even the stable of hollow concrete no longer vexed us with its broken roof – it was covered with roofing paper and inside the carpenters were finishing the building of a hoghouse. According to Sherre's calculations it should house a hundred and fifty hogs.

Life at the new colony was not very tempting, especially in winter. In the old colony we had more or less settled down, and everything was in such good order that we scarcely noticed either the bleak brick buildings, or the aesthetic shortcomings of our daily life. Mathematical order, cleanliness and scrupulous neatness in the most insignificant details, compensated for the absence of beauty. The new colony, despite its wild beauty in the loop of the Kolomak, the high riverbanks, the orchard, the large, handsome buildings, had not yet been wrested from the chaos of ruin; it was still littered with building debris, and broken up by lime pits, and everything was so overrun with tall weeds, that I often wondered if we should ever be able to deal with them.

Nothing here was really quite ready for life – the dormitories were good ones, but there was no proper kitchen or dining room. And when the kitchen was more or less in order, there was no cellar. Worst of all was the matter of personnel there was no one to set things going in the new colony.

As a result of all this, the members of the colon, who had with such eagerness and fervour accomplished the enormous work of restoring the new colony, had no desire to live in it. Bratchenko, who was ready to cover twenty kilometres a day between one colony and the other, and to put up with insufficient food and sleep, considered that transference to the new colony would have been a disgrace. Even Osadchy declared: "I'd rather leave the colony than go to live at Trepke."

All the more vivid personalities in the old colony had by this time formed such a close circle, that not one of them could have been wrenched from it without a painful shock. To have transferred them to the new colony would have meant risking both the new colony and the individualities concerned. The boys themselves thoroughly realized this.

"Our lads are like good horses," Karabanov wouid say, "just harness a fellow like Burun properly, and cluck to him in the right way, and he'll go like anything, and be quite perky, but give him his head and he'll rush headlong down some hill, break his neck and smash the cart."

For this reason a collective of quite another tone and value began to form itself in the new colony. It contained boys who were neither so vivid, so active, nor so difficult. It had a kind of rawness, as regards the collective itself – the result of selection along pedagogical lines.

Any interesting personalities had got there by chance, having only lately emerged from the little ones, or unexpectedly turned up in a batch of new arrivals, and so far such personalities had had no time to make themselves felt, and were lost in the commonplace crowd of Trepke dwellers.

The Trepke lot as a whole were such as more and more to depress me, the teachers, and the other members of the colony. They were lazy, grubby, and even inclined to the mortal sin of begging. They regarded the old colony with envy, and mysterious rumours were rife among them as to what was had for dinner and supper there, what was brought to the larder in the original colony, and why this was not brought to them. They were incapable of strong, outspoken protest, and could only whisper sullenly in corners and cheek our official representatives.

The boys of the original colony had already begun to adopt a somewhat scornful attitude towards the Trepke dwellers. Zadorov or Volokhov would bring some grumbler from the new colony and thrust him into the kitchen of the old colony, with the words:

"Feed this starving fellow, do!"

The "starving fellow," would, of course, out of false pride, refuse to be fed. As a matter of fact the boys in the new colony were better fed. Our truck garden was nearer to it, there were things to be bought at the mill, and, finally, there were our own cows. It was difficult to send milk to the old colony: the distance was an impediment, and there never seemed to be a horse to spare.

A collective of shirkers and grumblers was formed in the new colony. As has already been pointed out, many circumstances were to blame for this, chief among which were the lack of the right people to form a true nucleus, and the poor work of the teaching staff.

Teachers did not wish to come and work in our colony – the pay was wretched and the work was hard. The Department of Public Education, moreover, sent us the first people who came to hand – men like Rodimchik, and after him, Deryuchenko. They arrived with their wives and children and occupied the best rooms in the colony. I made no protest, being thankful that even such people were to be found.

It could be seen at a glance that Deryuchenko was a typical follower of Petlyura. He "did not know" Russian, adorned all the rooms of the colony with cheap reproductions of Shevchenko's portrait, and immediately settled down to the only business for which he was fit – the singing of Ukrainian songs.

Deryuchenko was still young. He was curly all over, like the knave of clubs in Ukrainian national costume – his moustache was curly, his hair was curly, and his necktie, tied round the upright collar of his embroidered Ukrainian blouse, was curly too. And such a man had to perform tasks which – what a blasphemy! – had no connection with "the cause of the Great Ukraine": going on colony duty, making visits of inspection to the hoghouse, checking the arrival for work of mixed detachments, and, on his day of work duty, working alongside the boys. All this was pointless and unnecessary work in his eyes, and the whole colony was a completely futile phenomenon, bearing not the slightest relation to cosmic problems.

Rodimchik was just as useless in the colony as Deryuchenko, and even more repulsive....

Rodimchik had been in this world for thirty years, and had formerly worked in all sorts of departments – the Criminal Investigation Department, Co-operative Societies, the railway, – and at last he had turned to the business of educating the young in children's homes. His face, ruddy, creased and wrinkled, was strangely reminiscent of some ancient leather pouch. The flattened, crooked nose inclined sideways, the ears were pressed against the skull in lifeless, flabby folds, the mouth, vaguely awry, seemed to be worn out, jagged, and even torn in places, as if from long and slovenly use.

Arriving at the colony and installing himself and his family in a renovated apartment, Rodimchik hung around for a week, and then suddenly disappeared, sending me a note in which he explained that he had gone on most important business. Three days later he returned in a farm wagon, with a cow tied to the tail of the cart. Rodimchik told the boys to put the cow in with our own. Even Sherre was a trifle taken aback by this unexpected development.

In another two days Rodimchik came to me with the complaint.

"Little did I think that there would be such an attitude to employees here! They seem to have forgotten that the old days are over. My children and I have just as much right to milk as anyone else. The fact that I showed initiative and did not wait for government milk, but, as you know, did my best, and bought a cow out of my slender means and brought it to the colony myself, is, you'd think, worthy of approval, and not abuse. And how is my cow treated? There are several haystacks in the colony, and in addition to this the colony gets bran, chaff, and so on from the mill at reduced prices. And just look – all the cows are fed, and mine goes hungry, and the boys answer me so rudely – 'supposing everyone was to have his own cow!' they say. The other cons are cleaned, and mine hasn't been cleaned for five days, and it's dirty all over. I suppose my wife is expected to go and clean up after the cow herself. And she would, too, but the boys don't give her spades, or forks, and they don't give her straw for bedding either. If a trifle like straw is made such a fuss about, I warn you I shall have to take decisive measures. What if I'm not in the Party any more! I used to be in the Party, and I deserve better treatment for my cow."

I stared blankly at this individual, wondering if a way of dealing with him could be found.

"Excuse me, Comrade Rodimchik, I don't quite understand," I began, "that cow of yours is private property – how can it be kept with the others? And then – you're a pedagogue, aren't you? Look what a position you are putting yourself into in the eyes of your charges!"

"Why? I'm not asking for anything," gabbled Rodimchik. "I'm perfectly willing to pay for the fodder and for the labour of the boys, if it's not too clear. And I never said a word about my child's tam-o'-shanter being stolen, and of course it was stolen by one of the boys."

I sent him to Sherre.

The latter had by that time regained his wits and sent Rodimchik's cow out of the cattle yard. In a few days it disappeared altogether – its owner had apparently sold it.

Two weeks passed. Volokhov raised the question at a general meeting: "What's the meaning of this? Why is Rodimchik digging potatoes in the colony truck garden? We have no potatoes for our kitchen, and Rodimchik is digging them up for himself. What right has he?"

The other boys supported Volokhov. Zadorov said:

"It's not the potatoes that matter. He has a family – if he'd asked in the right place nobody would have grudged him potatoes, but what's the good of that Rodimchik altogether? He sits all day in his room, or goes off to the village. The kids go dirty, they never see him, they live like savages. You go to him to get a report signed, and he's not to be found – he's either asleep or having dinner, or he's busy – and you must wait. What's the good of him?"

"We know how the staff should work," put in Taranets. "And that Rodimchik! He goes out with a mixed detachment on working day, stands about with a hoe half an hour, and then says: 'Well, I must be off for a little while!' And that's the last of him, and two hours later you see him coming away from the village with something in a sack for his family."

I promised the boys I would take measures. The next day I summoned Rodimchik to my office. He came towards evening, and when we were alone I began to rate him, but he interrupted me immediately, almost foaming at the mouth in his indignation.

"I know whose work that is, I know quite well who is trying to trip me up – it's all that German! You would do better to find out, Anton Semyonovich, what sort of a man he is. I have already – there wasn't any straw to be found for my cow even for money, I sold my cow, my children go without milk, it has to be brought from the village. And now just you ask what Sherre feeds his Milord on! What does he feed him on – do you know? No, you don't! He takes millet intended for the poultry – and makes a mash for Milord! Out of millet! He makes it himself and gives it to the dog to eat, and doesn't pay a kopek. And the dog eats the colony millet on the sly, free of charge, all because that man takes advantage of being the agronomist and of your trust in him."

"How- do you know all this?" I asked.

"Oh, I would never say such a thing without grounds. I'm not that sort of fellow. Just you look...."

He unwrapped a little packet which he had drawn from an inner pocket. In the packet there was something blackish-white, a strange sort of mixture.

"What is it?" I asked in astonishment.

"This will prove everything I say. It's Milford's excrements. His excrements, d'you understand? I went on and on till I got it. D' you see what he excretes? Real millet! And d' you think he buys it? Of course he doesn't, he simply takes it out of the larder."

"Look here, Rodimchik," I said. "You'd better quit the colony."

"How d' you mean – quit?"

"Quit as soon as possible. I'll discharge you in today's Order. Give in an application for voluntary resignation, that'll be the best way."

"I'm not going to leave matters like this!"

"All right. You don't – but I'm going to discharge you!"

Rodimchik went away. He did "leave matters like this," and in three days he was gone.

What was to be done about thie new colony? The Trepke dwellers were turning out to be bad colonists, and this could not be tolerated any longer. Every now and then fights broke out among them, and they were always stealing from one another – an obvious sign of something wrong in the collective.

Where is one to find people for this accursed business? Real human beings! Not so easy, damn it!

27
THE STORMING OF THE KOMSOMOL

In 1923 the regular columns of the Gorkyites approached a new stronghold, which, strange as it may sound, had to be taken by storm – the Komsomol.

The Gorky Colony had never been an exclusive organization. From the year 1921 our ties with the so-called "surrounding population" had been extremely varied and extensive. Our nearest neighbours were, owing both to social and historical causes, our foes, against whom we struggled to the best of our abilities, but with whom we carried on economic relations, largely thanks to our workshops. The economic relations of the colony, however, extended far beyond the boundaries of the hostile section, since we did work for the village on a fairly wide radius, penetrating by our industrial services lands so remote as Storozhevoye, Machukhi, Brigadirovhka. By 1923, contacts with the big villages nearest to us – Goncharovka, Pirogovka, Andryushevka, Zabiralovka – had been established, and they were not merely of all economic nature. The very first sallies of our Argonauts, pursuing aims or an aesthetic nature, such as a review of local feminine beauty, or the demonstration of personal attainment as in the sphere of hairdressing, figure, bearing, and smiles – even these first voyagings into the ocean of village life led to a considerable extension of social ties. And it was precisely here that the members of the colony made their first acquaintance with Komsomol members.

The forces of the Komsomol in thee villages were extremely weak both as to quantity and quality. The village Komsomols themselves were mainly interested in girls and drink, and as often as not exerted a pernicious influence on our boys. It was only when the Lenin Agricultural Artel began to be organized opposite the new colony, on the right bank of the Komosol, and found itself, as it were involuntarily, in a state of grave hostility with our Village Soviet and the whole farmstead group, that we discovered a fighting spirit in the ranks of the Komsomols and began to make friends with the younger members of the artel.

Our boys knew thoroughly, down to the smallest detail, all the affairs of the new artel, and all the difficulties against which its organizers had had to contend in setting it up. In the first place the artel struck a violent blow at the kulak territories, thus evoking from the members of the farmstead united and furious resistance. The artel did not gain its victory easily.

The owners of farmsteads at that time represented a great force and had a certain pull in the town, while their essentially kulak nature was for some reason a secret to many of the town authorities. In this struggle the town offices were the principal battlefield, and the principal weapon – the pen, so that the members of the colony could take no direct part in the struggle. But when the matter of acreage was settled, to be followed by inventory operations of extreme complexity, much interesting work was found for both our own boys and the lads in the artel, in the course of which contacts became still closer.

The Komsomols did not play a leading role in the artel, being on a lower intellectual level than our older boys. Our school studies had proved a great asset to our members, greatly intensifying their political consciousness. The members of the colony had begun proudly to consider themselves proletarians, and thoroughly understood the difference between their own position and that of the village youth. Intensive, and often onerous, work on the land did nothing to disturb their profound conviction that quite different activities lay ahead of them.

The oldest of them were already able to describe in some detail what they expected from their future, and what they aspired to. And it was the youthful forces of the town and not of the village, which played the leading role in the crystallization of these dreams.

Not far from the railway station were situated great engine workshops. For our boys they represented the most cherished collection of valued individuals and objects. The engine workshops had a glorious revolutionary past, and contained a powerful Party collective. The boys dreamed of these shops as of something miraculous – a fairy palace. Within this palace was something more splendid than the luminous columns of "The Blue Bird" – the powerful swooping of cranes, steam hammers with their concentrated force, intricate turret lathes, which seemed to he endowed with a complex cerebral apparatus. About the palace the people – the masters – moved to and fro, noble princes, clad in precious attire, shining with train oil, and fragrant with the aromas of steel and iron. They had the right to touch the sacred surfaces, the cylinders and the cones, all the wealth of the palace. And they themselves were special people. The combed, red beards and fat, greasy faces of the farmstead dwellers were not to be found among them. They had wise, subtle faces, shining with knowledge and power – the power over machinery and engines, the knowledge of all the complex laws governing the use of switches, props, levers, and steering wheels. And among these people were many Komsomols, compelling our admiration by a new and wonderful hearing; here we could observe confident cheerfulness, could hear the strong salty idiom of the worker.

The engine workshops! They represented the utmost aspirations of many of our boys during the year 1922. Rumours of still more splendid human creations came to their ears – the Kharkov and Leningrad plants, all those legendary Putilov, Sormovo works. Ah, well – the world is full of wonders, and the dreams of a humble member of a provincial colony cannot soar to such heights. But we gradually began to get more intimate with the engine shop workers, whom we had opportunities of seeing with our own eyes, whose charms we could feel through all our senses, not excluding that of touch.

They were the first to come to us, and it was their Komsomols that came. One Sunday Karabanov rushed into my office, shouting:

The Komsomols had heard much good of the colony, and had come to make our acquaintance. There were seven of them. The boys surrounded them at affectionately in a dense crowd, and spent the whole day with them in the closest of contacts, showing them the new colony, our horses, our implements, our pigs, Sherre, the hothouse, feeling to the very depths of their beings the in significance of our wealth in comparison with the engine workshops. They were greatly struck by the fact that the Komsomols, far from putting on airs with us, or demonstrating their superiority, actually seemed to be impressed, and even a little touched by what they saw.

Before going back to town the Komsomols came to me to have a talk. They wanted to know why we had no Komsomol organization in the colony. I gave them a brief outline of the tragic history of this matter. We had been trying to organize a Komsomol nucleus in the colony ever since 1922, but the local Komsomol forces had come out absolutely against this – our colony was for delinquents, so how could there be Komsomol in it? To all our requests, arguments, adjurations the same answer was given – our members were delinquents. Let them leave the colony, let it be certified that they had reformed, then only could the acceptance in the Komsomol of individual boys be discussed.

The engine shop workers sympathized with our situation, and promised to support our cause in the town Komsomol organizations. And the very next Sunday one of them came again to the colony, but merely to give us discouraging news. Both the gubernia and town committees said: "Quite right – how can there be Komsomols in the colony so long as there are so many former Makhno followers, ex-criminals and other shady characters among them?"

I explained to him that we had very few Makhno followers, and that even these could hardly be taken seriously as such. Finally, I explained to him that the word "reformed" could not be used in the formal sense given it in the town. It was not enough for us to "reform" a boy, we had to re-educate him on new lines, that is to say, in such a manner that he should become not merely a harmless member of society but also an active worker in the new epoch. And how is such a one to be educated, if, when he aspires to become a Komsomol, he is not admitted, and everyone begins to bring up old, and after all, childish, crimes against him? The engine shop worker both agreed and disagreed with me. The question of a boundary line seemed to him the most difficult. When could a member of the colony be received into the Komsomol, and when not? And who was to decide this question?

"Who? Why, the colony Komsomol organization, of course!"

The Komsomol from the engine shops continued to visit us frequently, but at last I realized that their interest in us was not quite a healthy one. They regarded us, first and foremost, as criminals; they attempted with the utmost curiosity to delve into the boys' pasts, and were ready to acknowledge our successes, with, however, the sole qualification: but still yours are no ordinary boys. I had the utmost difficulty in getting individual Komsomols over to my point of view.

Our position on this question had remained unaltered from the very first day of the colony. I considered that the principal method for the reeducation of delinquents should be based upon a complete ignoring of the past, especially past crimes. It had been by no means easy for me to carry this method out in its entirety, for among other obstacles I had to combat my own instincts. There was always a sneaking desire to find out what a boy had been sent to the colony for, what he had really done. The usual pedagogical logic at that time aped medicine, adopting the sage adage: "In order to cure a disease, it must first be known." This logic sometimes seduced even me, not to mention my colleagues and the Department of Public Education.

The Commission for Juvenile Delinquency used to send us the personal records of our charges, in which were minutely described the various interrogations, confrontations, and all that rot, which were supposed to help in studying the disease.

I was able to get all my colleagues in the colony on to my side, and as far back as 1922 I had asked the Commission not to send me any more personal records. We quite sincerely ceased to interest ourselves in the past offences of our charges, and with such success that the latter soon began to forget them themselves. I rejoiced exceedingly to see how all retrospective interest was gradually disappearing from the colony, how the very memory of days which had been vile, diseased and alien to us had disappeared. In this respect we attained the limits of our ideal – even new arrivals were ashamed to talk about their feats.

And suddenly, in connection with such a wonderful undertaking as the organization of a Komsomol nucleus in the colony, we were forced to remember our past and to revive the words so hateful to us – "reform," "delinquency," "personal records."

The boys' aspirations to join the Komsomol hardened, thanks to the opposition they met, into stubborn determination, and they were even ready to fight for it. Those inclined to compromise, like Taranets proposed a roundabout way – to give those desiring to enter the Komsomol certificates showing that they had "reformed," but to leave them, of course, in the colony. The majority was against resorting to such a trick. Zadorov reddened with indignation, saying:

"None of that! You're not dealing with muzhiks, we don't have to fool anyone. We've got to work for a Komsomol nucleus in the colony, and the Komsomol will know itself who's fit for it, and who isn't."

The boys went very often to the Komsomol organizations in the town in their endeavours to attain their object, but on the whole without success.

In the winter of 1923 we got into friendly relations with yet another Komsomol organization. This happened quite by chance.

Anton and I were returning home one day, towards evening. Mary, her well-nourished skin gleaming, was harnessed to a sleigh. Just as we were going down the hill we met with a phenomenon unusual in our latitudes – a camel. Mary, unable to overcome her natural feeling of disgust, trembled, reared, kicked between the shafts, and went off into a wild gallop. Anton dug his feet into the front of the sleigh, but could not check the mare. A certain inherent defect of our sleigh, which Anton, it is true, had often pointed out – the shortness of the shafts – determined the further course of events and brought us nearer to the afore-mentioned Komsomol organization. Breaking into a frenzied gallop, Mary struck with her hind legs against the iron front of the sleigh, and, now quite panic-stricken, carried us towards inevitable catastrophe with terrifying rapidity. Anton and I tugged at the rains together, but this only made matters worse – Mary tossed up her head and grew more and more frantic. I could already make out, the spot at which everything was destined to come to a more or less disastrous end – -at the turn of the road were a number of peasants with their sleighs, crowding round the hydrant to water their horses. It seemed as if there could be no escape, for the road was barred. But by a kind of miracle Mary galloped between the drinking trough and the group of sleighs belonging to people from the town. There was a sound of cracking wood, and shouts, but we were already a long way off. The hill came to an end, we flew over the smooth, straight road less furiously, and Anton was even able to look back and shake his head: "We've smashed someone's sleigh up. We must get away!"

He began to wave the whip over Mary, who was trotting ahead at full speed, but I restrained his too eager arm.

"You can't get away! Look what a devil they have!"

Indeed, a splendid trotter was overtaking us with calm forceful strokes of his hoofs, while from over its croup a man with crimson tabs was gazing steadily after the unsuccessful runaways. We came to a stop. The possessor of the crimson tabs was standing up in his sleigh, holding on to the driver's shoulders; there was nowhere for him to sit, for the back seat and the back of the sleigh itself had been converted into a kind of trembling latticework, while the bespattered and splintered fragments of various sleigh appurtenances trailed behind it in the road.

"Follow!" barked out the military man.

We obeyed, Anton beaming. He was delighted with the improvements in the turnout which had been made by our troublous passage. In ten minutes we found ourselves in the commandant's office of the GPU, and only then did Anton's countenance display signs of discomfited wonderment.

"Just look!" he exclaimed. "We ran into the GPU!"

We were surrounded by people with crimson tabs, one of whom started shouting at me:

"Naturally – they have a mere lad for a driver – how could he be expected to hold the horse in? You'll be answerable yourself."

Anton writhed with mortification and, almost in tears, shook his head at his offender:

"A mere lad, indeed! If you didn't let camels go about the roads – letting all these brutes swarm all over the place! How could the mare bear it? How could she?"

"What brutes?"

"That camel!"

The crimson tabs laughed.

"Where are you from?" I answered.

"The Gorky Colony," I said.

"Oh, so it's the Gorky fellows! And who are you – the director? We've landed some fine fish today!" laughed a young man, calling to those around him, and pointing to us as if we were welcome guests.

A crowd formed around us. They teased their own driver, and bombarded Anton with questions about the colony.

"We've been meaning to go to the colony for a long time. They say you're a fighting lot, there. We'll come and see you on Sunday."

Then up came the supply manager and started angrily drawing up some sort of a statement. But everyone shouted him down.

"Drop your red tape! What are you writing it all down for?"

"What for? Have you seen what they've done to the sleigh? Now let them repair it!"

"They'll repair it without your deposition. You will, won't you? Go on – tell us about things in the colony! They say you don't even have a lockup."

"A lockup – what for? Have *you* got one?" inquired Anton.

Once again everyone burst out laughing.

"We'll be sure to come to you on Sunday. We'll bring you the sleigh for repair."

"And what'll I drive in till Sunday?" barked the supply manager.

But I calmed him down.

"We have another sleigh," I assured him. "Send someone with us to take it."

And so our colony gained some more good friends. On Sunday the Cheka Komsomols came to the colony. And once again the accursed question came up for discussion – why couldn't the members of our colony become Komsomols? The Cheka-men unanimously took our side on this question.

"What on earth do they mean?" they said to me. "Criminals, indeed! What rubbish! They ought to be ashamed of themselves! And they call themselves serious people! We'll take the matter up – in Kharkov, if we can't do it here."

At that time our colony had been put under the direct authority of the Ukrainian People's Commissariat for Education, as a "Model Delinquents' Institution." We began to be visited by inspectors from the People's Commissariat for Education. These were no longer shallow, fatuous provincials, believing in social education as a kind of emotional springtide. The Kharkov folk did not regard social education as a pageant of youthful souls unfolding, the right of the individual, and similar poetical claptrap. What they were looking for were new organizational forms and a new approach. The nicest thing about them was that they did not pose as Fausts, in quest of a single moment of bliss, but showed a friendly spirit of equality with us, seeking for what was new, and rejoicing in every grain of the new they discovered.

The Kharkov people were greatly astonished by our Komsomol mishaps.

"D'you mean you're working without a Komsomol nucleus? You are not allowed to form one? Who says so?"

In the evenings they got together with the elder boys, and stood about in groups, exchanging sympathetic nods.

Thanks to the representations of the People's Commissariat for Education and of our friends in the town, the question was decided with lightning speed in the Central Committee of the Ukrainian Komsomol, and in the summer of 1923 Tikhon Nestorovich Koval was appointed political instructor.

Tikhon Nestorovich was of peasant stock. He had managed to get the twenty-four years of his life filled with many an interesting event, chiefly from the struggle in the villages, and had accumulated strong reserves of political activity, and, besides all this, was a wise person and imperturbably good-natured. From the first moment he spoke to the members of our colony on equal terms like a comrade, and showed himself an expert both in the field and on the threshing floor.

A Komsomol nucleus was organized in the colony to the number of nine persons.

28
THE CEREMONIAL MARCH BEGINS

A sentry guards the Gorky Colony banners

Suddenly Deryuchenko began to speak Russian. This unnatural occurrence was connected with a series of unpleasant incidents in the Deryuchenko nest. It all began when Deryuchenko's wife, who was, by the way, completely indifferent to the Ukrainian cause, decided that the moment had arrived for the delivery of her child. Much as the prospect of perpetuating his glorious Cossack lineage moved Deryuchenko, it had not as yet succeeded in upsetting his equilibrium. In the purest Ukrainian he demanded horses from Bratchenko for the journey to the midwife. Bratchenko could not forego the satisfaction of expressing certain axioms anent the birth of the young Deryuchenko, who had not been provided for in the colony's transport schedule, and the calling of a midwife from town, since, in Anton's opinion – "It'll be all the same, with a midwife, or without a midwife." Still, he did let Deryuchenko have horses. The next day it appeared that it was necessary to take the expectant mother to town. Anton was so upset that he lost all sense of reality and declared: "I'm not going to give you horses!"

But Sherre and I, supported by public opinion in the colony, criticized Bratchenko's conduct so sharply and energetically, that he had to give in. Deryuchenko listened patiently to Anton's harangues, and tried, in his usual florid and magniloquent style, to persuade him.

"Inasmuch as the matter is urgent," he said, "it cannot he put off for an hour, Comrade Bratchenko."

Anton armed himself with mathematical data, in the persuasive powers of which he had a firm belief.

"Was a pair of horses sent for the midwife? It was. The midwife was taken back to town – again a pair of horses.... D' you think the horses care who's going to have a baby?"

"But, Comrade–"

"You and your 'buts'. Supposing everyone started such goings on!"

By way of protest Anton harnessed for these obstetrical matters the least beloved and slowest of the horses, vowed the phaeton was out of order, and sent out the gig, with Soroka on the box – an obvious sign that the turnout was no great shakes. But it was only when Deryuchenko again demanded horses, this time to go and fetch the newly-made mother home, that Anton really let himself go.

Deryuchenko was not destined to he a happy father – his firstborn, hastily given the name of Taras, only survived for one week, when he died in the maternity ward, having added nothing of importance to Deryuchenko's glorious Cossack race. Deryuchenko's face wore an expression of becoming grief, and his accents were somewhat subdued, but there was nothing particularly tragic about his sorrow, and he stubbornly continued to express himself in the Ukrainian language. Bratchenko, for his part, could find words in no language at all, so intense were his indignation and impotent rage. Only half-comprehensible, broken phrases issued from his lips:

"Sent the horses all for nothing! There are plenty of cabs... no hurry... could easily have waited an hour... people will always have babies... and all for nothing!..."

Deryuchenko brought the ill-starred mother back to the nest, and Bratchenko's sufferings ceased for some time. At this point Bratchenko drops out of this mournful story, which, however, had by no means come to an end. Taras Deryuchenko had not yet been born, when a seemingly irrelevant theme crept into the story, but one which subsequently turned out to be not so irrelevant after all. This theme was also a mournful one for Deryuchenko.

The teaching and other staff of the colony received their food ready-cooked from the same source as that which provided the pupils. But for some time now, in recognition of the special requirements of family life, and desirous of easing the work of the kitchen a little, I had allowed Kalina Ivanovich to issue uncooked rations to certain persons. Deryuchenko was one of three. It so happened that I once obtained in the town a minute quantity of butter. It was so little that it would only last in the common stock for a few days. Naturally it never entered into anyone's head that this butter could be included in the uncooked rations. But Deryuchenko was greatly disturbed to learn that for the last three days this precious substance had formed part of the general fare. Me hastened to rearrange matters, and sent in a declaration for transference to the general kitchen, abandoning his claims to uncooked rations. Unfortunately, by the time this transference had been accomplished, the whole supply of butter in Kalina Ivanovich's storeroom had been used up, a circumstance which sent Deryuchenko running to me in violent protest.

"You have no right to make a fool of people! Where's the butter?"

"Butter?" I repeated. "There isn't any more – it's all eaten up."

Deryuchenko wrote a declaration that he and his family would take their rations in uncooked form. Very well! But in two days' time Kalina Ivanovich brought some butter again, and again in the same small quantity. Deryuchenko, setting his teeth, bore up under this reverse too, and did not even go over to the general kitchen. But something seemed to have happened in our Department of Public Education – a long-drawn-out process of the gradual introduction of butter into the organisms of workers in the field of people's education and their charges, seemed to have set in. Every now and then, Kalina Ivanovich, arriving from town, drew out from under the seat a small tub, its top covered with a piece of clean butter muslin. Things got to a point when Kalina Ivanovich would not think of going to town without his tub. More often than not, however, the tub returned without any top covering, and Kalina Ivanovich tossed it carelessly on to the straw in the bottom of the gig, with the words:

"Such an ignorant lot! Can't you give a man something he can look at! What's this supposed to be for, anyway – you parasites? Is it to eat, or to smell?"

But Deryuchenko could no longer bear it, and he again went over to the general kitchen. He was, however, one who could never follow the dynamics of daily life; he failed to see the significance of the steadily rising curve of fats in the colony and, possessing but the feeblest political sense, he had no idea that, at a certain phase, quantity is bound to become quality. And this transformation suddenly burst over the heads of his family. All1 of a sudden we began to get butter in such abundance that I found it possible to issue a fortnight's supply with the uncooked rations. Wives, grandmothers, daughters, mothers-in-law, and other persons of secondary importance, carried away from Kalina Ivanovich's storeroom to their homes the golden-yellow blocks, reaping the reward of their patient endurance, while Deryuchenko, who had incautiously eaten up his fat ration in the imperceptible and unattractive form given it by the colony kitchen, got none. Deryuchenko actually grew pale from misery and the bad luck by which he was dogged. Thoroughly shaken, he wrote out a declaration of his desire to receive uncooked rations. His grief was profound, and evoked universal sympathy, but he still bore himself like a man and a Cossack, and did not give up his native Ukrainian language.

The theme of fats coincided chronologically with the unsuccessful attempt to prolong the Deryuchenko strain.

Deryuchenko and his wife were patiently chewing the cud of their mournful memories of Taras, when fate decided to restore the balance and bestowed upon Deryuchenko a long-merited joy – in the colony order for the day were directions to issue uncooked rations "for the previous fortnight," and butter once again figured in these rations. Deryuchenko went joyously to Kalina Ivanovich with his market bag. The sun was shining, and all living things rejoiced. But this did not last long. Half an hour later Deryuchenko came running to me, very much upset, and wounded to the depths of his soul. The strokes dealt by fate on his hard skull had become intolerable, he had gone completely off the rails and his wheels were beating over the sleepers in the purest Russian.

"Why haven't I been issued fats for my son?"

"What son?" I asked in astonishment.

"What son? Taras! This is arbitrary conduct, Comrade Director! Rations are supposed to be issued for each member of a family – so kindly do so!"

"But you have no son Taras!"

"It's none of your business whether he exists or not. I gave in a certificate showing that my son Taras was born on June the 2nd and died June the 10th – so you are bound to give him rations for eight days...."

Kalina Ivanovich, who had come to watch proceedings, took Deryuchenko cautiously by the elbow.

"Comrade Deryuchenko – who would be fool enough to feed a tiny infant butter? Ask yourself if a baby could stand such food!"

I looked from one to the other in amazement.

"Kalina Ivanovich!" I exclaimed. "What's the matter with you today? This baby died three weeks ago!"

"Oh – so he died? What d' you want then? Butter would no more help him, than incense would help a corpse. Oh, but he *is* a corpse, if I may say so."

Deryuchenko thrashed about the room in his rage, sawing the air with the palms of his hands.

"For a period of eight days my family included a fully entitled member, and you're bound to issue rations for him."

"Fully entitled? He's only theoretically entitled – in practice he hardly existed. It made no difference whether he was there or not."

But Deryuchenko had gone off the rails, and his subsequent movements were wild and disorderly. He lost all sense of style, even the specific tokens of his existence seemed to have become uncurled and droop – his moustache, his hair, his necktie. In this state he at last turned up in the office of the Chief of the Gubernia Department of Public Education, producing there the most unfavourable impression. The Chief of the Gubernia Department of Public Education sent for me.

"One of your employees has been to me with a complaint," he said. "Look here – such people must be got rid of! How can you keep such an intolerable cadger in your colony? He talked such indescribable nonsense – all about some Taras, butter, and God knows what!"

"But it was you who appointed him!"

"Impossible! Chuck him out this minute!"

To such pleasant results had the gradual interlocking of two themes – Taras and butter – led! Deryuchenko and his wife left by the same road that Rodimchik had taken before them. I rejoiced, the members of the colony rejoiced, and the small plot of Ukrainian landscape which had been the scene of the events described, seemed to rejoice, too. But my joy was mixed with anxiety. The same old problem – where to find a real human being – was more acute than ever, for there was not a single teacher in the new colony. But the Gorky Colony was undoubtedly in luck, and I, quite unexpectedly, came across the real human being for whom we thirsted. Such things do happen! I simply came across him in the street. He was stranding on the pavement, his back to the window of the Department of Public Education's supply section, idly regarding ihe simple objects on the dusty, dung-and-straw-littered street.

Anton and I were taking sacks of grain out of the depo. Anton caught his foot in a hollow in the ground, and fell. The real human being hastened to the scene of the catastrophe, and he and I together finished loading the aforesaid sack on to our cart. As I thanked the stranger took note of his well-knit figure, his intelligent youthful countenance, and the dignity with which he smiled in reply to my thanks. A white Cossack cap was perched on his head with the ease and confidence characteristic of the military.

"You're a military man, aren't you?" I asked.

"You're right!" smiled the stranger.

"Cavalryman?"

"Yes."

"Then what can there be to interest you in the Department of Public Education?"

"The Chief. They told me he'd be there soon, so I'm waiting."

"Are you looking for work?"

"Yes. I've been promised work as a physical culture instructor."

"Have a talk with me first."

"All right."

We had a talk. He clambered on to our cart and we drove home. I showed Pyotr Ivanovich over the colony, and by nightfall the question of his appointment was decided.

Pyotr Ivanovich brought with him to the colony a veritable wealth of most fortunate endowments. He had precisely what we needed – youth, vigour, almost superhuman powers of endurance, sobriety and cheerfulness, and there was nothing about him that we did not require – not a hint of pedagogical prejudices, not the slightest posing in front of the boys, no petty selfishness. And Pyotr Ivanovich had yet other qualities – he loved military training, could play the piano, had a certain poetic gift, and was exceedingly strong. Under his rule the new colony took on a new tone the very next day. By jokes, by orders, by chaff, and by example, Pyotr Ivanovich began to get the boys to form a collective. He took on trust all my pedagogical principles, and right up to the end never doubted anything, thus delivering me from futile pedagogical arguments and chatter.

The life of our two colonies began to forge ahead like a well-regulated train. I began to enjoy a sense of reliability and solidity with my staff, a new experience to me. Tikhon Nestorovich, Sherre and Pyotr Ivanovich began, like our experienced veterans, to serve the cause in good earnest.

There were up to eighty members in the colony at that time. The original members of 1920 and 1921 had formed a very close group, and frankly took the lead in the colony, composing at every step, for every newcomer, an inflexible framework of steely will, which it was practically impossible to resist. It was not often, however, that I observed any attempts to show resistance. The colony impressed the newcomers and disarmed them by what struck them as the beauty of its outward appearance, by the precision and simplicity of its daily life, by its many and varied traditions and customs, the origin of which was not always clear even to the oldest members. The duties of each member of the colony were laid down in harsh and inflexible terms, but they were all strictly defined in our constitution, making almost impossible the slightest arbitrariness or display of obstinate despotism in the colony. At the same time the whole colony was constantly confronted with a task as to the need of which there could not be the slightest doubt – the finishing of repairs in the new colony, the concentration of all in one place, the extension of our economic enterprises. That this task was an obligatory one for us, and that we were quite sure to fulfil it, was questioned by no one. Therefore it was that we all reconciled ourselves to countless privations, made all sorts of sacrifices in the sphere of private amusements, better clothes, food, and saved up every spare kopek for hog breeding, seeds, a new harvester. Our attitude to these sacrifices was so calm and good-natured, so cheerful and confident, that I allowed myself a humourous ebullition al the general meeting, when one of the youngsters raised the question of having new trousers made.

"We'll finish up the new colony," I said, "and get rich, and then we'll have new clothes made for everybody – the boys will have velvet blouses with a silver girdle, the girls will have silk dresses and patent-leather shoes, every detachment will have its own car, and every member of the colony will have a bicycle as well. And we'll plant the colony with thousands of rosebushes. D' you get me? And in the meantime let's buy a fine Siementhal cow with these three hundred rubles."

The boys laughed heartily, and after this the cotton patches on their trousers, and their grease-stained grey blouses no longer seemed so very shabby.

The heads of the colony collective were still open to occasional criticism for straying from the path of strict virtue, but who is there in the whole world immune from such strictures? And in our hard task these "heads" proved a very smooth and precise mechanism. What I particularly appreciated in them was the fact that the main tendency of their work had somehow unnoticeably become their own extinction as "heads," and the drawing in of the whole colony.

These "heads" included almost all our old friends – Karabanov, Zadorov, Vershnev, Bratchenko, Volokhov, Vetkovsky, Taranets, Burun, Gud, Osadchy, Nastya Nochevnaya; but more recently new names had crept into the list – Oprishko, Georgievsky, Zhorka Volkov and Alyoshka Volkov, Stupitsyn and Kudlaty.

Oprishko had assimilated many of Anton Bratchenko's qualities: his fervour, his love of horses, and his superhuman capacity for work. He was not so talented in a creative way, nor so vivid, but he had qualities peculiar to himself alone – a fine flow of animal spirits, coupled with a certain gracefulness and purposefulness in all his movements.

In the eyes of colony society Georgievsky was a dual personality. On the one hand his whole outward appearance tempted us to call him a gipsy. His dusky face, his prominent black eyes, his dry lazy humour, a mischievous laxity in regard to private property, all held something gipsy-like. Georgievsky, on the other hand, was obviously the offspring of educated people – he was well-read, well-groomed, and handsome in a towny way, and there was something almost aristocratic in his way of speaking, and his pronunciation of the letter "r." The boys declared that Georgievsky was the son of a former governor of Irkutsk. Georgievsky himself denied the very possibility of such a disgraceful origin, and his papers bore not the slightest trace of so damning a past, but in such cases I was always inclined to believe the boys. He went to the new colony as a commander, and distinguished himself immediately – no one worked so much on his detachment as the commander of the sixth. Georgievsky read aloud to his fellow members, helped them to dress, saw that they washed themselves, was never tired of convincing, persuading and adjuring them. In the Commanders' Council he always stood for the idea of love and care for the little ones. And he had many achievements to boast of. Into his hands were put the dirtiest, most ill-conditioned boys, and by a week he had turned them into dandies, their hair slicked, pursuing their way with the utmost precision along the paths of the colony's life of toil.

There were two Volkovs in the colony – Zhorka and Alyoshka. They had not a single feature in common, though they were brothers. Zhorka had made a bad start in the colony, displaying an unconquerable laziness, a distressing sickliness, a quarrelsome and spiteful nature. He never smiled and but seldom spoke, and I was afraid he would never become one of ourselves, but would run away. His transformation took place without any fuss and without pedagogical efforts. In the Commanders' Council it suddenly appeared that only one possible combination remained for the digging of an ice pit – Galatenko and Zhorka. Everyone laughed.

Nobody could want to put two such shirkers to work together.

There was still more merriment when somebody proposed an interesting experiment: to make a mixed detachment of them and see what came of it, and how much they would dig. After some deliberation Zhorka was chosen as commander, Galatenko being still worse. Zhorka was called before the Council and I addressed him as follows:

"Look here, Volkov. You've been elected commander of a mixed detachment for making an icehouse, and Galatenko will be your helper. Only we're a bit afraid you won't be able to manage him."

After a moment's thought, Zhorka muttered:

"I'll manage him."

The next day an excited monitor ran up to me.

"You simply must come! It's ever so amusing to watch Zhorka drilling Galatenko! Only take care – if they hear us everything will be spoiled!"

We crept up to the field of action in the shelter of the bushes. On the cleared space in the remains of what had been a garden, was the rectangular base of the future icehouse. One end of it was Galatenko's allotment, the other, Zhorka's. Which was which could be seen at a glance both by the disposition of the forces, and by an obvious difference in the productivity of the workers. Zhorka had already dug up several square metres, while Galatenko had only done a narrow strip. But Galatenko was by no means asleep – he was clumsily driving his thick foot against the intractable spade, sticking it into the earth, and continually turning his heavy head, with an effort which was apparent, towards Zhorka. If Zhorka was not looking, Galatenko would stop working, keeping his foot on the spade, ready at the first alarm to plunge it into the earth. It was obvious that Volkov was thoroughly sick of all these tricks.

"D' you think I'm going to stand over you and beg you to work? I have no time to fuss about with you!"

"Why should you work so hard?" grumbled Galatenko.

Without answering Zhorka went over to Galatenko.

"I'm not going to talk to you, d' you understand?" he said. "But if you don't dig from here to here, I'll throw your dinner on to the garbage heap."

"Who's going to let you throw it out? What would Anton say?"

"He can say what he likes, but throw it out I will, so now you know!"

Galatenko looked steadily into Zhorka's eyes and read in them that Zhorka meant business. Galatenko muttered.

"I'm working, aren't I? Can't you leave me alone?"

His spade began moving more briskly in the earth, and the monitor touched my elbow.

"Enter it in your report," I whispered.

That evening the monitor's report concluded with the words:

"I wish to draw attention to the good work of 3-I, mixed detachment under command of Volkov senior."

Karabanov encircled Volkov's head with his powerful arm, exclaiming:

"Oho! Not every commander gets honoured like that!"

Zhorka smiled proudly. Galatenko also bestowed a smile upon us from the door of the office, adding huskily:

"Oh, yes, we worked today – we worked like hell!"

From this moment Zhorka was a changed creature, he went full steam ahead towards perfection, and in two months' time the Commanders Council transferred him to the new colony with the special purpose of brisking up the lazy seventh detachment.

Everybody liked Alyoshka Volkov from the first day. He was far from handsome, his face being covered with spots of every possible shade, and his forehead was so low, that his hair seemed to grow forward instead of upwards; but Alyoshka was no fool, in fact he was exceedingly clever, and soon everyone realized this. There was no better commander of a mixed detachment than Alyoshka – he could plan work skilfully, find the right place for each of the younger boys, and was always discovering new ways and methods of doing things.

Kudlaty, with his broad Mongol face, and wiry stocky frame, was a clever boy, too. He had been a simple farm hand before he came to us, but always went by the nickname "kulak" in the colony; indeed, had it not been for the colony, which led Kudlaty in due time to Party membership, he *would* have become a kulak, for a sort of animal and at the same time profoundly possessive instinct, a love for property, for carts, for harrows, for horses, for manure and a ploughed field, for all sorts of farmyard work in sheds, in barns, were ruling passions with him. Kudlaty was unassailable in argument, unhurried in speech, and had the firm foundations of the serious and thrifty accumulator of property. As a former farm hand, however, he detested the kulaks with sane determination, believing wholeheartedly in the worth of our commune, as he did in that of all communes, on principle. Kudlaty had long been Kalina Ivanovich's right hand in the colony, and by the end of 1923 a considerable share of the economic administration had been laid on his shoulders.

Stupitsyn was also of a practical turn of mind, but he was quite a different type. He was a true proletarian. He could trace his origin to the workshops of Kharkov, and knew where his father, his grandfather, and his great-grandfather had worked. Members of his family had long adorned the ranks of the proletariat in the factories of Kharkov, and his eldest brother had been exiled for participation in the revolution of 1905. Stupitsyn was, moreover, a handsome fellow. He had finely pencilled brows and small, keen, black eves. On either side of his mouth was a fine knot of subtle mobile muscles, his face was extremely expressive, and its changes were abrupt and interesting. Stupitsyn represented one of our most important agricultural branches – the new colony hoghouse, in which the inmates had begun to increase and multiply at an almost fantastic rate. A special detachment – the tenth – worked in the hoghouse, and its commander was Stupitsyn. He managed to make of his detachment an energetic unit, its members having little in common with the traditional swineherd. They were seldom without a book, their heads were filled with figures, their hands with pencils and writing pads; on the doors of the pens were inscriptions, there were diagrams and regulations ail over the hoghouse, and each pig had its own document. What didn't they have in that hoghouse?

Alongside the leading group were two large groups much akin to it – its reserve. These consisted, on the one hand, in active veterans, splendid workers and comrades, strong, calm individuals without, however, outstanding organizational talent. These were Prikhodko, Chohot, Soroka, Leshy, Gleiser, Schneider, Ovcharenko, Koryto, Fedorenko and many others. On the other hand were the younger boys, a real reserve, even now beginning to show the marks of future organizers. Their youth prevented them as yet from gathering up the reins of government, besides, their seniors were in the ruling posts, and they loved and respected their seniors. They had, however, many advantages over them, having tasted of colony life at an earlier age, and assimilated its traditions more thoroughly, so that they believed still more strongly in the incontrovertible worth of the colony, and above all, were better educated, what knowledge they had being a more active possession. They were our old friends Toska, Shellaputin, Zhevely, Bogoyavlensky, but there were some new names – Lapot, Sharovsky, Romanchenko, Nazarenko, Veksler. These were all the future commanders and active workers of the epoch of the conquest of Kuryazh. And they were already beginning to be nominated commander of mixed detachments.

These groups of colonists composed the greater part of our collective. They were strong in the spirit of optimism, in energy, in knowledge and in experience, and the rest were drawn along irresistibly in their wake. The colonists themselves divided these latter under three headings – the "swamp," the "small fry," and the "rabble."

To the "swamp" belonged those who had in no way distinguished themselves, who were inarticulate, as if they were themselves not quite sure that they belonged to the colony. It must, however, be added, that outstanding personalities did sometimes emerge from it and that it represented a mere phase itself. For a time it consisted, to a great extent, of boys from the new colony. Of little ones we had over a dozen, regarded by the rest as raw material, whose chief function it was to learn to wipe their noses. The little ones, themselves, moreover, did not aspire to any outstanding activities, contenting themselves with games, skating, boating, fishing, sleighing, and other trifles. I considered that they were perfectly right.

There were only about five persons in the "rabble" – Galatenko, Perepelyatchenko, Evgenyev, Gustoivan, and a few others. They were relegated to the "rabble" by common consent as soon as a striking weakness was discovered in any one of them. Galatenko, for example, was a glutton and a shirker; Evgenyev showed himself to be a hysterical liar and chatterer; Perepelyatchenko was a sickly, whimpering cadger; while Gustoivan was "psychic," a sort of God's fool, ever praying to the Blessed Virgin, and dreaming of entering a monastery. In time the "rabble" shook off some of these unfortunate attributes, but it was a long and tedious process.

Such was the collective in our colony at the end of 1923. In appearance, all its members with few exceptions were equally spruce, and all flaunted a military bearing. We already had splendid marching columns, their vanguard adorned by four buglers and eight drummers. We had a banner, too, a lovely silk one, and embroidered in silk – a present from the Ukrainian People's Commissariat for Education, on the occasion of our third anniversary.

On proletarian holidays the colony marched into town to the roll of drums, astonishing the town dwellers and impressionable pedagogues by their austere rhythm, iron discipline and distinguished bearing. Always the last to come to the square, so as not to have to wait for anyone, we would stand at attention, till the buglers sounded a salute to all the town workers, the colonists raising their hands. Then our columns would break up in search of holiday impressions, leaving the standard-bearer and a small guard at attention in front, and a little ensign at the back to mark the lines of the rear. And this was so impressive that no one ever ventured to occupy the place we had marked out for ourselves. We overcame our sartorial limitations by ingenuity and audacity. We were determined opponents of cotton suits, that gruesome feature of children's homes. But we did not possess suits of better quality. Nor had we new and handsome footwear. For this reason we went on parade barefoot, but managed to make it look as if this was intentional. The boys wore shirts of dazzling whiteness. Their black trousers were of good quality, rolled up below the knees, snow-white undergarments turned up over them. Their shirt sleeves were also rolled above their elbow. The effect was smart and gay, striking a slightly rural note.

On the 3rd of October, 1923, such a column streamed across the colony drill ground. By then a most complex operation, which had taken three weeks to accomplish,, had been brought to all end. According to the resolution passed at a combined session of the Pedagogical Council and the Commanders' Council, the Gorky Colony was concentrated in one place – the former Trepke estate – putting its old estate on Lake Rakitnoye at the disposal of the Gubernia Department of Public Education. By the 3rd of October, everything had been transferred to the new colony. Work shops, sheds, stables, storerooms, dining room, kitchen and school were all there, and the belongings of the staff had been moved. By the morning of the 3rd of October, only fifty boys, the banner, and myself, remained in the old colony.

At twelve noon, a representative of the Gubernia Department of Public Education signed the deed for the handing over of the estate of the Gorky Colony, and stood aside. I gave the order:

"To the colours – attention!"

The boys drew themselves up for the salute, the drums thundered, the bugles sounded for the march past the colours. The flag brigade brought the banner out of the office. Bearing it on our right flank, we bade no farewell to the old place, though we harboured not the slightest hostility to it. We just didn't like looking back. Nor did we glance back when the columns of our colony, shattering the silence of the fields with its drumbeats, passed Lake Rakitnoye, and Andrei Karpovich's stronghold on the village street, and descended to the grassy valley of the Kolomak, marching towards the new bridge built by the members of our colony.

The whole staff and a number of villagers from Goncharovka were gathered in the yard at Trepke, and the columns of the new colony members, in all their glory, stood to attention in honour of the Gorky banner. We had entered upon a new era.

Made in the USA
Monee, IL
01 November 2019

16207942R00138